AF440107

HEALING THROUGH THE SHADOWS

DENISE GILMORE

How to Use This Book for Healing

Welcome to "Healing Through the Shadows: A Year of Grief and Renewal." This devotional is designed to be your companion on the journey of grief, providing daily readings, reflections, and prayers that offer comfort, insight, and perspective. As you embark on this transformative path, here's how you can make the most of this book to nurture your healing process:

1. **DEDICATE TIME FOR REFLECTION:** Carve out a quiet space in your day, free from distractions. Consider setting a specific time, whether it's in the morning, during lunch breaks, or before bed, to engage with the devotional. This intentional time allows you to fully immerse yourself in the readings and reflections, creating a meaningful rhythm for your healing journey.

2. **JOURNAL YOUR THOUGHTS AND FEELINGS:** After each reading, take a few moments to journal your thoughts, feelings, and insights. Writing can be a therapeutic tool that helps you process your emotions and track your personal growth. Your journal becomes a sacred space to explore your grief, record moments of clarity, and witness your healing unfold over time.

3. **CREATE A SACRED SPACE:** Designate a physical space where you can engage with the devotional. It could be a cozy corner with a comfortable chair, a special candle, or meaningful mementos. This space becomes a sanctuary where you can disconnect from the external world and connect with the messages of comfort and hope within the devotional.

4. **CHOOSE READINGS BASED ON YOUR NEEDS:** While this devotional follows a structured journey, feel free to adapt it to your unique healing process. Some days, a specific reading might resonate more deeply, while on others, you might find solace in revisiting previous entries. The flexibility to choose readings that align with your current emotions allows the devotional to be tailored to your evolving needs.

5. **SHARE WITH SUPPORTIVE INDIVIDUALS:** If you're comfortable, consider sharing the devotional journey with friends, family, or a grief support group. Engaging with the reflections together can spark meaningful conversations and foster a sense of shared understanding. Connecting with others who are also navigating grief can be a powerful source of validation and comfort.

Remember that healing is a gradual process, and each day's reading is a stepping stone towards renewal. As you embrace the reflections, prayers, and scriptures within this book, may you find comfort in the wisdom it offers, gain insight into your grief journey, and discover the enduring hope that arises from walking through the shadows of loss.

NAVIGATING THE LANDSCAPE OF GRIEF

Acknowledging Your Grief

SCRIPTURE: *Psalm 34:18 – "The Lord is near to the brokenhearted and saves the crushed in spirit."*

REFLECTION: Grief is a journey that begins with the courageous act of acknowledging the pain that resides within. It's not just a feeling; it's a process that unfolds in its own time. Today, as you open the pages of this devotional, take a deep breath and let yourself be in this moment.

Grief is not a sign of weakness but a testament to the depth of love and connection we share with those we've lost. The pain you feel is a reflection of the significance of that bond. You are not alone on this path – God is with you, walking beside you in the midst of your brokenness. As you navigate this chapter of your life, remember that acknowledging your grief is the first step towards healing. Be gentle with yourself.

PRAYER: Heavenly Father, as I begin this healing journey, help me embrace the pain I feel. I trust You are near, offering comfort and solace in my time of need. Amen.

DAY 2

Honoring Your Emotions

SCRIPTURE: *Ecclesiastes 3:4 – "A time to weep and a time to laugh, a time to mourn and a time to dance."*

REFLECTION: Emotions are the language of the heart, and grief can stir up a whirlwind of feelings within us. Today, take a moment to honor your emotions, whether they be sadness, anger, confusion, or even fleeting moments of joy. Each emotion you experience is valid and a part of your healing journey.

Just as there is a time for weeping and mourning, there will also come a time for laughter and dancing. Your grief does not define you, but it is a part of your story. In allowing yourself to feel, you open the door to understanding and growth. Remember, even in the depths of sorrow, there is room for hope.

PRAYER: Gracious God, I lay my emotions before You. Help me navigate the ever-changing landscape of my feelings. Grant me the strength to embrace both the tears and the smiles, knowing that through it all, You are shaping my healing heart. Amen.

DAY 3

Finding Comfort in Community

SCRIPTURE: *Galatians 6:2 – "Bear one another's burdens, and so fulfill the law of Christ."*

REFLECTION: Grief can shroud us in solitude, but the scripture from Galatians 6:2 reminds us of the transformative power of community. As we open ourselves to others, sharing the weight of our sorrow, we embody Christ's teachings of compassion and solidarity. In the act of bearing each other's burdens, we create a space where pain is understood, and healing becomes a collective journey.

The community becomes a refuge where our grief finds resonance. Whether it's a friend, family member, or a support group, the empathetic presence of others reminds us that we are not alone in our struggles. By letting others into our pain and offering our presence in return, we weave a tapestry of shared strength. In these connections, the essence of Christ's love is palpable, fulfilling the law of compassion and reminding us that healing is not a solitary endeavor but a bond that unites us in our brokenness.

PRAYER: Loving God, in times of grief, guide me towards the comfort of a caring community. Grant me the courage to share my burdens and the openness to receive the solace offered by others. Through our interconnectedness, may we embody Christ's love and find healing through shared empathy. Amen.

Embracing Vulnerability

SCRIPTURE: *2 Corinthians 12:9 – "My grace is sufficient for you, for my power is made perfect in weakness."*

REFLECTION: In a world that often encourages strength and resilience, embracing vulnerability can feel counterintuitive. Yet, in our moments of weakness, we find a unique space where divine grace can work wonders. The scripture from 2 Corinthians 12:9 reminds us that God's power is most profound when we acknowledge our limitations. It's through our vulnerabilities that we allow the light of grace to shine through, illuminating the path of healing with its gentle radiance.

When we open ourselves to vulnerability, we let go of the facade of invulnerability and humbly stand before the infinite strength of God. It's a transformative act of surrender, where we admit that we cannot heal on our own, and in doing so, we invite the power of God's grace to mend our brokenness. As we navigate grief's turbulent waters, remember that it's okay to be vulnerable, for it's in those moments that we experience the profound truth that our weaknesses can become conduits for divine strength.

PRAYER: Gracious God, in my moments of vulnerability, help me find strength in your grace. Teach me to let go of the need to be strong at all times and embrace the power of your perfect love in my weakness. May I find solace in the understanding that your grace is sufficient to carry me through the depths of my grief and lead me toward healing. Amen.

Seeking Clarity in the Chaos

SCRIPTURE: *Psalm 18:28 - "For it is you who light my lamp; the Lord my God lightens my darkness.*

REFLECTION: Amid the chaos and confusion that often accompany grief, we yearn for moments of clarity and understanding. The scripture from Psalm 18:28 assures us that even in our darkest moments, God's presence shines like a guiding light. Just as a lamp pierces through the darkness, God's wisdom and grace illuminate our path, providing insight and direction as we navigate the intricate landscape of grief.

When life feels like a labyrinth of emotions, it's comforting to know that there is a source of unwavering light to guide us. The verse invites us to seek solace in the assurance that, no matter how bewildering our journey may seem, God's divine light is there to dispel the shadows of confusion. As you grapple with the complexities of grief, take a moment to pause and allow the light of God's wisdom to reveal the way forward.

PRAYER: Heavenly Light, in moments of chaos and confusion, I turn to you for clarity. Illuminate my path with your divine wisdom so that I may find understanding and insight as I journey through grief's challenges. Just as you lighten the darkness, may your guidance lead me toward healing and renewal. Amen.

Letting Go of Guilt

SCRIPTURE: *Romans 8:1 – "There is therefore now no condemnation for those who are in Christ Jesus.*

DEVOTIONAL: Guilt often intertwines with grief, weaving a web of self-condemnation that hinders healing. The scripture from Romans 8:1 serves as a gentle reminder that in Christ, we find freedom from the burden of guilt. It's a declaration that we are not defined by our mistakes or perceived shortcomings. The embrace of Christ's love absolves us from self-condemnation, inviting us to release the weight of guilt and move forward toward healing.

When we cling to guilt, we hinder our ability to heal and grow. Christ's sacrifice offers us a fresh start, a chance to learn and transform. As you journey through grief, remember that forgiveness extends not only from God but also from yourself. Embrace the truth that you are worthy of compassion and renewal, and let go of guilt to make space for healing to flourish.

PRAYER: Loving God, I surrender my guilt to your boundless grace. In moments of self-condemnation, remind me of your unwavering love. Help me release the weight of guilt that hinders my healing journey. May I find solace in the freedom you offer and move forward with a heart unburdened by condemnation. Amen.

Remembering with Gratitude

SCRIPTURE: *Philippians 1:3 – "I thank my God in all my remembrance of you."*

DEVOTIONAL: Grief can evoke a bittersweet longing for the ones we've lost, yet within the ache of remembrance lies a wellspring of gratitude. The scripture from Philippians 1:3 reminds us that even in our recollections, we can find reasons to give thanks. Each memory becomes a tribute, a moment to cherish and honor the legacy of those we've loved.

As you navigate the path of grief, allow gratitude to weave through your remembrances. Instead of focusing solely on the void left by their absence, remember the moments that brought joy, love, and connection. These memories are a testament to the impact they had on your life. Expressing gratitude for their presence can help you find solace and celebrate the unique imprint they've left on your heart.

PRAYER: Gracious God, as I remember those I've lost, help me discover gratitude amidst the grief. May the remembrance of their presence fill my heart with thankfulness. Allow me to celebrate the moments we shared and find healing through the warmth of cherished memories. Amen.

DAY 8

Embracing Solitude

SCRIPTURE: *Mark 1:35 - "And rising very early in the morning, while it was still dark, he departed and went out to a desolate place, and there he prayed."*

DEVOTIONAL: Amid the tumult of grief, there is value in seeking solitude. The scripture from Mark 1:35 highlights a moment of solitude that Jesus sought for prayer and reflection. In a world filled with noise and distractions, embracing solitude allows us to create a sacred space where we can connect with our own thoughts and emotions and with God.

Solitude doesn't mean isolation; it's a deliberate choice to step away from the noise and busyness. In solitude, we find a quiet refuge where we can process our feelings, seek guidance, and find renewal. Just as Jesus found solace in a desolate place, we, too, can find solace in the quiet corners of our hearts. In moments of solitude, allow your grief to speak and your soul to heal.

PRAYER: Holy One, guide me towards moments of solitude where I can find respite from the noise of the world. In those quiet spaces, may I encounter your presence and discover the depths of my own heart. Grant me the strength to embrace solitude as a means of healing and growth during my journey of grief. Amen.

DAY 9

Finding Meaning in Loss

SCRIPTURE: *Romans 8:28 – "And we know that for those who love God all things work together for good, for those who are called according to his purpose."*

DEVOTIONAL: Amid the pain of loss, it's natural to question the purpose behind our suffering. The scripture from Romans 8:28 offers a perspective of hope, reminding us that God can bring forth good even from the most difficult circumstances. While we may not immediately see the reasons behind our grief, we can trust that God is working in the midst of our pain.

In the tapestry of life, moments of loss are interwoven with moments of growth and transformation. Though the path may be unclear, the belief that God's purpose is at work can provide comfort. As you grapple with the questions that loss raises, remember that even in the midst of heartache, your grief can be a catalyst for deeper understanding, compassion, and connection.

PRAYER: Compassionate God, in the midst of my grief, helps me find meaning and purpose. Illuminate the ways in which you are working through my pain for my ultimate good. May my journey through loss lead me to a deeper connection with your purpose and a greater sense of compassion for myself and others. Amen.

DAY 10

Navigating Triggers

SCRIPTURE: *1 Corinthians 10:13 – "No temptation has overtaken you that is not common to man. God is faithful, and he will not let you be tempted beyond your ability, but with the temptation he will also provide the way of escape, that you may be able to endure it."*

DEVOTIONAL: Grief has its triggers – moments, places, and memories that stir up waves of emotion. The scripture from 1 Corinthians 10:13 reminds us of God's faithfulness in providing a way to endure challenges. While grief's triggers can be overwhelming, this verse reassures us that we possess the inner strength to face them.

When triggers arise, it's easy to feel consumed by the intensity of emotions they evoke. But the same triggers can also be moments of opportunity. Instead of avoiding them, we can navigate them with resilience. Just as God promises a way of escape from temptation, He offers us a path through our triggers, guiding us toward healing and growth.

PRAYER: Gracious God, as I encounter triggers that stir my grief, grant me the strength to face them with courage. May I trust in your faithfulness and the inner resources you've provided. Help me recognize these triggers as opportunities for healing and transformation, knowing that you walk alongside me through each challenging moment. Amen.

DAY 11

Embracing the Waves of Grief

SCRIPTURE: *Psalm 42:7 - "Deep calls to deep at the roar of your waterfalls; all your breakers and your waves have gone over me."*

DEVOTIONAL: Grief often resembles the ebb and flow of ocean waves. Just as the waves rise and recede, grief's intensity waxes and wanes. The scripture from Psalm 42:7 vividly portrays the deep emotional currents that can engulf us. Yet, within this portrayal, there's a powerful metaphor for finding equilibrium.

Just as waves balance between the force of their rise and retreat, we, too, can navigate our grief with balance. It's about acknowledging the waves of emotion without being overwhelmed by them. Like seasoned surfers, we learn to ride these waves, finding moments of stability in between. The waves of grief are part of the journey, and by embracing them and finding balance, we can navigate their impact with resilience.

PRAYER: Compassionate Creator, as I encounter the waves of grief, teach me the art of balance. Help me find strength in the rise and retreat of my emotions. May I learn to ride the waves of sorrow with grace, finding moments of peace and stability within the tumult. Guide me through the tides of grief's journey, knowing that you are with me every step of the way. Amen.

Connecting with Nature's Healing

SCRIPTURE: *Psalm 19:1 - "The heavens declare the glory of God, and the sky above proclaims his handiwork."*

DEVOTIONAL: Amid the weight of grief, nature holds a profound gift of solace and renewal. The scripture from Psalm 19:1 reminds us that the beauty of the world around us is a testament to the Creator's artistry. When we connect with nature's rhythms, from the rustling leaves to the vast expanse of the sky, we find a space where healing begins to unfold.

In the presence of nature's splendor, we can glimpse the grandeur of a world that continues to bloom and transform despite the pain of loss. Nature's cyclical patterns mirror the journey of grief – moments of darkness followed by the emergence of light. When you feel weighed down, step outside, breathe in the fresh air, and let the beauty of creation breathe life back into your spirit.

PRAYER: Divine Artist, in the embrace of nature, I discover a healing balm. May the beauty of the world around me remind me of your ongoing work of creation and renewal. As I connect with the rhythms of nature, it brings solace to my heart and renewal to my soul. Help me find comfort in the presence of your handiwork, allowing nature's beauty to infuse my healing journey with hope. Amen.

Vulnerability

SCRIPTURE: *2 Corinthians 12:9 - "My grace is sufficient for you, for my power is made perfect in weakness."*

DEVOTIONAL: Vulnerability is often seen as a sign of weakness, but the scripture from 2 Corinthians 12:9 unveils a different truth. It tells us that God's strength is magnified in our moments of weakness. When we're open and authentic about our grief, we create a space for God's grace to shine through, infusing us with emotional resilience.

In our vulnerability, we open ourselves to the possibility of healing and growth. When we share our pain, we allow others to offer comfort and support. And in that exchange, we're reminded that we are not alone in our struggles. God's grace, like a gentle tide, flows into the spaces of our vulnerability, transforming them into wellsprings of emotional strength.

PRAYER: Gracious God, in my moments of vulnerability, help me find strength through your grace. Teach me that being open about my grief doesn't make me weak but allows your strength to shine through. May my willingness to be vulnerable become a source of healing and connection as I experience your power perfected in my weaknesses. Amen.

DAY 14

Embracing Rituals of Remembrance

SCRIPTURE: *Ecclesiastes 3:1 – "For everything there is a season, and a time for every matter under heaven."*

DEVOTIONAL: Grief invites us to weave threads of remembrance into our healing journey. The scripture from Ecclesiastes 3:1 reminds us of life's changing seasons, each with its own purpose. In the tapestry of grief, creating rituals of remembrance becomes a way to honor and cherish the lives of those we've lost.

Rituals have a unique way of grounding us, connecting us to the past while guiding us through the present. Whether it's lighting a candle, visiting a special place, or sharing stories, these rituals carve out spaces for reflection and connection. They're not meant to erase the pain but to create a bridge between what was and what remains.

PRAYER: Eternal Creator, in the rhythm of seasons, I find inspiration for meaningful rituals of remembrance. Guide me in crafting practices that honor the lives of those I've lost. May these rituals become bridges that connect me to cherished memories, and in their embrace, may I find solace and a continued sense of connection with those who have passed on. Amen.

Embracing God's Presence

SCRIPTURE: *Psalm 139:10 - "Even there your hand shall lead me, and your right hand shall hold me.*

DEVOTIONAL: Grief can be a lonely journey, but the scripture from Psalm 139:10 assures us of God's unwavering presence. In the depths of sorrow, God's hand guides and upholds us, a reminder that we are not alone in our grief journey. Even in the darkest moments, we are held by divine love.

When the weight of grief feels overwhelming, remember that God's presence is a constant refuge. You are not left to navigate this journey on your own. In the midst of your pain, God walks beside you, offering strength and solace. Embrace this truth and find comfort in the assurance that, even in your grief, you are held in the loving embrace of the Creator.

PRAYER: Loving God, in my moments of grief, help me to recognize your presence. May I find comfort in the knowledge that your hand guides and holds me, even in the midst of sorrow. As I journey through this season of loss, may I draw strength from your unwavering love and find solace in your constant companionship. Amen.

FINDING SOLACE IN SCRIPTURE

Seeking Comfort in Times of Sorrow

SCRIPTURE: *Psalm 34:18 - "The Lord is near to the brokenhearted and saves the crushed in spirit."*

DEVOTIONAL: In the depths of sorrow, when our hearts are broken, and spirits are crushed, the scripture from Psalm 34:18 offers a gentle reminder of God's nearness. In the midst of our pain, God draws close to us, extending a hand of comfort and healing. The Creator understands the depths of our grief and is present to offer solace.

Amid the storms of sorrow, we are not abandoned. Instead, we are embraced by a love that transcends our pain. The Lord walks with us through the shadows, offering hope and strength. As you navigate the waves of sorrow, know that God's nearness is a constant source of comfort and refuge.

PRAYER: Gracious God, in moments of sorrow, helps me feel your nearness. In the midst of my brokenness, may I find solace in your presence. Lift me up when my spirit is crushed, and fill my heart with the assurance of your comforting love. Thank you for being a refuge for my soul in times of sorrow. Amen.

Embracing the Promise of Peace

SCRIPTURE: *John 14:27 - "Peace I leave with you; my peace I give to you. Not as the world gives do I give to you. Let not your hearts be troubled, neither let them be afraid."*

DEVOTIONAL: In the midst of grief's turmoil, Jesus offers a gift of peace unlike any the world can give. The scripture from John 14:27 reminds us that Christ's peace is a calming balm for troubled hearts. It's a peace that surpasses understanding, gently soothing the ache of loss and comforting our fears.

This peace isn't the absence of pain but a presence that walks alongside us. It's a reassurance that even in the depths of grief, we are held in a divine embrace that transcends our circumstances. As you navigate the complexities of mourning, allow Christ's promise of peace to infuse your heart with comfort and hope.

PRAYER: Prince of Peace, in my grief-stricken moments, help me discover the tranquility you offer. Your peace is a beacon of hope amidst the storms of sorrow. May your presence quiet my troubled heart and ease my fears, allowing me to find solace in your unwavering love. Thank you for the peace that surpasses all understanding. Amen.

DAY 18

Finding Strength

SCRIPTURE: *2 Corinthians 12:10 – "For when I am weak, then I am strong."*

DEVOTIONAL: In the paradox of human weakness and divine strength, we find a profound truth. The scripture from 2 Corinthians 12:10 reveals that when we admit our vulnerability, God's power shines more brilliantly. Our moments of weakness become fertile ground for the seeds of divine strength to take root.

Grief can strip us of our usual sources of strength, leaving us feeling fragile and exposed. Yet, it's precisely in these moments that God's strength is most evident. As we surrender our burdens to the Creator, we find ourselves carried by a power beyond our own. In embracing our weakness, we open the door for God's strength to flow through us.

PRAYER: Almighty God, in my moments of weakness, I turn to you for strength. Teach me that acknowledging my vulnerability doesn't diminish me but allows your power to shine within me. As I journey through grief, may I find solace in the assurance that your strength is perfected in my weakness, leading me toward healing and renewal. Amen.

Restoring Joy in the Mourning

SCRIPTURE: *Psalm 30:5 - "For his anger is but for a moment, and his favor is for a lifetime. Weeping may tarry for the night, but joy comes with the morning."*

DEVOTIONAL: The journey through grief is marked by nights of weeping and days of sorrow. Yet, the scripture from Psalm 30:5 reminds us that just as the darkness of night gives way to the dawn, so too does mourning yield to the emergence of joy. In the midst of our pain, God's grace has the power to transform our tears into the blossoms of joy.

Grief doesn't erase the possibility of joy; rather, it shapes our capacity to appreciate it. The moments of mourning are a part of our human experience, but they are not the entirety. With time, as healing takes root, we find that joy has a way of weaving itself into the tapestry of our hearts, reminding us that even in the midst of sorrow, there is hope for restoration.

PRAYER: God of Restoration, in my moments of mourning, help me hold onto the promise of joy. Your grace turns the tides of sorrow, bringing light to my darkness. As I journey through grief's night, guide me towards the morning of joy that you have prepared. May I find solace in the knowledge that healing can lead to the renewal of joy in my heart. Amen.

Embracing God's Comforting Word

SCRIPTURE: *Psalm 119:50 - "This is my comfort in my affliction, that your promise gives me life.*

DEVOTIONAL: In the depths of affliction and grief, the scriptures become a sanctuary of solace. The verse from Psalm 119:50 speaks of the comfort found in God's promises, reminding us that His word has the power to breathe life into our weary souls.

When sorrow weighs heavy, turning to God's word can provide a lifeline. The pages of the Bible are filled with stories of resilience, hope, and the enduring promise of God's love. They offer us guidance, assurance, and a reminder that we are not alone in our suffering. Embrace His comforting word as a source of strength and renewal during your journey through grief.

PRAYER: Compassionate God, in my affliction, your promises breathe life into my weary heart. Your word offers comfort and solace when grief threatens to overwhelm you. As I turn to your scriptures, may I find the strength and hope I need to navigate this journey. May your word be a guiding light, leading me towards healing and renewal. Amen.

DAY 21

Nurturing Self-Compassion

SCRIPTURE: *Psalm 103:13 – "As a father shows compassion to his children, so the Lord shows compassion to those who fear him."*

DEVOTIONAL: Compassion is a gift from God, both given and received. The scripture from Psalm 103:13 beautifully illustrates how God, like a loving father, extends compassion to His children. In our journey through grief, we are called to embrace this divine compassion and learn to extend it to ourselves.

Self-compassion is often overlooked in times of sorrow. Yet, just as God offers comfort and kindness to us, we must also treat ourselves with gentleness. Be patient with your own grieving heart, for you are a beloved child of the Creator. Nurture self-compassion as you would a fragile bud, allowing it to bloom and offer solace amidst the storms of grief.

PRAYER: Gracious God, teach me the art of self-compassion. Help me to extend the same kindness to myself that you lavish upon me. In moments of grief, may I remember that your compassion knows no bounds, and may I learn to treat my own heart with the same loving care. Amen.

Dwelling in God's Presence

SCRIPTURE: *Psalm 16:11 – "You make known to me the path of life; in your presence there is fullness of joy; at your right hand are pleasures forevermore.*

DEVOTIONAL: In the depths of grief, the scripture from Psalm 16:11 beckons us to find solace and joy in the presence of God. Though our hearts may be heavy with sorrow, God's presence offers a sanctuary of fullness and enduring pleasures.

In moments of profound loss, it's easy to feel disconnected from joy. Yet, even amid grief's shadows, God's presence is a wellspring of hope and fulfillment. As you navigate your journey, remember that joy can coexist with sorrow, and in God's presence, you can find moments of profound joy and solace.

PRAYER: Divine Presence, in the midst of my grief, help me dwell in your joy. Remind me that in your presence, there is a fullness of joy, even in the darkest moments. May I find comfort and fulfillment in your nearness, knowing that you are a constant source of solace and hope. Amen.

The Power of Renewal

SCRIPTURE: *Isaiah 40:31 – "But they who wait for the Lord shall renew their strength; they shall mount up with wings like eagles; they shall run and not be weary; they shall walk and not faint."*

DEVOTIONAL: In the journey through grief, the scripture from Isaiah 40:31 offers a promise of renewal. When we wait upon the Lord, our strength is not depleted but replenished. Just as eagles soar to great heights, we, too, can rise above the weight of sorrow and find renewed vigor.

Grief can be exhausting, both physically and emotionally. Yet, in the quiet moments of waiting upon the Lord, we discover a wellspring of strength that enables us to continue our journey. God's promise is not just to help us endure but to empower us to run, walk, and even soar with resilience and hope.

PRAYER: Almighty Renewer of Strength; in my moments of weariness, I turn to you for renewal. Help me to wait patiently upon you and discover the strength to rise above my grief. As I journey through this season of loss, may I find solace in your promise of renewal and restoration. Amen.

DAY 24

Facing Fear with Faith

SCRIPTURE: *Psalm 56:3 - "When I am afraid, I put my trust in you."*

DEVOTIONAL: Fear can be an unwelcome companion on the journey of grief. It sneaks in during the quiet moments, whispering doubts and worries. But the scripture from Psalm 56:3 encourages us to confront fear with faith. When we are afraid, we can choose to place our trust in God.

In the presence of fear, faith becomes our anchor. It reminds us that we are not alone in our struggles and that God walks with us through the valleys of grief. As you face the uncertainties and anxieties that accompany loss, remember that faith is your shield, and trust in the Creator is your refuge.

PRAYER: Faithful God, in moments of fear, I choose to trust in you. When grief casts shadows and doubts arise, help me remember that you are with me. May my faith in your unwavering love and presence be a source of strength and courage as I journey through the unknown. Amen.

Embracing the Light of Hope

SCRIPTURE: *Psalm 119:105 - "Your word is a lamp to my feet and a light to my path."*

DEVOTIONAL: In the midst of grief's darkness, the scripture from Psalm 119:105 reminds us that God's word is a guiding light. When the path ahead seems shrouded in uncertainty, His word illuminates the way, offering both guidance and hope.

Grief can be disorienting, leaving us feeling lost and overwhelmed. Yet, as you immerse yourself in God's word, you'll discover a steady light that leads you forward. It's a light that doesn't promise the absence of pain but assures you that you're not walking this path alone. Embrace this guiding light, and you'll find hope even in the darkest of moments.

PRAYER: Divine Light, in my moments of grief, I turn to your word as my guide. Illuminate my path with your wisdom and hope. May your word be a lamp to my feet, showing me the way forward, even when the road is challenging. Thank you for being the light that leads me through the shadows. Amen.

Finding Healing Through Forgiveness

SCRIPTURE: *Colossians 3:13 - "Bearing with one another and, if one has a complaint against another, forgiving each other; as the Lord has forgiven so you also must forgive."*

DEVOTIONAL: Grief can sometimes be entangled with feelings of resentment or unforgiveness. The scripture from Colossians 3:13 calls us to explore the liberating power of forgiveness on the journey of healing. Just as the Lord has forgiven us, we are encouraged to extend forgiveness to others.

Forgiveness doesn't negate the pain of loss, but it untangles the knots of bitterness that can hinder our healing. It's an act of grace that releases the weight of grievances, allowing us to move forward with lighter hearts. As you navigate your grief, consider the profound healing that forgiveness can bring, both to yourself and to others.

PRAYER: Merciful God, grant me the strength to forgive as I have been forgiven. In my journey through grief, help me release the burdens of resentment and find healing through the liberating power of forgiveness. May your grace guide my heart toward greater compassion and understanding. Amen.

DAY 27

Embracing the Comforter

SCRIPTURE: *John 14:16 – "And I will ask the Father, and he will give you another Helper, to be with you forever."*

DEVOTIONAL: In times of grief, the Holy Spirit is our ever-present Helper and Comforter, as promised in John 14:16. When the weight of sorrow bears down upon us, we are not left to navigate it alone. The Holy Spirit is a constant source of solace and guidance.

As you journey through grief, open your heart to the gentle presence of the Comforter. The Holy Spirit comes alongside us, whispering words of hope and offering a balm for our wounded souls. In moments of despair, turn to the One who is with you forever, finding solace and strength in His unfailing companionship.

PRAYER: Divine Comforter, in my grief, I turn to you for solace. Thank you for the promise of your presence, a constant source of comfort and guidance. May I be attuned to your gentle whispers of hope, finding solace in the knowledge that I am never alone on this journey. Amen.

Walking in the Footsteps of Love

SCRIPTURE: *1 Corinthians 13:7 – "Love bears all things, believes all things, hopes all things, endures all things."*

DEVOTIONAL: Love is a faithful companion on the journey through grief. The scripture from 1 Corinthians 13:7 reminds us that love is enduring and all-encompassing. It bears our burdens, believes in our healing, and offers hope when we are in despair.

Even in the face of loss, love persists. It may take different forms—memories, the support of friends and family, or the love of a Higher Power—but it remains a guiding light through the darkness of grief. Embrace the love that surrounds you and walks with you on this journey, for it is a steadfast companion that endures all things.

PRAYER: Eternal Love, in my moments of grief, help me recognize the enduring nature of love. May I find solace in the love of others, and in turn, may I be a vessel of love to those who mourn alongside me. Thank you for the love that bears, believes, hopes, and endures through all the seasons of life. Amen.

Trusting God's Timing

SCRIPTURE: *Ecclesiastes 3:2 – "A time to be born, and a time to die; a time to plant, and a time to pluck up what is planted."*

DEVOTIONAL: Grief often leads us to question the timing of life's events. The scripture from Ecclesiastes 3:2 reminds us that there is a time and season for everything. In our journey through loss, finding peace requires trusting in the rhythm of God's timing.

Though we may not understand why certain things happen when they do, we can take solace in the knowledge that God is sovereign over all seasons of life. Even in the pain of loss, there is a purpose and a plan. As you navigate the complexities of grief, may you find comfort in trusting God's timing, knowing that He holds all things in His hands.

PRAYER: Sovereign God, in my moments of grief, help me trust in your timing. Even when I cannot see the purpose, may I find peace in knowing that you hold all seasons of life in your hands. Guide me through this journey with faith in your divine plan, and grant me the strength to endure and grow through every season. Amen.

DAY 30

Discovering Strength in Surrender

SCRIPTURE: *Matthew 11:28 - "Come to me, all who labor and are heavy laden, and I will give you rest."*

DEVOTIONAL: In the midst of grief's labor and heavy burdens, the scripture from Matthew 11:28 extends an invitation from Christ: "Come to me, and I will give you rest." It is in surrendering our burdens to Him that we discover a wellspring of strength and solace.

Grief can be exhausting, both physically and emotionally, and it's easy to carry the weight alone. But Jesus offers a different way—a way of surrender. As you come to Him with your burdens, you find rest for your weary soul. In surrender, you discover that His strength is sufficient to carry you through every trial.

PRAYER: Compassionate Saviour, in my moments of grief, I come to you with my burdens. Thank you for the promise of rest and strength in your presence. As I surrender my pain and sorrow to you, may I discover the solace and renewal that only you can provide. Grant me the courage to release my burdens and find rest in your loving embrace. Amen.

Embracing the Comfort of God's Love

SCRIPTURE: *Zephaniah 3:17 - "The Lord your God is in your midst, a mighty one who will save; he will rejoice over you with gladness; he will quiet you by his love; he will exult over you with loud singing."*

DEVOTIONAL: In the depths of grief, we can find comfort in the unshakeable love of God. The scripture from Zephaniah 3:17 reminds us that the Lord is in our midst, rejoicing over us with gladness, quieting us with His love, and singing over us with exultant joy.

Amidst the tempest of sorrow, God's love remains a steadfast anchor. It is a love that embraces us in our brokenness, offering solace and healing. As you journey through grief, rest in the assurance that you are cherished by the Creator, who sings songs of love over your weary heart.

PRAYER: Heavenly Father, in my moments of grief, I find solace in your unwavering love. Thank you for being in my midst, rejoicing over me with gladness, and quieting me with your love. May I rest in the assurance of your presence and find comfort in the knowledge that I am deeply loved by you. Amen.

Finding Shelter in God's Wings

SCRIPTURE: *Psalm 91:4 - "He will cover you with his pinions, and under his wings you will find refuge; his faithfulness is a shield and buckler."*

DEVOTIONAL: In moments of grief, when the storms of sorrow rage, we can find refuge in the shelter of God's wings. The scripture from Psalm 91:4 beautifully illustrates His protective embrace, a place of security and solace.

Under the wings of the Almighty, we discover a haven of peace. It's a refuge where we can lay down our burdens and find shelter from the tempests of life. God's faithfulness is our shield and defense, assuring us that even in the fiercest storms, we are held securely in His loving embrace.

PRAYER: Heavenly Protector, in my times of grief, I seek refuge under your wings. Thank you for being a shield of faithfulness and a sanctuary of peace. May I find solace in the knowledge that I am secure in your loving care, even in the midst of life's storms. Amen.

DAY 33

Transforming Suffering into Glory

SCRIPTURE: *Romans 8:18 - For I consider that the sufferings of this present time are not worth comparing with the glory that is to be revealed."*

DEVOTIONAL: In the midst of grief and suffering, the scripture from Romans 8:18 offers a profound perspective. It reminds us that the trials of this present time, no matter how painful, are incomparable to the glory that will be revealed.

Grief can feel all-encompassing, like a shadow that obscures our view of the future. Yet, in the heart of suffering, God is at work, weaving a tapestry of redemption and renewal. Your current pain, though deep, is not the final chapter of your story. In your journey through grief, hold onto the promise that glory and healing await, and they will ultimately outweigh the sorrows of today.

PRAYER: Heavenly Father, in moments of suffering and grief, help me see beyond the present pain. Strengthen my faith to believe in the glory that is to be revealed. May I find solace in the assurance that your purpose for me goes beyond my current struggles, leading me toward healing and restoration. Amen.

Embracing Divine Understanding

SCRIPTURE: *Psalm 139:1 – "O Lord, you have searched me and known me!"*

DEVOTIONAL: In the depths of grief, we may feel as though no one truly understands our pain. But the scripture from Psalm 139:1 reminds us that God intimately knows us and searches our hearts. He understands the intricacies of our grief in ways no human can.

Take solace in the knowledge that even when you can't put your grief into words, God comprehends your heart's deepest cries. He is intimately acquainted with your pain and suffering. In your moments of sorrow, lean into the divine understanding that offers comfort and solace beyond measure.

PRAYER: Compassionate God, thank you for searching and knowing me in the midst of my grief. Even when I struggle to find the words, you understand the depths of my heart. May I find comfort in your divine understanding, knowing that I am never alone in my pain. Amen.

Restoring the Brokenhearted

SCRIPTURE: *Psalm 147:3 – "He heals the brokenhearted and binds up their wounds."*

DEVOTIONAL: In the aftermath of loss and grief, the scripture from Psalm 147:3 shines as a beacon of hope. It reminds us that God is the Healer of the brokenhearted, the One who tenderly binds up our wounds.

Grief leaves us with emotional wounds that seem impossible to mend. Yet, in God's hands, there is a promise of restoration. He is the Divine Physician who knows how to mend the most shattered of hearts. As you journey through your grief, embrace the assurance that healing is not only possible but is being actively carried out by the One who loves you deeply.

PRAYER: Divine Healer, in my brokenness and grief, I turn to you for restoration. Thank you for being the One who heals the brokenhearted and binds up our wounds. May I find solace in the knowledge that you are actively at work in my healing journey. Grant me the patience and faith to trust in your loving care. Amen.

DAY 36

The Gift of God's Peace

SCRIPTURE: *Philippians 4:7 - "And the peace of God, which surpasses all understanding, will guard your hearts and your minds in Christ Jesus."*

DEVOTIONAL: Grief often brings turmoil to our hearts and minds. In those moments, the scripture from Philippians 4:7 reminds us of the precious gift of God's peace, a peace that transcends all understanding.

God's peace is not contingent upon our circumstances but is grounded in His unfailing love. It is a peace that stands as a guardian over our hearts and minds, even in the most turbulent times. As you navigate the complex emotions of grief, seek the peace that can only be found in Christ, trusting that it will sustain you beyond understanding.

PRAYER: Heavenly Father, in my moments of grief, I yearn for your peace that surpasses all understanding. Guard my heart and mind with your divine tranquillity, especially when I cannot comprehend the depths of my sorrow. May your peace become a steadfast companion on this journey, offering solace and hope. Amen.

Rejoicing in God's Salvation

SCRIPTURE: *Psalm 13:5 – "But I have trusted in your steadfast love; my heart shall rejoice in your salvation."*

DEVOTIONAL: Amidst grief, the choice to rejoice may seem counterintuitive. However, the scripture from Psalm 13:5 teaches us that even in the darkest moments, we can trust in God's steadfast love and find cause for rejoicing in His salvation.

Grief can feel all-consuming, but it doesn't have the final say. In trusting God's love and His redemptive work, we discover a wellspring of joy that transcends our circumstances. Rejoicing in His salvation doesn't mean denying our pain but recognizing that even in our sorrow, God offers a path to healing and restoration.

PRAYER: Gracious God, in the midst of my grief, help me trust in your steadfast love. May my heart find reasons to rejoice in the assurance of your salvation, even when sorrow surrounds me. Grant me the strength to see beyond the shadows of grief and embrace the joy that your love brings. Amen.

The Promise of Everlasting Life

SCRIPTURE: *John 3:16 – "For God so loved the world, that he gave his only Son, that whoever believes in him should not perish but have life."*

DEVOTIONAL: In the depths of grief, the promise of eternal life, as expressed in John 3:16, offers profound comfort. It reminds us that God's love is so vast that He gave His Son to grant us life that transcends the boundaries of this world.

Grief can make us acutely aware of mortality's fragility. However, the promise of eternal life is a beacon of hope that pierces through the darkness of sorrow. It assures us that death is not the end but the beginning of a life with God that is eternal and free from suffering.

PRAYER: Eternal God, in my moments of grief, I find solace in the promise of eternal life through your Son, Jesus Christ. May this assurance bring comfort to my heart and perspective to my sorrow. Help me to live in the light of this promise, trusting that your love endures beyond the boundaries of this world. Amen.

DAY 39

Embracing the Light of the World

SCRIPTURE: *John 8:12 - "Again Jesus spoke to them, saying, 'I am the light of the world. Whoever follows me will not walk in darkness, but will have the light of life."*

DEVOTIONAL: In times of grief, when darkness seems to envelop us, Jesus offers the profound declaration in John 8:12 that He is the light of the world. Whoever follows Him will not remain in darkness but will have the light of life.

Grief can cast shadows over our hearts, leaving us feeling lost and alone. Yet, in following Jesus, we discover a guiding light that leads us out of the darkness. His light not only illuminates our path but also infuses us with the light of life, offering hope and guidance even in the bleakest of moments.

PRAYER: Light of the World, in the midst of my grief, I turn to you for guidance and hope. Thank you for being the source of light that dispels the darkness of sorrow. May I follow you faithfully, knowing that in your light, I find life and renewed hope. Amen.

The Hope of a New Creation

SCRIPTURE: *Revelation 21:4 - "He will wipe away every tear from their eyes, and death shall be no more, neither shall there be mourning, nor crying, nor pain anymore, for the former things have passed away."*

DEVOTIONAL: On this journey of healing through grief, meditate on the promise found in Revelation 21:4. It paints a vivid picture of a future where God Himself wipes away every tear from our eyes. In this new creation, there will be no more death, mourning, crying, or pain, for the former things will have passed away.

Grief is a journey that can seem endless, but this scripture invites us to envision a future where sorrow is no more. God's promise of a new creation is a source of eternal hope, reminding us that the pain we endure in this life is temporary. Let this promise infuse you with renewed hope and the assurance that one day, all tears will be wiped away.

PRAYER: Heavenly Father, along this journey of healing through grief, I hold onto the promise of a new creation. Thank you for the hope of a future where sorrow will be no more. May this assurance sustain me in my moments of grief, reminding me that you are making all things new. Amen.

The Power of God's Word

SCRIPTURE: *Isaiah 40:8 - "The grass withers, the flower fades, but the word of our God will stand forever."*

DEVOTIONAL: In the ever-changing seasons of life, there is a profound solace to be found in the unchanging nature of God's Word. Isaiah beautifully captures this truth: "The grass withers, the flower fades," reminding us of the transitory nature of our world. But in the midst of this impermanence, there is an anchor of enduring strength—the Word of our God. It stands as an unwavering source of wisdom, comfort, and guidance.

God's Word is not confined by time or circumstance. It remains a constant, a foundation on which we can build our lives. In moments of grief and uncertainty, when everything else seems to crumble, the promises and truths found within the Scriptures remain resolute. They offer solace as we navigate life's unpredictable landscapes.

PRAYER: Heavenly Father, we are grateful for the constancy of Your Word. In a world of change, it is our rock and our refuge. As we face the challenges of life, may Your Word continue to bring solace to our hearts. Help us to find strength and comfort in the unchanging truths it holds. In Jesus' name, we pray. Amen.

DAY 42

Divine Guidance

SCRIPTURE: *Psalm 119:105 - "Your word is a lamp to my feet and a light to my path."*

DEVOTIONAL: In the darkest of nights, a single lamp can guide our steps and illuminate our path. Similarly, in the uncertainties of life, God's Word serves as a radiant light to guide our way. Psalm 119:105 reminds us of this truth, portraying His Word as a lamp that not only brightens the immediate path at our feet but also lights the broader journey ahead.

Seeking divine guidance is a humbling yet profound endeavor. It means acknowledging our need for direction and understanding that, in God's Word, we find answers to life's complex questions. When we turn to the Scriptures, we gain clarity and insight, much like a traveler using a lamp to navigate through darkness.

As you face the twists and turns of life, remember that God's Word is your constant companion, a dependable source of direction. In moments of confusion or doubt, take solace in the fact that His light is always there to lead you forward.

PRAYER: Heavenly Father, we thank You for the guiding light of Your Word. May it continue to shine brightly on our path, granting us wisdom and clarity in every step we take. Help us to seek Your guidance daily, knowing that in Your Word, we find the answers we need. In Jesus' name, we pray. Amen.

DAY 43

The Word of Healing

SCRIPTURE: *Proverbs 4:20-22 - "My son, be attentive to my words; incline your ear to my sayings... for they are life to those who find them, and healing to all their flesh."*

DEVOTIONAL: In times of distress, we often seek healing for our bodies and souls. Proverbs 4:20-22 reminds us that God's Word is a source of profound healing. It's not just a collection of words; it's life itself. When we attentively listen to His Word, we open ourselves to the healing power contained within it. His words bring comfort to the weary, strength to the weak, and restoration to the afflicted. Just as a skilled physician can mend a broken body, God's Word has the ability to mend our spirits and restore our well-being. In moments of distress, turn to His Word, for it holds the promise of healing for your body and soul.

PRAYER: Heavenly Father, in times of distress, we seek the healing power of Your Word. May Your words bring life and restoration to our weary souls and bodies. Incline our hearts to listen and grant us the healing we so desperately need. In Jesus' name, we pray. Amen.

DAY 44

Wisdom from Above

SCRIPTURE: *James 3:17 - "But the wisdom from above is first pure, then peaceable, gentle, open to reason, full of mercy and good fruits, impartial and sincere."*

DEVOTIONAL: In life's complex and often turbulent waters, we yearn for wisdom to navigate the challenges that come our way. James 3:17 reveals to us the nature of divine wisdom. This wisdom is unlike any other; it is pure, peaceable, gentle, open to reason, full of mercy, and marked by sincerity. It's a wisdom that provides not only solace but also a compass for our journey.

God's Word is a treasure trove of this heavenly wisdom. As we delve into His teachings, we find guidance for every aspect of our lives. His wisdom brings clarity to confusion, calm to chaos, and direction to uncertainty. In times of perplexity, we can trust that His Word offers not only solace but also the profound wisdom needed to make the right choices.

PRAYER: Heavenly Father, we seek the wisdom from above, which brings solace and clarity to our lives. May Your Word continue to guide us on this journey, offering us the heavenly wisdom we so desperately need. Help us to apply Your wisdom to our daily decisions and challenges. In Jesus' name, we pray. Amen.

DAY 45

The Bread of Life

SCRIPTURE: *John 6:35 – "Jesus said to them, 'I am the bread of life; whoever comes to me shall not hunger, and whoever believes in me shall never thirst.'"*

DEVOTIONAL: In our physical lives, we need sustenance to survive, and Jesus, in John 6:35, offers a profound parallel to our spiritual lives. He proclaims Himself as the "bread of life," the sustenance that nourishes our souls. Just as we hunger for physical food, our spirits hunger for the presence and teachings of Christ.

In God's Word, we find the spiritual nourishment we need. It satisfies the deep hunger and thirst within us, providing comfort, guidance, and solace. When we come to Jesus and believe in Him, we partake in the eternal banquet of His wisdom and love. As you meditate on His Word, may you find your spiritual hunger satisfied and your soul refreshed.

PRAYER: Lord Jesus, You are the bread of life, and in Your presence, we find sustenance for our souls. As we delve into Your Word, may it satisfy our deepest spiritual hunger and thirst. Nourish us daily with Your teachings and presence so that we may find solace and strength in You. In Your name, we pray. Amen.

A Refuge in Troubled Times

SCRIPTURE: *Psalm 46:1 - "God is our refuge and strength, a very present help in trouble."*

DEVOTIONAL: Life often presents us with moments of trouble, turmoil, and uncertainty. In these times, we yearn for a place of refuge, a source of strength to carry us through. Psalm 46:1 reminds us that God is our refuge and strength, an ever-present help in times of trouble. His Word serves as a sanctuary in which we find solace and shelter.

When life's storms rage, we can turn to the Scriptures for comfort and assurance. God's promises offer peace amid chaos and strength in the face of adversity. He is a refuge we can run to, a steadfast anchor in troubled waters. As you face the challenges of life, know that His Word provides a haven where you can find solace, strength, and unwavering support.

PRAYER: Heavenly Father, in times of trouble and uncertainty, we find refuge and strength in Your Word. May Your presence be a constant comfort and Your promises a source of unwavering strength. Help us to turn to You for solace and shelter in every trial we face. In Jesus' name, we pray. Amen.

The Comforter's Promises

SCRIPTURE: *John 14:26 - "But the Helper, the Holy Spirit, whom the Father will send in my name, he will teach you all things and bring to your remembrance all that I have said to you."*

DEVOTIONAL: In moments of need and confusion, we find solace in the promise of the Holy Spirit. John 14:26 reminds us that the Father has sent the Helper, the Holy Spirit, to be with us. This divine presence is our teacher, our guide, and our source of comfort.

God's Word reveals the profound promises of the Holy Spirit. Through His guidance, we gain understanding, wisdom, and the ability to recall Christ's teachings. He comforts us in our trials, reminding us of God's unfailing love and promises. As you meditate on Scripture, allow the promises of the Holy Spirit to bring you comfort, guidance, and a deep sense of God's abiding presence.

PRAYER: Heavenly Father, we are grateful for the promise of the Holy Spirit, our Helper and Comforter. May Your Word continue to reveal His promises to us, bringing comfort and guidance in our times of need. Help us to rely on His presence and teachings in our daily lives. In Jesus' name, we pray. Amen.

DAY 48

The Armour of God

SCRIPTURE: *Ephesians 6:17 – "And take the helmet of salvation, and the sword of the Spirit, which is the word of God."*

DEVOTIONAL: Life can sometimes feel like a battlefield, with challenges and trials testing our faith and resolve. Ephesians 6:17 introduces us to a powerful piece of spiritual armor—the sword of the Spirit, which is the word of God. In the midst of life's battles, this sword becomes our source of strength and protection.

God's Word serves as both our defense and our offense. It guards our minds, represented here by the helmet of salvation, and equips us with the sword of the Spirit to stand firm in our faith. When we immerse ourselves in Scripture, we wield the weapon of truth, capable of cutting through doubt, fear, and falsehood. It's not just a passive defense; it's an active tool for spiritual warfare.

PRAYER: Heavenly Father, thank You for the spiritual armor You provide, including the sword of the Spirit, which is Your Word. Help us to equip ourselves daily, drawing strength and guidance from Your Scriptures. May we use the truth of Your Word to defend our faith and overcome the challenges we face. In Jesus' name, we pray. Amen.

A Lamp Unto My Feet

SCRIPTURE: *Psalm 119:105 - "Your word is a lamp to my feet and a light to my path."*

DEVOTIONAL: Life's journey often leads us through shadowy valleys and uncertain terrain. In such moments, we yearn for light to guide our way. Psalm 119:105 reassures us that God's Word is that guiding light, a lamp that illuminates our path, dispelling the darkness and uncertainty.

As you navigate life's twists and turns, remember that God's Word offers clarity, direction, and solace. It not only lights the path immediately before you but also reveals the broader journey ahead. In times of confusion, His Word serves as a steadfast guide. It shows you where to step and how to navigate life's challenges. Allow His Word to be a radiant light that brightens your path, providing comfort and guidance along the way.

PRAYER: Heavenly Father, we thank You for Your Word, which serves as a lamp to our feet and a light to our path. In times of darkness and uncertainty, may Your Word illuminate our way, providing clarity and direction. Help us to trust in Your guidance and to walk confidently in the light of Your truth. In Jesus' name, we pray. Amen.

Finding Peace in God's Promises

SCRIPTURE: *Isaiah 26:3 - "You keep him in perfect peace whose mind is stayed on you because he trusts in you."*

DEVOTIONAL: In a world filled with turmoil and anxiety, we yearn for peace that transcends our circumstances. Isaiah 26:3 reminds us that perfect peace is found in God when our minds are steadfastly focused on Him, rooted in trust.

God's promises, as revealed in His Word, offer a profound source of peace. They reassure us of His presence, His love, and His faithfulness, regardless of the storms we face. As you immerse yourself in Scripture, let His promises become an anchor for your soul, a reminder that even in the midst of chaos, you can find peace by trusting in Him.

PRAYER: Heavenly Father, we seek the perfect peace that comes from keeping our minds steadfastly focused on You and Your promises. May Your Word be a source of unshakable peace in our lives, reminding us of Your unwavering love and faithfulness. In moments of turmoil, help us to trust in You and find the tranquillity that only You can provide. In Jesus' name, we pray. Amen.

DAY 51

Unwavering Love

SCRIPTURE: *Psalm 119:76 - "Let your steadfast love comfort me according to your promise to your servant."*

DEVOTIONAL: Life often brings us moments of longing for comfort and solace. In Psalm 119:76, we see a plea for God's steadfast love to be a source of comfort in accordance with His promises.

God's Word is filled with promises of His unwavering love and comfort. When we turn to His Word, we discover that His love is a steadfast anchor in the storms of life. His promises assure us that we are never alone and that His love will always be there to provide solace and strength. As you meditate on His Word, allow His steadfast love to bring you the comfort and assurance you seek.

PRAYER: Heavenly Father, we thank You for Your steadfast love and the comfort it brings. May Your promises, found in Your Word, be a source of reassurance and strength in our times of need. Help us to rely on Your unwavering love as we navigate life's challenges. In Jesus' name, we pray. Amen.

The Healing Word

SCRIPTURE: *Psalm 107:20 – "He sent out his word and healed them, and delivered them from their destruction."*

DEVOTIONAL: In times of pain and suffering, we long for healing and deliverance. Psalm 107:20 reveals the profound healing power of God's Word. His Word goes forth, bringing healing and rescue to those in distress.

God's Word is a balm for our wounded souls and bodies. It carries within it the power to mend, restore, and rescue us from the depths of suffering. As you immerse yourself in Scripture, remember that His Word is not just a collection of verses but a source of healing and deliverance. Let His Word be the salve that soothes your wounds and the light that guides you out of destruction.

PRAYER: Heavenly Father, we are grateful for the healing power of Your Word. In times of pain and suffering, may Your Word go forth to heal and deliver us. Bring restoration to our wounded hearts and bodies and guide us out of destruction. We trust in Your Word's power to bring healing and hope. In Jesus' name, we pray. Amen.

Strength in Weakness

SCRIPTURE: *2 Corinthians 12:9 – "My grace is sufficient for you, for my power is made perfect in weakness."*

DEVOTIONAL: In moments of weakness, we often seek strength beyond our own. 2 Corinthians 12:9 reminds us that God's grace is sufficient, and His power shines brightest in our weakness.

God's Word is a testament to His grace and strength. It reassures us that when we are at our lowest, His grace lifts us up, and His strength becomes evident. In times of struggle, His Word reminds us that we need not rely solely on our own power. Instead, we can draw upon His unending grace, finding the strength to endure, overcome, and grow through our weaknesses.

PRAYER: Heavenly Father, in our moments of weakness, we find strength in Your abundant grace. May Your Word continue to remind us of Your power made perfect in our frailty. Help us to lean on Your grace, knowing that it is sufficient for every trial we face. In Jesus' name, we pray. Amen.

DAY 54

Abiding in God's Love

SCRIPTURE: *John 15:9 - "As the Father has loved me, so have I loved you. Abide in my love."*

DEVOTIONAL: God's love is a profound source of solace and security. In John 15:9, Jesus invites us to abide in His love, a love that mirrors the boundless love of the Father.

God's Word is a testament to His love. It reminds us that His love is constant, unwavering, and unconditional. As we immerse ourselves in His Word, we find solace in the knowledge that we are deeply loved by our Creator. His love provides comfort, assurance, and a sense of belonging. It is a refuge we can turn to in times of need, a love that offers unwavering support.

PRAYER: Heavenly Father, we are grateful for the love You offer us, as demonstrated in Your Word. May Your love be a source of solace and security in our lives. Help us to abide in Your love, finding comfort and strength in the knowledge that we are deeply cherished by You. In Jesus' name, we pray. Amen.

The Path of Righteousness

SCRIPTURE: *Psalm 23:3 – "He restores my soul. He leads me in paths of righteousness for his name's sake."*

DEVOTIONAL: Life's journey can often lead us through challenging terrain, where our souls yearn for restoration and guidance. In Psalm 23:3, we find solace in the assurance that God restores our souls and leads us along the paths of righteousness.

God's Word is a map for this journey, offering guidance and comfort. When we seek His leading, He restores our weary souls and directs us in the way of righteousness. As you immerse yourself in Scripture, trust that God is your faithful guide, leading you in the paths that honor His name. His presence and Word are sources of restoration and righteous living.

PRAYER: Heavenly Father, we thank You for the restoration and guidance You provide. May Your Word be our compass, leading us along paths of righteousness for Your name's sake. Restore our souls, Lord, and lead us in Your ways. In Jesus' name, we pray. Amen.

The Assurance of Salvation

SCRIPTURE: *Romans 8:38-39 – "For I am sure that neither death nor life...nor anything else in all creation, will be able to separate us from the love of God in Christ Jesus our Lord."*

DEVOTIONAL: In life's uncertainties, we long for assurance, especially in matters of faith and salvation. Romans 8:38-39 assures us that nothing—neither death nor life nor anything else in all creation—can separate us from the love of God in Christ Jesus our Lord.

God's Word is a steadfast anchor for our souls, providing unwavering assurance of His love and our eternal security in Him. As you engage with His Word, take solace in the unbreakable bond you have with God. No matter

the trials you face, His love remains constant, and His promises of salvation
are sure.

PRAYER: Heavenly Father, we find deep assurance and solace in Your unbreakable love. Your Word reminds us that nothing can separate us from Your
love in Christ Jesus. Help us to cling to this truth, finding comfort and
strength in our unshakable bond with You. In Jesus' name, we pray. Amen.

DAY 57

The Rock of Our Salvation

SCRIPTURE: *Psalm 18:2 - "The Lord is my rock and my fortress and my deliverer,
my God, my rock, in whom I take refuge, my shield, and the horn of my salvation, my stronghold."*

DEVOTIONAL: Life can be turbulent, and in the midst of storms, we seek refuge
and stability. Psalm 18:2 beautifully portrays God as our unshakable rock,
fortress, and deliverer.

God's Word is a testament to His steadfastness and reliability. As we delve
into His Word, we discover that He is the unchanging foundation upon
which we can build our lives. He is our refuge and stronghold in times of
trouble. When the world around us feels uncertain, His Word reminds us
that we can find security and stability in Him.

PRAYER: Heavenly Father, we thank You for being our rock and refuge. In
times of uncertainty, help us to anchor ourselves in Your Word and find
stability in Your unchanging nature. May Your Word continue to be our
source of strength and confidence. In Jesus' name, we pray. Amen.

The God of All Comfort

SCRIPTURE: *2 Corinthians 1:3 - "Blessed be the God and Father of our Lord Jesus Christ, the Father of mercies and God of all comfort."*

DEVOTIONAL: In times of distress and sorrow, we yearn for comfort. 2 Corinthians 1:3 reminds us that God is the source of all comfort and mercy.

God's Word is a treasure trove of His comforting presence. It reassures us that He is the Father of mercies and the One who provides solace beyond measure. As you engage with His Word, let His comforting presence wash over you, filling your heart with peace and assurance. In every trial and tribulation, remember that you can find true and lasting comfort in God, as revealed in His Word.

PRAYER: Heavenly Father, we praise You as the God of all comfort. May Your Word be a source of solace and peace in our lives. In times of distress, help us to turn to You, knowing that Your comfort surpasses all understanding. We seek refuge in Your loving arms. In Jesus' name, we pray. Amen.

DAY 59

The Light in the Darkness

SCRIPTURE: *Psalm 27:1 - "The Lord is my light and my salvation; whom shall I fear? The Lord is the stronghold of my life; of whom shall I be afraid?"*

DEVOTIONAL: In the darkest moments of life, we yearn for a glimmer of hope. Psalm 27:1 reminds us that the Lord is our light and salvation, a fortress that dispels fear.

God's Word is a beacon of hope in times of darkness. It reassures us that we need not be afraid because the Lord is our steadfast protector. As you immerse yourself in His Word, remember that His presence is the light that banishes fear. With Him as our stronghold, we can face any challenge with courage and hope.

PRAYER: Heavenly Father, we thank You for being our light and salvation. In moments of darkness and fear, help us to turn to Your Word, finding hope and courage in Your presence. May we live without fear, knowing that You are our unfailing protector. In Jesus' name, we pray. Amen.

DAY 60

The Shelter in the Storm

SCRIPTURE: *Psalm 91:2 – "I will say to the Lord, 'My refuge and my fortress, my God, in whom I trust.'"*

DEVOTIONAL: Life's storms can be relentless, and we seek a place of refuge. Psalm 91:2 affirms that the Lord is our refuge and fortress, the One in whom we can trust.

God's Word is an enduring testament to His faithfulness as our shelter in life's storms. It reminds us that, in Him, we find a safe haven. As you engage with His Word, allow it to strengthen your trust in God as your refuge. When the winds of adversity blow and the rains of trials pour, remember that He is your fortress, offering protection and peace.

PRAYER: Heavenly Father, we declare that You are our refuge and fortress, our trustworthy God. In the midst of life's storms, help us to find shelter and peace in Your presence. May Your Word continually remind us of Your faithfulness as our refuge. In Jesus' name, we pray. Amen.

The Fountain of Living Water

SCRIPTURE: *John 4:14 – "But whoever drinks of the water that I will give him will never be thirsty again. The water that I will give him will become in him a spring of water welling up to eternal life."*

DEVOTIONAL: In the parched moments of life, we long for something to quench our spiritual thirst. John 4:14 reminds us that in Christ, we find living water that satisfies our deepest needs and offers eternal life.

God's Word is a wellspring of this living water. As you delve into His Word, consider the refreshment and renewal it offers. Just as a spring continually bubbles up with life-giving water, Christ's presence in our lives nourishes us and leads to eternal life. His Word is an invitation to drink deeply from His well of grace and find lasting satisfaction.

PRAYER: Heavenly Father, we thank You for the living water that Christ offers. May Your Word remind us of the refreshment and renewal found in Him. Help us to continually drink from this well of grace and experience the satisfaction that leads to eternal life. In Jesus' name, we pray. Amen.

The Anchor of Our Hope

SCRIPTURE: *Psalm 42:11 – "Why are you cast down, O my soul, and why are you in turmoil within me? Hope in God; for I shall again praise him, my salvation and my God."*

DEVOTIONAL: Life can often leave us feeling cast down and in turmoil. Psalm 42:11 reminds us to place our hope in God, finding solace in His Word as we await His salvation.

God's Word is our anchor in times of turmoil. It speaks of hope and restoration, even in the midst of trials. As you immerse yourself in His Word, let it be a lifeline that steadies your soul. In the face of adversity, remember to put your hope in God, for He is your salvation and your refuge.

PRAYER: Heavenly Father, when our souls are troubled, help us to find solace in Your Word. May it be an anchor of hope that keeps us steady in the midst of life's storms. We place our trust in You, our salvation, and our God. In Jesus' name, we pray. Amen.

DAY 63

The God of Comfort

SCRIPTURE: *2 Corinthians 1:4 - "Who comforts us in all our affliction, so that we may be able to comfort those who are in any affliction, with the comfort with which we ourselves are comforted by God."*

DEVOTIONAL: Life often brings afflictions that weigh heavy on our hearts. In 2 Corinthians 1:4, we find solace in the God who comforts us in our afflictions and equips us to comfort others.

God's Word is a testament to His comforting presence in our lives. As you engage with His Word, consider the comfort it provides, knowing that the same comfort empowers you to be a source of solace for others. In times of affliction, remember that God's comfort is not only for you but also a gift you can share, uplifting those who face trials.

PRAYER: Heavenly Father, we thank You for being the God of comfort. May Your Word remind us of the solace You provide in our afflictions. Help us to be vessels of Your comfort, offering support and empathy to those in need. In Jesus' name, we pray. Amen.

The Joy of the Lord

SCRIPTURE: *Nehemiah 8:10 - "...the joy of the Lord is your strength."*

DEVOTIONAL: Life can be draining, and we often seek strength to carry on. Nehemiah 8:10 reminds us that the joy of the Lord is our source of strength.

God's Word is filled with reasons for joy. As you immerse yourself in His Word, consider the joy that comes from knowing the Lord. It is a profound source of strength, lifting us up in difficult times. In moments of weariness, let the joy of the Lord be your solace and fortification.

PRAYER: Heavenly Father, we find strength and solace in Your joy. As we engage with Your Word, may the joy of knowing You lift our spirits and provide the strength we need for each day. In times of weariness, remind us of the joy that is our anchor. In Jesus' name, we pray. Amen.

The Anchor of Hope

SCRIPTURE: *Hebrews 6:19 - "We have this as a sure and steadfast anchor of the soul, a hope that enters into the inner place behind the curtain..."*

DEVOTIONAL: In the turbulent sea of life, we yearn for something unshakable to anchor our souls. Hebrews 6:19 speaks of hope as a steadfast anchor that reaches beyond the veil.

God's Word offers this hope as an unwavering source of solace. As you delve into His Word, consider the profound hope found in Christ. It's an anchor for your soul, unyielding in the face of life's storms. When uncertainty abounds, let this hope be your refuge and strength.

PRAYER: Heavenly Father, we are grateful for the steadfast hope found in Christ. May Your Word continually remind us of this unshakable anchor for our souls. In times of turbulence, help us to find solace and strength in the hope that transcends all understanding. In Jesus' name, we pray. Amen.

The Power of Prayer

SCRIPTURE: *Philippians 4:6-7 - "Do not be anxious about anything, but in everything by prayer and supplication with thanksgiving let your requests be made known to God. And the peace of God, which surpasses all understanding, will guard your hearts and your minds in Christ Jesus."*

DEVOTIONAL: In times of anxiety and worry, we turn to prayer for solace. Philippians 4:6-7 reminds us that through prayer, we find a peace that transcends understanding.

God's Word affirms the power of prayer as a source of solace and peace. As you engage with His Word, consider the comfort that comes from laying your concerns before Him in prayer. It's a peace that stands guard over your heart and mind, even in the midst of life's storms.

PRAYER: Heavenly Father, we thank You for the incredible power of prayer. May Your Word remind us of the solace and peace that come from placing our worries in Your hands. In moments of anxiety, help us to turn to You in prayer, experiencing the peace that surpasses all understanding. In Jesus' name, we pray. Amen.

The Comfort of Community

SCRIPTURE: *1 Thessalonians 5:11 - "Therefore encourage one another and build one another up, just as you are doing."*

DEVOTIONAL: Life's burdens can feel lighter when we have a supportive community. 1 Thessalonians 5:11 emphasizes the importance of encouragement and building each other up.

God's Word reminds us of the comfort and solace found in the community. As you engage with His Word, reflect on the strength that comes from caring relationships. In times of need, lean on your community for support and be a source of comfort to others.

PRAYER: Heavenly Father, we are grateful for the comfort of the community. May Your Word remind us of the solace found in encouraging and supporting one another. In moments of difficulty, help us to be both recipients and givers of comfort within our community. In Jesus' name, we pray. Amen.

DAY 68

The Beauty of Creation

SCRIPTURE: *Psalm 19:1 - "The heavens declare the glory of God, and the sky above proclaims his handiwork."*

DEVOTIONAL: Amid life's challenges, the beauty of creation often offers solace and awe. Psalm 19:1 reminds us that the heavens proclaim the glory of God.

God's Word directs our attention to the splendor of His creation. As you immerse yourself in His Word, take time to reflect on the solace and inspiration found in the natural world. In moments of weariness, find comfort in the beauty that surrounds you, a testament to the Creator's handiwork.

PRAYER: Heavenly Father, we find solace and awe in the beauty of Your creation. May Your Word remind us of the wonder found in the world You've crafted. In moments of weariness, help us to take refuge in the beauty that declares Your glory. In Jesus' name, we pray. Amen.

The Gift of Grace

SCRIPTURE: *Ephesians 2:8 - "For by grace you have been saved through faith. And this is not your own doing; it is the gift of God..."*

DEVOTIONAL: In times of reflection, we often find solace in God's unmerited grace. Ephesians 2:8 reminds us that we are saved by grace, a precious gift from God.

God's Word emphasizes the beauty of His grace. As you engage with His Word, ponder the comfort and gratitude that come from knowing His grace. In moments of doubt or struggle, remember that His grace is a gift that brings solace and salvation.

PRAYER: Heavenly Father, we are grateful for the gift of Your grace. May Your Word remind us of the solace and gratitude found in this unmerited favor. In moments of uncertainty, help us to rest in Your grace, knowing that it is a source of salvation and comfort. In Jesus' name, we pray. Amen.

The Love That Never Fails

SCRIPTURE: *1 Corinthians 13:8 - "Love never ends..."*

DEVOTIONAL: In moments of uncertainty, we often seek solace in the assurance of love. 1 Corinthians 13:8 declares that love never ends.

God's Word reassures us of the enduring love of our Creator. As you immerse yourself in His Word, contemplate the comfort and security found in His unfailing love. In times of doubt or fear, remember that God's love is a constant presence, offering solace and assurance.

PRAYER: Heavenly Father, we find solace and assurance in Your unfailing love. May Your Word remind us of the constancy of Your love, which never ends. In moments of doubt or fear, help us to rest in Your love, knowing it is a source of everlasting comfort. In Jesus' name, we pray. Amen.

The Power of Forgiveness

SCRIPTURE: *Colossians 3:13 – "Bearing with one another and, if one has a complaint against another, forgiving each other; as the Lord has forgiven you, so you also must forgive."*

DEVOTIONAL: In the journey of healing, forgiveness holds remarkable power. Colossians 3:13 reminds us of the liberating command to forgive as the Lord has forgiven us.

God's Word teaches us about the transformative power of forgiveness. As you immerse yourself in His Word, reflect on the solace and freedom found in letting go of grudges and extending forgiveness. In times of hurt or bitterness, remember that forgiveness is a path to healing and peace.

PRAYER: Heavenly Father, we acknowledge the profound power of forgiveness in our healing journey. May Your Word remind us of the solace and liberation that come from forgiving others as You have forgiven us. In moments of hurt or anger, help us to choose the path of forgiveness, experiencing the healing it brings. In Jesus' name, we pray. Amen.

The Comfort of God's Presence

SCRIPTURE: *Psalm 16:11 – "You make known to me the path of life; in your presence there is fullness of joy; at your right hand are pleasures forevermore."*

DEVOTIONAL: Amid life's challenges, we find solace in the promise of God's presence. Psalm 16:11 reveals that in His presence, there is fullness of joy.

God's Word assures us of the comfort and fulfillment found in His presence. As you engage with His Word, reflect on the joy that comes from being near Him. In times of loneliness or despair, remember that God's presence is a source of unending joy and solace.

PRAYER: Heavenly Father, we find comfort in the assurance of Your presence.

May Your Word remind us of the joy and fulfillment found in being close to You. In moments of loneliness or despair, help us to seek Your presence, knowing that it is a wellspring of solace and joy. In Jesus' name, we pray. Amen.

DAY 73

The Assurance of God's Providence

SCRIPTURE: *Romans 8:28 - "And we know that in all things God works for the good of those who love him, who have been called according to his purpose."*

DEVOTIONAL: In times of uncertainty, we seek solace in the assurance of God's providence. Romans 8:28 affirms that in all things, God is working for the good of those who love Him.

God's Word offers us the comforting knowledge that His providence is at work in every circumstance. As you immerse yourself in His Word, reflect on the solace found in knowing that God's purpose is unfolding, even in challenging times. In moments of doubt or confusion, remember that God's providence is a source of reassurance and peace.

PRAYER: Heavenly Father, we find solace in the assurance of Your providence. May Your Word remind us that You work for the good of those who love You, even in challenging circumstances. In moments of doubt or confusion, help us to trust in Your unfolding purpose, finding solace in Your divine plan. In Jesus' name, we pray. Amen.

The Comfort of Knowing God

SCRIPTURE: *Jeremiah 9:24 - "But let him who boasts boast in this, that he understands and knows me, that I am the Lord who practices steadfast love, justice, and righteousness in the earth..."*

DEVOTIONAL: Jeremiah 9:24 invites us to boast in our understanding and knowledge of the Lord, who exemplifies steadfast love, justice, and righteousness.

God's Word reveals the depth of His character. As you immerse yourself in His Word, reflect on the profound comfort that arises from truly knowing God. In moments of challenge or distress, remember that knowing Him intimately is a wellspring of enduring solace.

PRAYER: Heavenly Father, we take comfort in the knowledge of Your character, characterized by steadfast love, justice, and righteousness. May Your Word continually draw us into a deeper understanding and knowing of You. In moments of challenge or distress, help us to find enduring solace in the richness of our relationship with You. In Jesus' name, we pray. Amen.

DAY 75

The God Who Hears

SCRIPTURE: *Psalm 34:17 - "When the righteous cry for help, the Lord hears and delivers them out of all their troubles."*

DEVOTIONAL: Psalm 34:17 reminds us that when the righteous cry for help, the Lord hears and delivers them from all their troubles.

God's Word assures us of His attentive ear. As you delve into His Word, reflect on the solace found in knowing that God hears our cries. In moments of distress or despair, remember that God is the one who listens and delivers, offering us comfort and peace.

PRAYER: Heavenly Father, we take solace in the knowledge that You are the God who hears our cries for help. Your Word reminds us that You deliver us from troubles. In moments of distress or despair, help us to trust in Your attentive and caring presence. May we find comfort and peace in the assurance of Your response. In Jesus' name, we pray. Amen.

DAY 76

The Refuge in Times of Trouble

SCRIPTURE: *Nahum 1:7 - "The Lord is good, a refuge in times of trouble. He cares for those who trust in him."*

DEVOTIONAL: Nahum 1:7 beautifully reminds us that the Lord is not just good but also a refuge in times of trouble. He extends His caring hand to those who place their trust in Him.

God's Word reveals His nature as our safe haven. As you explore His Word, reflect on the immense comfort of finding refuge in God during life's storms. In times of trouble, may you find solace in the loving embrace of your Heavenly Father.

PRAYER: Gracious God, Your Word assures us that You are our refuge in times of trouble. We find great comfort in the knowledge that You care for those who trust in You. In moments of uncertainty or distress, may we find refuge in Your loving presence and trust in Your care. In Jesus' name, we pray. Amen.

DAY 77

The Source of True Comfort

SCRIPTURE: *2 Corinthians 1:3-4 - "Blessed be the God and Father of our Lord Jesus Christ, the Father of mercies and God of all comfort, who comforts us in all our affliction..."*

DEVOTIONAL: Amidst life's trials and tribulations, we often seek comfort from various sources, but 2 Corinthians 1:3-4 reminds us that true comfort originates from the Father of mercies and God of all comfort.

As you journey through the pages of His Word, consider the profound solace found in recognizing God as the ultimate source of comfort. In moments of distress, may you turn to Him, finding reassurance and peace in His everlasting care.

PRAYER: Heavenly Father, we acknowledge You as the ultimate source of true comfort. In times of trial, may we find solace in Your unwavering love and care. Help us to turn to You as our refuge and receive the comfort that only You can provide. In Jesus' name, we pray. Amen.

DAY 78

The Promise of Peace

SCRIPTURE: *Isaiah 26:3 - "You keep him in perfect peace whose mind is stayed on you, because he trusts in you."*

DEVOTIONAL: Isaiah 26:3 speaks of the perfect peace that envelops those whose minds are steadfastly fixed on God, rooted in trust.

As you immerse yourself in God's Word, consider the profound solace that can be found in the promise of perfect peace. In a world often filled with turmoil and uncertainty, may you find tranquillity in trusting the One who offers peace beyond understanding.

PRAYER: Gracious God, Your Word assures us of perfect peace when our trust is in You. In moments of turmoil and uncertainty, help us anchor our minds on You. May Your peace, which surpasses all understanding, guard our hearts and minds. In Jesus' name, we pray. Amen.

DAY 79

The Healing Touch of God

SCRIPTURE: *Psalm 147:3 - "He heals the brokenhearted and binds up their wounds."*

DEVOTIONAL: Psalm 147:3 reminds us of the tender care of our Heavenly Father, who not only heals the brokenhearted but also binds up their wounds.

In your journey through God's Word, reflect on the deep solace found in His healing touch. Just as a loving parent comforts a wounded child, God cares for His children with boundless compassion. In moments of pain and brokenness, may you find comfort in knowing that His healing touch is always near.

PRAYER: Heavenly Father, Your Word reassures us that You heal the brokenhearted and bind up their wounds. In times of hurt and pain, may we experience Your comforting touch and find solace in Your love. Heal our wounds, Lord, and restore us. In Jesus' name, we pray. Amen.

The Strength to Endure

SCRIPTURE: *1 Corinthians 10:13 – "No temptation has overtaken you that is not common to man. God is faithful, and he will not let you be tempted beyond your ability, but with the temptation, he will also provide the way of escape, that you may be able to endure it."*

DEVOTIONAL: Life often presents challenges that seem overwhelming. During these moments, it's easy to feel alone in our struggles. However, 1 Corinthians 10:13 reminds us that our trials are not unique; they are shared by humanity. What brings solace is God's unwavering faithfulness. He knows our limits, weaknesses, and fears. He promises not to let us face more than we can bear.

Moreover, this scripture assures us that God provides a way out of our difficulties. This doesn't always mean an escape from the situation itself, but rather, a path guided by His grace and strength. It's a way to endure and overcome the trials that confront us.

Reflect on times when you've felt overwhelmed by grief, loss, or adversity. In those moments, God's faithfulness sustained you. He gave you the strength to endure and emerge stronger.

PRAYER: Heavenly Father, we're grateful for Your unfailing faithfulness. In times of weakness, help us remember that You are with us, offering the strength to endure and overcome. We find solace in Your love. In Jesus' name, we pray. Amen.

The God Who Restores

SCRIPTURE: *Joel 2:25 – "I will restore to you the years that the swarming locust has eaten, the hopper, the destroyer, and the cutter, my great army, which I sent among you."*

DEVOTIONAL: Life often takes us through seasons of loss and devastation, leaving us feeling as if precious time has been stolen from us. Yet, Joel 2:25 offers a powerful promise of restoration. The imagery of locusts devouring everything in their path serves as a metaphor for life's challenges that seem to consume our years of joy and peace.

God assures us that He is the ultimate restorer. Even in the face of trials that have left us broken and weary, He can renew what was lost. His grace and power have the ability to mend the broken pieces of our lives and breathe new life into them.

As you reflect on your journey through grief, remember that God is the great Restorer. In His time, He can transform the years of sorrow into seasons of joy and abundance.

PRAYER: Heavenly Father, we come before You with gratitude for Your promise of restoration. In times of loss and sorrow, help us trust in Your power to renew our lives and bring joy from our pain. May Your restoration work be evident in our hearts. In Jesus' name, we pray. Amen.

The Blessing of God's Presence

SCRIPTURE: *Exodus 33:14 - "And he said, 'My presence will go with you, and I will give you rest.'"*

DEVOTIONAL: In the midst of grief and the trials of life, we often long for a sense of rest and reassurance. Exodus 33:14 reminds us of God's promise to be with us and grant us rest through His abiding presence.

The journey of grief can be exhausting, both physically and emotionally. We may feel overwhelmed and burdened, but God offers us solace. His presence is our refuge, a safe haven where we can find rest for our weary souls. In His company, there is comfort and peace that surpasses understanding.

Take a moment today to dwell on the assurance of God's presence. In His nearness, there is rest for your heart, peace for your mind, and strength for your spirit. Embrace the blessing of His company as you navigate the landscape of grief.

PRAYER: Heavenly Father, we thank You for the promise of Your presence and the rest it brings. In the midst of our grief and struggles, help us to feel Your nearness and find solace in Your embrace. Grant us the strength to continue on this journey with You by our side. In Jesus' name, we pray. Amen.

The God Who Gives Strength

SCRIPTURE: *Psalm 28:7 - "The Lord is my strength and my shield; in him my heart trusts, and I am helped; my heart exults, and with my song I give thanks to him."*

DEVOTIONAL: In the midst of grief, we often find ourselves feeling weak and vulnerable. Yet, Psalm 28:7 reminds us that the Lord is not only our strength but also our shield. In Him, our hearts can find trust, help, and even the ability to rejoice.

When the weight of sorrow bears down upon us, we can turn to God, our unshakable source of strength. He doesn't just offer us physical or emotional fortitude; He also shields us from the full brunt of life's challenges. Trusting in Him means finding solace in His unwavering support and knowing that we are never alone in our trials.

Today, as you reflect on this verse, allow your heart to trust in the Lord's strength. Let His presence be your shield, and even in the midst of grief, may your heart find reason to exult and give thanks.

PRAYER: Heavenly Father, we come before You, acknowledging that You are our strength and our shield. In times of grief and weakness, help us to place our trust in You and find solace in Your presence. May our hearts exult and overflow with gratitude for Your unfailing love. In Jesus' name, we pray. Amen.

The Comforter's Presence

SCRIPTURE: *John 14:16 – "And I will ask the Father, and he will give you another Helper, to be with you forever."*

DEVOTIONAL: In our journey through grief, we often long for someone to come alongside us to offer comfort, understanding, and guidance. In John 14:16, Jesus promises the gift of the Holy Spirit, our Helper, who is with us always.

The Holy Spirit is not a distant, ethereal force; He is a present and loving companion, offering solace in our times of need. When we feel overwhelmed by the weight of sorrow, He brings the comfort only God can provide. He understands our pain intimately, interceding for us with groanings too deep for words (Romans 8:26).

As you reflect on this verse, remember that you are never alone in your grief. The Holy Spirit is your constant Helper, offering solace, strength, and guidance. Lean into His presence, and allow Him to bring you the comfort you need.

PRAYER: Heavenly Father, we thank You for the gift of the Holy Spirit, our Helper in times of grief. We find solace in His presence and the comfort He brings. Fill us with Your Spirit today so that we may be strengthened and guided through our journey. In Jesus' name, we pray. Amen.

The God of Compassion

SCRIPTURE: *Psalm 103:13 – "As a father shows compassion to his children, so the Lord shows compassion to those who fear him."*

DEVOTIONAL: In times of grief, it's easy to be hard on ourselves, expecting unwavering strength and unending faith. However, Psalm 103:13 reminds us of God's compassion, likening it to a father's love for his children.

God's compassion isn't contingent on our performance or the strength of our faith. It flows from His very nature. Just as a loving father tenderly cares for his children in their times of need, our Heavenly Father extends compassion to us in our grief. He understands our pain, our doubts, and our moments of weakness.

Today, find solace in the boundless compassion of God. Allow yourself to receive His love and care, just as a child receives comfort from a loving parent. And as you experience His compassion, extend it to yourself, knowing that it's okay to grieve and seek His comfort in your pain.

PRAYER: Heavenly Father, thank You for Your unending compassion. In times of grief, help us to receive Your love and kindness, knowing that Your compassion knows no bounds. Grant us the grace to extend this same compassion to ourselves and others. In Jesus' name, we pray. Amen.

DAY 86

The Joy of His Presence

SCRIPTURE: *Psalm 16:11 - "You make known to me the path of life; in your presence, there is fullness of joy; at your right hand are pleasures forevermore."*

DEVOTIONAL: In the depths of grief, joy might seem distant and unattainable. Yet, Psalm 16:11 reminds us that in God's presence, there is a fullness of joy. When we draw near to Him, we find solace not only in His comforting embrace but also in the joy that transcends our circumstances.

In your journey through grief, take moments to bask in the presence of the Lord. Seek Him through prayer, worship, or simply being still in His company. It's in these sacred moments that you can experience a joy that surpasses understanding. This joy isn't dependent on external happiness but is rooted in the unchanging character of God.

PRAYER: Heavenly Father, we thank You for the promise of joy found in Your presence. In times of grief, help us draw near to You and discover the fullness of joy that only You can provide. May this joy sustain us through our sorrows. In Jesus' name, we pray. Amen.

The Promise of Restoration

SCRIPTURE: *Joel 2:25 – "I will restore to you the years that the swarming locust has eaten, the hopper, the destroyer, and the cutter, my great army, which I sent among you."*

DEVOTIONAL: In times of grief, it can feel like life has been consumed by sorrow and loss, leaving you with a sense of emptiness. Yet, Joel 2:25 reminds us of God's promise of restoration. He is the master of rebuilding what has been broken, healing what has been wounded, and renewing what has been lost.

As you journey through the difficult terrain of grief, trust in God's ability to restore. Even when it seems like the locusts have devoured your years, God's redemptive power can breathe new life into your circumstances. He specializes in turning mourning into dancing and ashes into beauty.

PRAYER: Heavenly Father, we cling to Your promise of restoration in times of grief. You are the God who brings life from the ashes, and we trust in Your healing and renewal. Restore our hearts, our hope, and our joy, we pray. In Jesus' name, amen.

The God of All Comfort

SCRIPTURE: *2 Corinthians 1:3 – "Blessed be the God and Father of our Lord Jesus Christ, the Father of mercies and God of all comfort."*

DEVOTIONAL: In moments of grief, we long for comfort that transcends the temporary soothing of our pain. The words of 2 Corinthians 1:3 reveal to us that God is the ultimate source of all comfort. He is not just a comforter; He is the God of all comfort.

When we are overwhelmed by sorrow, it is essential to remember that God's comfort is abundant, unending, and perfectly tailored to our needs. He understands the depths of our grief, and His comforting presence is a balm for our wounded souls. In Him, we find solace that goes beyond human understanding.

PRAYER: Heavenly Father, we praise You as the God of all comfort. In our moments of grief, we seek Your comforting embrace. Wrap us in Your love, soothe our pain, and fill us with the peace that only You can provide. In Jesus' name, amen.

DAY 89

The Light in the Darkness

SCRIPTURE: *Psalm 27:1 - "The Lord is my light and my salvation; whom shall I fear? The Lord is the stronghold of my life; of whom shall I be afraid?"*

DEVOTIONAL: In times of darkness, when grief casts a long shadow over our hearts, it's easy to feel overwhelmed by fear and uncertainty. But the words of Psalm 27:1 remind us of the comforting truth that the Lord is our light and salvation.

Imagine a pitch-black night pierced by a radiant beam of light. That's the image of God's presence in our lives. He is the unwavering light that banishes the darkness of fear and doubt. In His light, we find not only hope but also salvation – a rescue from the depths of despair.

The Lord is also our stronghold, our refuge when grief's storms rage. When life feels fragile, He is our unshakable foundation. So, even in the darkest moments, remember that you are not alone. You have a Light that pierces the night, a Savior who brings hope, and a stronghold that stands firm. In Him, there's no need to be afraid.

PRAYER: Heavenly Father, You are our light and salvation. When grief surrounds us, and fear creeps in, help us to turn to You. May Your radiant presence dispel the darkness, and may we find our refuge and strength in You alone. In the name of Jesus, our Saviour, we pray. Amen.

The Shelter in the Storm

SCRIPTURE: *Psalm 91:1-2 - "He who dwells in the shelter of the Most High will abide in the shadow of the Almighty. I will say to the Lord, 'My refuge and my fortress, my God, in whom I trust.'"*

DEVOTIONAL: Life often presents us with storms—times of turmoil, uncertainty, and adversity. In these moments, we seek shelter, a place of safety and peace. Psalm 91 beautifully describes God as our shelter, our refuge, and our fortress.

Imagine a mighty fortress with towering walls impervious to the fiercest of storms. This is the image of God's protection and presence in our lives. When we dwell in the shelter of the Most High, we abide in His shadow, under His loving care. We can confidently declare, "My refuge and my fortress, my God, in whom I trust."

No matter how fierce the storm may be, when we place our trust in the Almighty, we find solace and security. God's shelter is not just a temporary hiding place; it's a dwelling, a place to reside continually. In Him, we discover the peace that surpasses all understanding, even in the midst of life's storms.

PRAYER: Heavenly Father, You are our shelter and fortress, a refuge in times of trouble. When life's storms rage, help us to trust in Your unwavering protection. May we find peace and solace in the shadow of Your presence. In Jesus' name, we pray. Amen.

The God Who Hears

SCRIPTURE: *Psalm 34:17 - "When the righteous cry for help, the Lord hears and delivers them out of all their troubles."*

DEVOTIONAL: In life's most challenging moments, when troubles surround us, and it feels like no one understands, there is a profound comfort in knowing that God hears our cries. Psalm 34:17 assures us that when the righteous cry for help, the Lord not only listens but also delivers them from all their troubles.

When we pour out our hearts to God, we're not just uttering words into the void; we're communicating with a God who cares deeply for us. He leans down from heaven to hear our cries, to understand our pain, and to offer His divine comfort. The troubles that seem insurmountable to us are under His sovereign control.

In the quiet moments of prayer, in the midst of tears and trials, remember that you have a God who not only listens but also responds. Find solace in the knowledge that He is working behind the scenes, orchestrating deliverance and transformation. As you cry out to Him today, trust that He hears, cares, and is moving on your behalf.

PRAYER: Heavenly Father, I thank You for being a God who hears my cries and delivers me from troubles. In my moments of despair, help me remember that You are with me, working all things together for my good. Grant me the peace that comes from knowing You are near. In Jesus' name, I pray. Amen.

The Source of True Comfort

SCRIPTURE: *Psalm 46:1 - "God is our refuge and strength, a very present help in trouble."*

DEVOTIONAL: In times of trouble, we often seek refuge and strength in various places – in friends, in distractions, in our own abilities. But Psalm 46:1 reminds us that the true source of refuge and strength is God Himself. He is not a distant deity but a very present help in our times of trouble.

When life's storms rage around us and we feel overwhelmed, God is our safe haven. He is our refuge, a place where we can find shelter and protection. In His presence, we discover a strength that goes beyond our own capabilities. It's a strength that carries us through even the most challenging circumstances.

So, as you face the trials of life, remember that you are not alone. God is with you, offering His refuge and strength. He is a very present help, ready to guide you through the storm. Find solace in the knowledge that in Him, you can weather any trouble that comes your way.

PRAYER: Heavenly Father, I thank You for being my refuge and strength, a very present help in times of trouble. In the midst of life's storms, help me turn to You for shelter and strength. May Your presence bring comfort and peace to my soul. In Jesus' name, I pray. Amen.

EMBRACING MEMORIES AND HEALING

DAY 93

Cherishing Memories

SCRIPTURE: *Psalm 77:11-12 - "I will remember the deeds of the Lord; yes, I will remember your wonders of old. I will ponder all your work, and meditate on your mighty deeds."*

DEVOTIONAL: Memories are the treasured keepsakes of our hearts, capturing the essence of our journey through life. In Psalm 77, the psalmist reminds us of the importance of remembering not only our own deeds but also the mighty works of the Lord. Our memories are like a mosaic of experiences, some joyful and others challenging, all contributing to the story of our lives.

As you reflect on your memories, take a moment to give thanks for the moments of grace, love, and strength that God has woven into your life. Cherish these memories, for they reveal the profound tapestry of His providence. Just as the psalmist ponders God's mighty deeds, may you find solace in the memories that affirm His presence and guidance.

PRAYER: Dear Lord, we thank You for the gift of memories, both the joyful and the challenging. Help us to remember Your mighty deeds in our lives, knowing that each memory is a testament to Your faithfulness. May our memories bring us comfort and inspiration as we journey through life with You. In Your name, we pray. Amen.

DAY 94

Letting Go of Regrets

SCRIPTURE: *Philippians 3:13 - "Brothers, I do not consider that I have made it my own. But one thing I do: forgetting what lies behind and straining forward to what lies ahead."*

DEVOTIONAL: Regrets can weigh heavy on our hearts, like anchors holding us back from embracing the future. Yet, as the apostle Paul reminds us in Philippians 3:13, our faith journey isn't about dwelling on past mistakes but about focusing on the path ahead.

God's grace offers us the incredible gift of forgiveness. When we confess our sins and ask for His forgiveness, He wipes the slate clean. It's as if He erases our regrets and replaces them with hope. As you reflect on your own regrets, remember that God's forgiveness is complete and unwavering. It's an invitation to release the burdens of the past and step forward into the promise of His grace.

PRAYER: Heavenly Father, we come before You burdened by our regrets. Help us, Lord, to fully accept Your forgiveness and let go of the mistakes and shortcomings that weigh us down. May we find solace in Your grace and, with hearts unburdened, strain forward toward the beautiful future You have prepared for us. In Jesus' name, we pray. Amen.

DAY 95

The Gift of Forgiveness

SCRIPTURE: *Colossians 3:14 – "And above all these put on love, which binds everything together in perfect harmony."*

DEVOTIONAL: Forgiveness is a profound act of love that brings harmony and healing to our lives. When we forgive, we release the grip of bitterness and resentment that can bind us. Colossians 3:14 reminds us that love is the thread that weaves together the torn fabric of relationships and hearts.

In forgiving others, we emulate the boundless love and forgiveness that God extends to us. It's not always easy, but it's a gift we can give not only to those who have wronged us but also to ourselves. Forgiveness sets us free from the weight of anger and hurt, allowing us to walk in the light of God's love.

PRAYER: Heavenly Father, Your love is our inspiration and model for forgiveness. Help us to let go of grudges and resentment, to extend grace and love to those who have wronged us, and to experience the healing power of forgiveness in our lives. May Your love bind us together in perfect harmony. In Jesus' name, we pray. Amen.

DAY 96

Redeeming the Past

SCRIPTURE: *Isaiah 43:19 - "Behold, I am doing a new thing, now it springs forth, do you not perceive it? I will make a way in the wilderness and rivers in the desert."*

DEVOTIONAL: It's a beautiful truth that God can bring new life from our past mistakes and failures. When we stumble, when we make wrong turns, God is there, offering us a chance to begin anew. Isaiah 43:19 reminds us that God is continually working, even in the wilderness moments of our lives. He makes a way where there seems to be no way and provides refreshment in our spiritual deserts.

Our past does not define our future when we walk with God. His grace is transformative, and He offers us a fresh start. Today, consider how God might be working in your life, redeeming your past and creating something new and beautiful from it.

PRAYER: Heavenly Father, we thank you for your promise to make all things new. Help us to let go of the weight of past mistakes and trust in your redemptive power. We look forward to the new beginnings you have in store for us. In Jesus' name, we pray. Amen.

DAY 97

Healing Through Gratitude

SCRIPTURE: *1 Thessalonians 5:18 - "Give thanks in all circumstances; for this is the will of God in Christ Jesus for you."*

DEVOTIONAL: Gratitude is a powerful balm for the wounded soul. In the midst of pain, sorrow, or regret, it might seem challenging to be thankful. Yet, 1 Thessalonians 5:18 reminds us that giving thanks, even in difficult circumstances, aligns with God's will for us.

When we express gratitude, we shift our focus from what we lack to the blessings we have. Gratitude has the remarkable ability to heal and restore, lifting our spirits and helping us see God's goodness even in the midst of trials. It doesn't mean we ignore our pain, but it allows us to find hope and comfort in the midst of it.

Today, try to find something, even something small, for which you can genuinely give thanks. Allow gratitude to be a healing salve, soothing your heart and drawing you closer to God.

PRAYER: Dear Lord, in both joy and sorrow, help us develop hearts of gratitude. Teach us to see the blessings that surround us, even in challenging times. May our thanksgiving bring healing and draw us closer to your loving presence. In Jesus' name, we pray. Amen.

DAY 98

Healing Broken Relationships

SCRIPTURE: *Matthew 5:23-24 - "So if you are offering your gift at the altar...first be reconciled to your brother, and then come and offer your gift."*

DEVOTIONAL: Broken relationships can be among the most painful experiences we face in life. Whether it's a family member, friend, or colleague, conflicts and misunderstandings can create deep wounds. Yet, in Matthew 5:23-24, Jesus provides a profound insight into healing these broken bonds.

He encourages us to prioritize reconciliation before offering our gifts at the altar. This means that repairing relationships takes precedence even over our religious duties. Why? Because God values the unity and love, we share with one another.

Reconciliation requires humility, forgiveness, and open communication. It's not always easy, but it's a path to healing that aligns with God's heart. Today, if you have broken relationships, consider taking the first step toward reconciliation. Reach out, listen, and seek understanding. As you do, you'll find God's healing grace working in your life and in your relationships.

PRAYER: Heavenly Father, grant us the wisdom and strength to reconcile with those we've had conflicts with. Help us to prioritize love and unity, following your example. May our actions reflect your grace and healing power in our relationships. In Jesus' name, we pray. Amen.

The Peace of Forgiving Yourself

SCRIPTURE: *Psalm 103:12 - "As far as the east is from the west, so far does he remove our transgressions from us."*

DEVOTIONAL: One of the most challenging forms of forgiveness is forgiving ourselves. Often, we cling to our past mistakes, letting guilt and shame define us. However, God's forgiveness is boundless and complete. As Psalm 103:12 beautifully puts it, God removes our sins "as far as the east is from the west."

Think about that for a moment. When you travel east, you never reach a point where you start heading west. It's an infinite separation. God's forgiveness is like that. Once He forgives us, our sins are eternally removed from us.

Today, embrace this truth and release the burdens of self-condemnation. Accept God's forgiveness with a grateful heart. Know that He not only forgives but also redeems and restores. As you forgive yourself, you'll find the peace that surpasses all understanding.

PRAYER: Heavenly Father, help us to fully grasp the depth of your forgiveness. Teach us to forgive ourselves, just as you have forgiven us. May your grace wash away our self-condemnation and fill our hearts with peace. In Jesus' name, we pray. Amen.

Reflecting on God's Faithfulness

SCRIPTURE: *Lamentations 3:22 – "The steadfast love of the Lord never ceases; his mercies never come to an end."*

DEVOTIONAL: Reaching this milestone reminds us of the faithfulness of our Heavenly Father. Just as Lamentations 3:22 proclaims, His steadfast love never ceases, and His mercies never run out. When we look back on the journey we've walked through these devotionals, we see a tapestry woven with threads of faith, hope, and healing.

Take a moment today to reflect on God's faithfulness in your life. Remember the times He lifted you out of despair, the moments when His Word brought comfort and the healing that His presence brought to your soul. Even in your grief and moments of weakness, His love never wavered.

As we look forward to the next leg of this journey, let's do so with hearts full of hope. God's faithfulness isn't just a theme in the past; it's a promise for the future. Whatever lies ahead, you can trust that His love and mercy will be there to guide and sustain you.

PRAYER: Heavenly Father, we thank you for your unwavering faithfulness. As we reflect on the past 100 days, we're reminded of your love and mercy. Help us to carry this assurance into the future, knowing that your faithfulness knows no end. In Jesus' name, we pray. Amen.

Healing from Loss

SCRIPTURE: *Psalm 34:18 - The Lord is near to the brokenhearted and saves the crushed in spirit.*

DEVOTIONAL: In the depths of loss and grief, it's often challenging to find solace. The pain can feel overwhelming, and it's in these moments that we need to remember Psalm 34:18. It reminds us that the Lord is near to the brokenhearted. His presence is a source of comfort, a steady hand to hold when our own strength falters.

Loss can leave us feeling crushed, as if our spirit is broken beyond repair. But here's the beautiful truth: God saves the crushed in spirit. He doesn't leave us in our brokenness. Instead, He offers healing, restoration, and the promise of a brighter tomorrow.

As you navigate the complex emotions of loss, take comfort in knowing that you're not alone. God is with you, ready to mend the pieces of your heart. His love is a balm for your wounded soul. In His presence, there is healing, hope, and the assurance that, though the night may be long, joy will come in the morning.

PRAYER: Heavenly Father, in times of loss and grief, we turn to you for comfort. We thank you for being near to the brokenhearted and for saving those who are crushed in spirit. Bring healing to our wounded hearts, Lord, and restore our hope. May we find solace in your loving presence. In Jesus' name, we pray. Amen.

Restoring Joy in Memories

SCRIPTURE: *Psalm 30:11 - "You have turned for me my mourning into dancing."*

DEVOTIONAL: Memories have a remarkable power to heal and restore. In our grief, it's easy to become overwhelmed by sadness, but as we reflect on cherished memories, we can find glimpses of joy even in the midst of mourning. Psalm 30:11 reminds us that God can transform our mourning into dancing. He takes our sorrow and, over time, replaces it with moments of happiness and gratitude for the times we shared with our loved ones. It's like finding treasures in the midst of a storm. These memories become a source of strength and healing.

Take time today to recall a cherished memory of your loved one. Embrace the joy it brings, knowing that God can use these moments to restore your spirit. Let the dance of gratitude replace the mourning of loss as you celebrate the love and joy that memory represents.

PRAYER: Gracious God, we thank you for the gift of cherished memories that bring joy even in times of grief. Help us to remember and celebrate the moments we shared with our loved ones. May these memories restore our spirits and bring healing to our hearts. In your loving presence, we find solace. Amen.

Learning from Past Mistakes

SCRIPTURE: *Proverbs 3:6 – "In all your ways acknowledge him, and he will make straight your paths."*

DEVOTIONAL: Life is a journey filled with experiences, both good and bad. Sometimes, we make mistakes along the way that bring us pain and regret. Yet, in those moments of reflection and humility, we have an opportunity to grow and learn.

Proverbs 3:6 encourages us to acknowledge God in all our ways. This means inviting His wisdom and guidance into every aspect of our lives, including acknowledging our mistakes. When we do this, we open ourselves to His grace and direction.

Learning from past mistakes is a sign of maturity and wisdom. It's an acknowledgment that we are not perfect, but we serve a God who offers forgiveness, guidance, and a path to healing. Take time today to reflect on a past mistake and the lessons you've learned from it. Ask God for His guidance in making better choices, and trust that He will make your path straight.

PRAYER: Heavenly Father, we acknowledge our past mistakes and seek your wisdom. Help us learn and grow from these experiences. Guide our steps and make our paths straight as we strive to make better choices. Thank you for your forgiveness and grace. In Jesus' name, we pray. Amen.

Renewing the Mind

SCRIPTURE: *Romans 12:2 - "Do not be conformed to this world, but be transformed by the renewal of your mind, that by testing you may discern what is the will of God, what is good and acceptable and perfect."*

DEVOTIONAL: Our minds are powerful instruments that can shape the course of our lives. They are where thoughts, beliefs, and perspectives take root. In today's fast-paced and often chaotic world, it's easy for our minds to become cluttered with worldly concerns and distractions.

Romans 12:2 urges us not to conform to the patterns of this world but to be transformed by renewing our minds. This renewal comes through prayer, meditation on God's Word, and seeking His wisdom. As we align our thoughts with God's truth, our perspective changes, and we gain clarity to discern His will.

Take time today to renew your mind. Reflect on scripture, meditate on God's promises, and pray for a transformed perspective. Ask God to guide your thoughts so you may better understand His will and live a life that is good, acceptable, and perfect in His sight.

PRAYER: Heavenly Father, we thank you for the power of transformation through renewing our minds with your Word. Help us not to be conformed to the patterns of this world but to seek your wisdom and understanding. Transform our thoughts and perspectives to align with your will. In Jesus' name, we pray. Amen.

The Healing Touch of Jesus

SCRIPTURE: *Mark 5:34 - "And he said to her, 'Daughter, your faith has made you well; go in peace, and be healed of your disease.'"*

DEVOTIONAL: In the Gospels, we encounter numerous accounts of people who were physically or spiritually healed by Jesus. One striking story is that of a woman who had suffered from a chronic illness for twelve years. She reached out to touch the fringe of Jesus' garment, believing that even a touch of His clothing would bring healing. Jesus, recognizing her faith, turned to her and said, "Daughter, your faith has made you well; go in peace and be healed of your disease." It was her faith in Jesus' healing power that made her whole.

This story reminds us that our faith in Jesus can bring healing and restoration. Just as this woman found physical healing through her faith, we, too, can find healing in Jesus. Whether we seek physical, emotional, or spiritual healing, Jesus invites us to come to Him in faith. Today, place your trust in Him and seek His healing touch in whatever areas of your life need restoration.

PRAYER: Lord Jesus, we come to you with our needs and concerns, seeking your healing touch. Just as the woman in the Gospels found healing through her faith, we trust that you can bring healing to our lives as well. Increase our faith, Lord, and grant us the peace that comes from knowing you are our healer. In your name, we pray. Amen.

Embracing Memories of God's Provision

SCRIPTURE: *Psalm 23:1 - "The Lord is my shepherd; I shall not want."*

DEVOTIONAL: The words of Psalm 23 remind us of God's unwavering provision and care throughout our lives. "The Lord is my shepherd; I shall not want." These simple yet profound words echo in the hearts of those who have walked with God, recounting His faithfulness. As we reflect on our memories, we can see countless instances where God provided for us, even in the midst of challenges. He is the shepherd who guides us through the valleys and leads us beside still waters. When we were in need, He was there. When we faced uncertainty, He provided clarity. When we were in despair, He brought comfort.

In embracing these memories of God's provision, we find peace and reassurance. We recognize that the same God who has been our shepherd in the past continues to lead and provide for us today and into the future. In gratitude, let us hold these memories close, knowing that we shall not want because our faithful Shepherd is with us.

PRAYER: Heavenly Father, we thank you for being our Shepherd and Provider. As we reflect on the memories of your provision in our lives, our hearts are filled with gratitude. Help us to trust you in all circumstances, knowing that you are faithful and that we shall not want. May our memories of your care bring us peace and assurance. In Jesus' name, we pray. Amen.

Embracing God's Healing Love

SCRIPTURE: *Isaiah 41:10 - "Fear not, for I am with you; be not dismayed, for I am your God; I will strengthen you, I will help you, I will uphold you with my righteous right hand."*

DEVOTIONAL: In moments of suffering and distress, we find solace in the loving embrace of our Heavenly Father. Isaiah 41:10 reminds us of God's unwavering presence and love, even in our most challenging times. "Fear not, for I am with you; be not dismayed, for I am your God; I will strengthen you, I will help you, I will uphold you with my righteous right hand." As we reflect on our journey through life, we can recall moments when God's healing love surrounded us, providing strength and comfort when we needed it most. In times of physical or emotional pain, His love has been our refuge. In the midst of uncertainty, His love has been our steady anchor. In moments of despair, His love has lifted us up.

Embrace the memories of God's healing love, for they remind us that we are never alone. The God who promises to strengthen, help, and uphold us is the same God who has carried us through every trial and will continue to do so. In His love, we find hope, restoration, and the assurance that we are cherished beyond measure.

PRAYER: Heavenly Father, your love is our refuge and strength. We thank you for the healing love that has carried us through difficult moments in our lives. As we reflect on these memories, may we find renewed hope and confidence in your abiding presence. Strengthen us, help us, and uphold us with your righteous right hand. In Jesus' name, we pray. Amen.

Trusting in God's Timing

SCRIPTURE: *Ecclesiastes 3:11 – "He has made everything beautiful in its time."*

DEVOTIONAL: In a world that often values speed and immediacy, God's timing can feel like a challenge. We might grow impatient, wondering why our prayers aren't answered, or our circumstances aren't changing as swiftly as we'd like. But in Ecclesiastes 3:11, we're reminded that God has a beautiful plan, and it unfolds in His perfect time.

Imagine a skilled artist working on a masterpiece. They don't rush through their creation; instead, they carefully choose each brushstroke, each color, and each detail to bring out the beauty of the painting. Likewise, God meticulously crafts the story of our lives. He knows when to add a stroke of joy, a hue of sorrow, or a touch of challenge. Every experience, whether joyful or painful, plays a part in making our lives beautiful in His time.

PRAYER: Heavenly Father, in moments of impatience, help us remember that your timing is perfect. Give us the faith to trust in your plan and the wisdom to appreciate the beauty you're creating in our lives. May we rest in the assurance that you make all things beautiful in your time. In Jesus' name, we pray. Amen.

The Comfort of God's Presence

SCRIPTURE: *Psalm 139:7 - "Where shall I go from your Spirit? Or where shall I flee from your presence."*

DEVOTIONAL: In our journey through life, there are moments that we treasure, moments we wish to forget, and moments that we hold dear in our hearts. Regardless of the nature of these memories, one constant remains - the presence of God. King David, who wrote this beautiful psalm, acknowledges the profound truth that there is no place on this earth where we can escape from God's presence. This means that as we reflect on our memories, whether joyous or challenging, God is right there with us. His presence is our comfort, our solace, and our assurance.

When we look back on cherished memories, we can be thankful for the times God's presence added extra joy to those moments. But it's in the recollection of difficult times that we might struggle to find comfort. Yet, even in the midst of trials and hardships, God was there, offering His unfailing presence to bring us through. As you reflect on your memories, whether filled with laughter or tears, take a moment to acknowledge God's presence throughout. It's a beautiful reminder that He has been with you every step of the way, and He continues to be with you today. So, find comfort in His enduring presence, for there is no memory or situation where His love and care cannot reach.

PRAYER: Dear Lord, thank You for Your constant presence in my life. As I reflect on my memories, I'm reminded that You've been there in every moment, both the joyous and the challenging. Help me find comfort in the assurance that Your presence is my steadfast companion, no matter where I go or what memories I recall. In Jesus' name, I pray. Amen.

Healing Through Worship

SCRIPTURE: *Psalm 103:1 - "Bless the Lord, O my soul, and all that is within me, bless his holy name.*

DEVOTIONAL: Worship has the remarkable ability to shift our focus from our pain to God's greatness. It lifts our spirits, soothes our hearts, and ushers in God's presence. When we worship with sincerity, we lay our burdens at the feet of the One who can heal and restore us. In these moments of worship, we're reminded of God's love, His faithfulness, and His sovereignty over our lives. It's in the act of blessing the Lord that we often find ourselves blessed, comforted, and renewed. As you reflect on your memories today, consider how worship can be a pathway to healing. Invite God into your thoughts and emotions, and allow Him to minister to your soul through praise and adoration. Let the words of your heart bless His holy name, and in doing so, may you find healing, restoration, and a deep sense of His comforting presence.

PRAYER: Heavenly Father, I come before You in worship, offering all that is within me to bless Your holy name. As I reflect on my memories, I ask for Your healing touch to mend any brokenness within my heart. May Your presence fill my worship, bringing comfort and renewal to my soul. In Jesus' name, I pray. Amen.

The Blessing of Family Memories

SCRIPTURE: *Psalm 127:3 - "Behold, children are a heritage from the Lord, the fruit of the womb a reward.*

DEVOTIONAL: Family memories hold a special place in our hearts. They are a collection of moments that weave together the tapestry of our lives, and in them, we find blessings beyond measure. Psalm 127:3 reminds us that children are a heritage from the Lord, a reward that fills our lives with love, laughter, and cherished memories.

In the chaos and busyness of life, it's easy to overlook the significance of these memories. Yet, they are a gift from God, a reminder of His faithfulness and grace. The laughter of children, the warmth of family gatherings, the shared meals and stories—all these are part of the rich heritage the Lord bestows upon us.

Take a moment today to cherish your family memories. Reflect on the joy, the love, and the moments that have shaped your family's unique story. Give thanks for the blessing of family, for in these memories, we glimpse the beauty of God's design for love and community.

PRAYER: Heavenly Father, I thank You for the gift of family and the precious memories we've created together. Help me cherish these moments, recognizing them as a heritage from You. May the love and joy that flow from these memories be a constant reminder of Your grace and faithfulness. In Jesus' name, I pray. Amen.

The Comfort of God's Word

SCRIPTURE: *Psalm 119:50 - "This is my comfort in my affliction, that your promise gives me life."*

DEVOTIONAL: The psalmist declares that God's promises are a wellspring of life and comfort. In the pages of the Bible, we find words of hope, assurance, and healing. They remind us that we are not alone in our afflictions and that God's presence is a constant source of strength. His promises offer the assurance of His love, guidance, and the hope of a better tomorrow.

As you face challenges and afflictions, turn to God's Word. Seek solace in His promises, for they breathe life into weary souls. Let His comforting words heal your heart and fill you with renewed strength.

PRAYER: Heavenly Father, thank You for the comfort found in Your promises. In times of affliction, help me turn to Your Word for solace and healing. May Your promises be a source of life and strength, reminding me of Your unwavering love and presence. In Jesus' name, I pray. Amen.

DAY 113

The Power of Testimonies

SCRIPTURE: *Psalm 66:16 – "Come and hear, all you who fear God, and I will tell what he has done for my soul."*

DEVOTIONAL: Sharing our testimonies is a powerful act of healing, both for ourselves and those who hear. When we share, we not only recall God's faithfulness but also bolster our own faith. And as others hear our stories, their faith is strengthened, too. In this way, the circle of God's goodness expands, touching hearts and bringing healing and hope.

Today, consider sharing a testimony of God's faithfulness with someone who needs to hear it. As you do, remember that in the act of sharing, healing, and hope flow not only to them but back to you as well.

PRAYER: Heavenly Father, thank You for the moments of grace and healing in my life. Help me to share these testimonies with others so that Your goodness may shine brightly in the lives of those who hear. May our stories bring healing, hope, and increased faith. In Jesus' name, I pray. Amen.

Rejoicing in God's Salvation

SCRIPTURE: *Psalm 13:5 – "But I have trusted in your steadfast love; my heart shall rejoice in your salvation.*

DEVOTIONAL: Life often presents us with moments of sorrow and distress, times when it feels as though the weight of the world rests upon our shoulders. In such moments, we can turn to Psalm 13:5 for guidance. It reminds us that even amid our struggles, we have reason to rejoice in God's salvation.

Choosing to rejoice doesn't mean we deny our feelings or circumstances. Instead, it means we trust in God's steadfast love and the promise of salvation. It's a conscious decision to find joy in the hope that God offers, even when our hearts are heavy with sorrow.

Today, if you're facing challenges or feeling burdened, remember this verse. Let it be a reminder that, in God's love and salvation, there is always a reason to rejoice, no matter the circumstances.

PRAYER: Heavenly Father, in moments of sorrow and struggle, help me to trust in Your steadfast love and to find joy in Your salvation. May my heart be lifted by the hope that only You can provide. In Your name, I pray. Amen.

Rejoicing in God's Love

SCRIPTURE: *Romans 5:8 – "But God shows his love for us in that while we were still sinners, Christ died for us."*

DEVOTIONAL: In the midst of life's challenges and sorrows, we find solace in the knowledge of God's incredible love. Romans 5:8 beautifully reminds us that God demonstrated His love for us when we were still far from perfect, still sinners. He didn't wait for us to be flawless or deserving but extended His love through Christ's sacrifice.

When we grasp the depth of God's love, it becomes a source of comfort and rejoicing even in the face of difficulties. It's a love that holds us when we're broken, forgives us when we fail, and carries us through every trial. Today, take a moment to reflect on this extraordinary love and let it bring you joy and peace, regardless of your circumstances.

PRAYER: Heavenly Father, Your love is beyond measure, and I am grateful for the way You've shown it to me through Christ's sacrifice. Help me find joy and solace in Your love, especially in times of sorrow and difficulty. In Jesus' name, I pray. Amen.

DAY 116

Embracing the Light of the World

SCRIPTURE: *John 8:12 – "Again Jesus spoke to them, saying, 'I am the light of the world. Whoever follows me will not walk in darkness, but will have the light of life."*

DEVOTIONAL: In a world often clouded by darkness—whether it's the darkness of confusion, despair, or sin—Jesus stands as the beacon of hope and light. His words in John 8:12 remind us that He is the light of the world. When we follow Him, we no longer stumble through the obscurity of life, for His light illuminates our path.

In times of confusion or despair, turn to Jesus, the Light of the World. He guides our steps, dispels the shadows, and brings clarity to our journey. His light brings hope, and in His radiance, we find solace and direction. Today, choose to follow Him, and you will discover the light of life that overcomes all darkness.

PRAYER: Lord Jesus, thank You for being the light that guides us through the darkness of this world. Help us follow You faithfully, finding hope and solace in Your presence. Illuminate our paths and fill our hearts with Your light. In Your name, we pray. Amen.

Our Safe Haven

SCRIPTURE: *Psalm 61:3 - "For you have been my refuge, a strong tower against the enemy."*

DEVOTIONAL: Life is often likened to a turbulent sea, filled with storms that can leave us feeling overwhelmed. In these moments, we yearn for a safe haven, a refuge where we can find solace and security. Psalm 61:3 reminds us that God is our refuge, a strong tower against the storms of life.

When the tempests of adversity threaten to engulf us, we can find comfort in knowing that God is our shelter. His loving embrace provides the peace and protection we desperately need. Like a fortress that stands unwavering against the fiercest gales, God's presence shields us from harm and becomes our safe haven amidst life's storms.

PRAYER: Heavenly Father, thank You for being our refuge, our strong tower, and our safe haven. In times of trouble and turmoil, we find solace in Your unwavering protection and love. Help us seek shelter in Your presence and find peace amidst life's storms. In Jesus' name, we pray. Amen.

The Blessing of Unity

SCRIPTURE: *Psalm 133:1 - "Behold, how good and pleasant it is when brothers dwell in unity."*

DEVOTIONAL: Unity is a precious gift from God, and it's often in our shared bonds of unity that we find solace and strength. Psalm 133:1 beautifully describes the goodness and pleasantness that come when people live together in harmony.

In moments of discord or strife, we can seek solace in the pursuit of unity. It's in unity that we find common purpose, support, and the fulfillment of Christ's prayer for us to be one (John 17:21). When we join together in love and understanding, the burdens of life become lighter, and we experience the blessing of fellowship and shared faith.

As you reflect on this verse, consider how you can contribute to unity in your community, family, or church. In unity, we discover a deep sense of solace as we strive to live in harmony with one another.

PRAYER: Dear Lord, we thank You for the blessing of unity. Help us to foster harmony and understanding in our relationships and communities. May we find solace in the goodness and pleasantness that unity brings. In Jesus' name, we pray. Amen.

DAY 119

His Eternal Embrace

SCRIPTURE: *Isaiah 66:13 – "As one whom his mother comforts, so I will comfort you; you shall be comforted in Jerusalem."*

DEVOTIONAL: In the midst of grief, we often find solace in the memories of our loved ones and the comfort they provide. In Isaiah 66:13, God's promise of comfort is likened to a mother's comforting embrace. Just as a mother tenderly consoles her child, God extends His comforting presence to us in times of sorrow.

Our cherished memories become a source of comfort as we remember the love, laughter, and warmth our loved ones brought into our lives. These memories serve as a reminder that the bonds of love are not broken by death but remain eternally cherished in our hearts.

As you reflect on your memories today, remember that God, the ultimate Comforter, is with you, offering solace and healing. Allow His presence to bring you peace and hope, knowing that you will find ultimate comfort in His eternal embrace.

PRAYER: Heavenly Father, in times of grief, we find solace in Your comforting presence. Thank you for the cherished memories that bring warmth to our hearts. May Your loving embrace provide us with the ultimate comfort, knowing that we will be eternally reunited with our loved ones. In Jesus' name, we pray. Amen.

The God of Comfort and Peace

SCRIPTURE: *2 Corinthians 1:3 – "Blessed be the God and Father of our Lord Jesus Christ, the Father of mercies and God of all comfort."*

DEVOTIONAL: When we grieve, we can turn to God for the peace that surpasses understanding, for He knows the depths of our sorrow. He is the One who can wrap us in His loving arms and bring a sense of calm to our troubled hearts. In His presence, we find a refuge from the storms of grief, a place where our tears are heard, and our pain is understood.

As you navigate the path of grief, take a moment today to meditate on God's comforting presence. He is the One who offers the peace that transcends all understanding. Lean on Him, pour out your heart, and allow His divine comfort to envelop you, knowing that you are held in the arms of the Father of mercies.

PRAYER: Gracious God, in moments of grief, we thank You for being our Father of mercies and the source of all comfort. Wrap us in Your loving arms and fill our hearts with Your peace that surpasses understanding. Help us find solace in Your presence as we navigate the path of grief. In Jesus' name, we pray. Amen.

Healing Through Community

SCRIPTURE: *Galatians 6:2 – "Bear one another's burdens, and so fulfill the law of Christ."*

DEVOTIONAL: Grief is a journey that can feel heavy and lonely, yet God, in His wisdom, has provided us with a gift—a Christian community. In Galatians 6:2, we are reminded of the importance of bearing one another's burdens. This is not just a suggestion but a calling for us as followers of Christ.

When we grieve, it can be easy to isolate ourselves, thinking that others won't understand our pain. However, God designed us to be in fellowship with one another, and it's within the embrace of a loving Christian community that we can find solace and healing.

In your time of grief, don't hesitate to reach out to your brothers and sisters in Christ. Share your burden, be it sorrow, confusion, or simply the weariness of the journey. In doing so, you not only allow others to fulfill the law of Christ by bearing your burden but also open yourself to receiving the love, prayers, and support of your community.

Today, take a step toward healing by connecting with your Christian brothers and sisters. Remember, you are not alone in your grief, and in the embrace of a caring community, you may find unexpected comfort and strength.

PRAYER: Heavenly Father, we thank You for the gift of the Christian community. Help us to bear one another's burdens and fulfill the law of Christ, especially in times of grief. May we find support, love, and healing through our relationships with fellow believers. In Jesus' name, we pray. Amen.

DAY 122

Embracing the Fruit of the Spirit

SCRIPTURE: *Galatians 5:22-23 "Love, joy, peace, patience, kindness, goodness, faithfulness, gentleness, self-control; against such things there is no law."*

DEVOTIONAL: When we allow the Holy Spirit to cultivate these fruits within us, we open ourselves to healing and transformation. Love and kindness bring comfort to our broken hearts. Patience helps us navigate the slow process of healing. Joy and peace fill the gaps left by grief. Faithfulness assures us of God's constant presence. Gentleness soothes the pain we carry, and self-control gives us the strength to move forward.

Today, as you journey through grief and healing, invite the Holy Spirit to bear these fruits in your life. Embrace them as God's gifts to guide you on your path of restoration.

PRAYER: Dear Lord, thank You for the fruit of the Spirit. As I seek healing, help me to embrace these qualities in my life. May Your love, joy, peace, and all the others bring comfort, strength, and transformation. In Jesus' name, I pray. Amen.

Healing Through Surrender

SCRIPTURE: *Matthew 11:29 – "Take my yoke upon you, and learn from me, for I am gentle and lowly in heart, and you will find rest for your souls."*

DEVOTIONAL: Grief can often feel like an overwhelming burden, one too heavy to bear. In these times, Christ extends an invitation: "Take my yoke upon you."

This yoke is not an additional burden but a partnership. When we surrender our grief, our pain, and our struggles to Christ, we share the load with the One who is gentle and lowly in heart. He understands our suffering intimately, and in His presence, we find rest for our weary souls.

Learning to surrender isn't a sign of weakness; it's an act of trust. It's acknowledging that we can't carry our burdens alone and entrusting them to the One who can. As we yield to Christ's yoke, we discover healing in the rest He provides.

Today, take a moment to surrender your grief to Christ. Lay it at His feet and find rest for your soul.

PRAYER: Lord, I surrender my grief and burdens to You. I trust that in Your gentleness, I will find the rest my soul so desperately needs. Thank You for carrying my load. In Your name, I pray. Amen.

The Renewing Hope of Healing

SCRIPTURE: *Psalm 147:3 – "He heals the broken-hearted and binds up their wounds."*

DEVOTIONAL: In the journey of healing from grief, we often long for renewal—a restoration of the joy that grief has taken away. The psalmist reminds us that our God is not only a healer but also a restorer. He specializes in healing the brokenhearted, binding up the wounds that life's trials have inflicted.

Grief can leave us feeling shattered, like a vessel irreparably broken. Yet, our Heavenly Father takes the pieces and meticulously restores us. His work is not rushed or hasty; it's a loving process of binding, healing, and renewing.

Today, let the promise of Psalm 147:3 fill your heart with hope. Whatever has broken your spirit, God stands ready to heal and restore. In your moments of despair, remember that He is the Master Restorer who can transform your pain into a testimony of His healing grace.

PRAYER: Gracious God, I bring my brokenness before You. Heal my wounds and restore my spirit. Thank You for Your promise to mend what is broken. May my life be a testament to Your healing grace. In Jesus' name, I pray. Amen.

DAY 125

The Path of Healing

SCRIPTURE: *Isaiah 30:21 - "And your ears shall hear a word behind you, saying, 'This is the way, walk in it,' when you turn to the right or when you turn to the left."*

DEVOTIONAL: On the path of healing from grief, we often encounter crossroads and uncertainties. It can be challenging to discern the way forward. Yet, Isaiah 30:21 assures us that God is our faithful guide. He whispers to us, directing our steps and providing clarity even when we feel lost.

Take a moment today to listen to that still, small voice within your heart. God is guiding you along the way of healing. Trust in His wisdom and let Him lead you toward restoration and peace. Remember that healing is a journey, and you are not walking it alone.

PRAYER: Heavenly Father, thank You for being my guide on this journey of healing. Help me to listen for Your voice and follow Your direction. When I'm unsure of the way, remind me that You are always with me. In Your loving guidance, I find hope and peace. Amen.

Healing Through Hope

SCRIPTURE: *Romans 15:13 – "May the God of hope fill you with all joy and peace in believing, so that by the power of the Holy Spirit you may abound in hope."*

DEVOTIONAL: In times of grief and pain, hope can feel like a distant star in the night sky. But Romans 15:13 reminds us that God is the source of our hope. He's not a God of despair but a God of hope. When we trust in Him, even in the midst of our struggles, He fills us with a profound sense of joy and peace.

Hope is the light that guides us through the darkest nights of our lives. It's the assurance that, in Christ, we can find healing, renewal, and a brighter tomorrow. As you navigate your journey of healing, remember that the God of hope is by your side, ready to fill you with His comforting presence.

PRAYER: Heavenly Father, I thank You for being the source of my hope. In moments of despair, help me to trust in Your promises. Fill me with Your joy and peace, and let the power of the Holy Spirit abound in my heart so that I may walk in hope and healing. In Jesus' name, I pray. Amen.

The Comforter's Presence

SCRIPTURE: *John 14:16 – "And I will ask the Father, and he will give you another Helper, to be with you forever."*

DEVOTIONAL: In times of sorrow and grief, we are never alone. Jesus, in John 14:16, promised to send us the Holy Spirit as our Helper. The Holy Spirit is our Comforter, our Counsellor, and our Guide. His presence is a constant source of solace in the midst of life's trials.

The Helper, the Holy Spirit, brings a unique kind of comfort that transcends our understanding. He whispers words of peace to our troubled hearts and leads us toward healing. As you navigate your journey of grief, take comfort in the knowledge that the Comforter is with you, ready to provide strength, peace, and solace.

PRAYER: Heavenly Father, I am grateful for the gift of the Holy Spirit, my Helper. In times of grief, help me to be aware of His comforting presence. May I find solace, strength, and guidance in Him as I journey toward healing. In Jesus' name, I pray. Amen.

DAY 128

The God Who Hears Our Prayers

SCRIPTURE: *Psalm 34:17 - "When the righteous cry for help, the Lord hears and delivers them out of all their troubles."*

DEVOTIONAL: In times of distress and sorrow, our hearts often turn to prayer. It's in these moments of vulnerability that we find solace in the knowledge that our cries for help are heard by the Almighty. Psalm 34:17 assures us that when the righteous cry out to the Lord, He not only hears but also delivers them from their troubles.

Knowing that God listens to our prayers and responds with deliverance can be a profound source of comfort during times of grief. We may not always understand His timing or methods, but we can trust in His unwavering faithfulness. Take comfort in the assurance that your prayers are not in vain, for the God who hears is also the God who delivers.

PRAYER: Heavenly Father, I thank You for being a God who hears my prayers, especially in times of trouble and grief. Your promise to deliver brings me solace and hope. Help me to trust in Your perfect timing and plan, even when I cannot see the way out of my troubles. In Jesus' name, I pray. Amen.

The Source of True Comfort

SCRIPTURE: *Psalm 46:1 – "God is our refuge and strength, a very present help in trouble."*

DEVOTIONAL: In the midst of life's storms and challenges, where do you seek refuge? Psalm 46:1 reminds us that our ultimate source of comfort and strength is found in God. He is not a distant or absent deity; He is a very present help in times of trouble.

When grief washes over us like a relentless tide, when the weight of sorrow threatens to overwhelm us, we can turn to the Lord as our refuge. His presence provides shelter from life's storms, a safe haven where we can find solace and renewal.

God's strength is not only a shield against adversity but also a wellspring of comfort. It is in His embrace that we discover the peace that surpasses understanding, a refuge where we can pour out our hearts in times of sorrow.

As you journey through your grief, remember that you are not alone. God, your refuge and strength, is with you, offering solace, shelter, and strength to carry you through.

PRAYER: Heavenly Father, I am grateful that in times of trouble, I can find comfort and strength in You. You are my refuge, my safe haven, and my source of peace. When grief overwhelms me, help me to turn to You and find solace in Your presence. In Your name, I pray. Amen.

The Healing Power of Scripture

SCRIPTURE: *Hebrews 4:12 - "For the word of God is living and active, sharper than any two-edged sword, piercing to the division of soul and of spirit, of joints and of marrow, and discerning the thoughts and intentions of the heart."*

DEVOTIONAL: The Bible is more than just words on paper; it's a dynamic force. Hebrews 4:12 describes it as living, active, and sharper than a double-edged sword. In times of grief and pain, God's Word provides comfort, guidance, and solace.

When you're hurting, turn to Scripture. It's not a passive text; it has the power to heal, transform, and reveal God's love. Let it penetrate your heart, discern your thoughts, and bring restoration. The Word of God can be a profound source of healing in your life.

PRAYER: Heavenly Father, thank You for the living power of Your Word. As I journey through healing, may it bring comfort and transformation to my heart. In Jesus' name, I pray. Amen.

DAY 131

God's Healing Presence

SCRIPTURE: *Exodus 33:14 - "And he said, 'My presence will go with you, and I will give you rest.'"*

DEVOTIONAL: In the midst of life's trials and tribulations, God's presence is our sanctuary. Exodus 33:14 reminds us that His presence accompanies us, offering a refuge of rest and solace. When we face grief or adversity, we don't journey alone; the Lord walks with us.

Find peace in the knowledge that God is always with you. In His presence, you discover a haven of healing and tranquillity. In times of distress, lean on Him for the rest only He can provide.

PRAYER: Heavenly Father, I am grateful for Your constant presence in my life. May I find comfort and rest in the assurance that You walk beside me, especially during times of healing and restoration. In Jesus' name, I pray. Amen.

Abundant Grace

SCRIPTURE: *James 4:6 - "But he gives more grace. Therefore it says, 'God opposes the proud but gives grace to the humble.'"*

DEVOTIONAL: In times of healing and restoration, we often seek solace in God's abundant grace. James 4:6 reminds us that His grace is ever-flowing, a balm for our wounds and strength for our spirits.

When we approach God with humility, acknowledging our need for His grace, we find comfort in His outpouring of love and mercy. Let His grace be your refuge, offering the healing and renewal only He can provide.

PRAYER: Heavenly Father, I humbly come before You, seeking Your abundant grace. In moments of healing, may Your grace be my source of strength and solace. Thank you for your unending love. In Jesus' name, I pray. Amen.

The Blessing of God's Restoration

SCRIPTURE: *Job 42:10 - "And the Lord restored the fortunes of Job when he had prayed for his friends. And the Lord gave Job twice as much as he had before."*

DEVOTIONAL: The story of Job is a profound testament to the blessing of God's restoration. Job faced unimaginable trials, losing his wealth, health, and loved ones. Yet, through his unwavering faith and prayer, God restored him.

In times of grief and loss, it may feel as if everything is crumbling. But like Job, we can find solace in knowing that God is the ultimate restorer. His promise is to bring beauty from ashes, to lift us from despair, and to bless us abundantly.

As we navigate life's challenges, let us remember that God's restoration knows no bounds. Through prayer and faith, He can turn our darkest moments into stories of His grace and redemption.

PRAYER: Heavenly Father, I thank You for the promise of restoration found in Your Word. In moments of despair and loss, help me to hold onto faith, knowing that You can turn my mourning into dancing. May Your restoration bring glory to Your name. In Jesus' name, I pray. Amen.

DAY 134

The Comfort of His Rod and Staff

SCRIPTURE: *Psalm 23:4 - "Even though I walk through the valley of the shadow of death, I will fear no evil, for you are with me; your rod and your staff, they comfort me."*

DEVOTIONAL: In life's darkest valleys, we often yearn for comfort and guidance. The imagery of God's rod and staff in Psalm 23 reminds us that even in the most challenging times, we are not alone. His rod serves as protection, warding off threats and dangers we may not even see. His staff gently leads and guides us, keeping us on the right path.

When we face uncertainty, grief, or fear, we can take solace in knowing that God is our ever-present Shepherd. His loving care and guidance provide a comforting presence in the midst of life's trials. We need not fear the shadows when we walk in the light of His love.

PRAYER: Heavenly Father, thank You for being our Shepherd and Protector. In times of darkness and uncertainty, may we find comfort in the assurance of Your presence. Guide us with Your staff, and protect us with Your rod. We trust in Your loving care. In Jesus' name, we pray. Amen.

The God of Healing and Wholeness

SCRIPTURE: *Psalm 147:3 – "He heals the brokenhearted and binds up their wounds."*

DEVOTIONAL: Life can be filled with moments that leave us broken and wounded. We may carry scars from past experiences or face fresh hurts that pierce our hearts. In these times of pain and brokenness, we can find solace in the promise of God as our Healer.

God is the mender of shattered hearts and the binder of wounds. His love and grace reach into the depths of our pain, offering healing and restoration. Just as a skilled physician tends to wounds with care, God tends to our wounded souls. His touch brings not only physical healing but also emotional and spiritual wholeness.

When you find yourself broken and hurting, turn to God in prayer. Lay your wounds before Him and trust in His promise to heal and restore. His love is a balm for your wounded heart.

PRAYER: Heavenly Father, we come before You with our brokenness and wounds. We thank You for Your promise to heal and restore. Pour out Your love and grace upon us, bringing wholeness to our hearts and lives. May we find solace and strength in Your presence. In Jesus' name, we pray. Amen.

The Peace That Comes from Trusting God's Plan

SCRIPTURE: *Proverbs 3:5-6 - "Trust in the Lord with all your heart, and do not lean on your own understanding. In all your ways acknowledge him, and he will make straight your paths."*

DEVOTIONAL: Life often takes unexpected turns, and we may find ourselves in situations we didn't anticipate. During these uncertain times, it's comforting to know that God has a plan for our lives—a plan filled with hope and a bright future.

Proverbs 3:5-6 reminds us to trust in the Lord with all our hearts and to avoid relying solely on our own understanding. This is a call to surrender control and place our confidence in God's wisdom and guidance. In doing so, we find solace and peace.

Trusting God's plan doesn't mean that everything will be easy or without challenges. It means that we have confidence in His wisdom and goodness, knowing that He is working all things for our welfare. In times of uncertainty, take comfort in the promise of a hopeful future that God has prepared for you.

PRAYER: Heavenly Father, we place our trust in Your loving plan for our lives. In moments of uncertainty, help us find solace and peace in the knowledge that You have a purpose and hope-filled future for us. Grant us the wisdom to follow Your guidance each day. In Jesus' name, we pray. Amen.

The Joy of the Lord as Our Strength

SCRIPTURE: *Nehemiah 8:10 - "Then he said to them, 'Go your way. Eat the fat and drink sweet wine and send portions to anyone who has nothing ready, for this day is holy to our Lord. And do not be grieved, for the joy of the Lord is your strength.'"*

DEVOTIONAL: Life often presents us with trials and challenges that can leave us feeling weak and weary. In these moments, it's easy to lose our sense of joy. However, Nehemiah reminds us that the joy of the Lord is our source of strength.

God's joy is not dependent on our circumstances. It's a deep and abiding gladness that flows from our relationship with Him. When we tap into this joy, we find solace and a renewed sense of strength to face whatever lies ahead.

Take time today to reconnect with the joy of the Lord through prayer, worship, and reflection on His goodness. In His joy, you will discover the strength needed to navigate life's challenges with resilience and hope.

PRAYER: Dear Lord, we thank You for the joy that comes from knowing You. In times of weakness and weariness, help us to draw strength from Your boundless joy. May we find solace and renewed energy in Your presence. In Jesus' name, we pray. Amen.

The God Who Sustains Us

SCRIPTURE: *Isaiah 41:10 - "Fear not, for I am with you; be not dismayed, for I am your God; I will strengthen you, I will help you, I will uphold you with my righteous right hand."*

DEVOTIONAL: Life can often be a daunting journey filled with challenges that test our strength and resolve. In these moments, it's comforting to know that we have a God who promises to sustain us. Isaiah 41:10 reassures us that God is with us, holding us up with His righteous right hand and providing the strength we need.

When you feel overwhelmed or anxious, take refuge in this promise. Embrace it as a source of comfort and solace. God is not only present in our trials but also actively working to sustain us through them. He is our source of strength, our help in times of need, and our unfailing support.

Today, as you face the challenges of life, remember that the God who upholds the universe is the same God who upholds you. Find peace in His presence and strength in His promises.

PRAYER: Heavenly Father, we thank You for being our constant source of strength and sustenance. In moments of fear and doubt, help us to remember Your promise to uphold us. May we find comfort and courage in Your presence, trusting in Your faithfulness. In Jesus' name, we pray. Amen.

DAY 139

The Power of Surrender and Trust

SCRIPTURE: *Psalm 9:10 - "And those who know your name put their trust in you, for you, O Lord, have not forsaken those who seek you."*

DEVOTIONAL: Surrendering control can be one of life's greatest challenges. We often think we know what's best, but Psalm 9:10 reminds us that putting our trust in the Lord is the path to peace. When we seek Him and acknowledge His name, we find assurance that He won't abandon us.

Today, in whatever you face, let go and trust the One who never forsakes those who seek Him. Surrender your understanding, and let His wisdom guide your steps. In His hands, you'll find strength and direction.

PRAYER: Dear Lord, we place our trust in You, knowing that You never forsake those who seek You. Help us surrender control and find peace in Your wisdom. Guide our steps today and always. In Jesus' name, we pray. Amen.

The Peace That Comes from Trust in God

SCRIPTURE: *Isaiah 26:3 – "You keep him in perfect peace whose mind is stayed on you because he trusts in you."*

DEVOTIONAL: In a world filled with uncertainty and turmoil, Isaiah 26:3 reminds us that perfect peace is found in unwavering trust in God. When our minds are steadfastly focused on Him, when we fix our gaze upon His unchanging character and promises, peace flows like a tranquil river.

Today, take a moment to quiet the anxieties and distractions around you. Trust in the Lord's faithfulness, His goodness, and His sovereignty. As you do, you'll find a peace that transcends circumstances, guarding your heart and mind, just as God has promised.

PRAYER: Heavenly Father, in a world filled with chaos, we place our trust in You. May our minds remain steadfastly fixed on Your unwavering character, and in that trust, may we find the perfect peace that only You can provide. In Jesus' name, we pray. Amen.

The Comfort of God's Presence in Our Lives

SCRIPTURE: *Psalm 16:11 – "You make known to me the path of life; in your presence, there is fullness of joy; at your right hand are pleasures forevermore."*

DEVOTIONAL: In the busyness and challenges of life, there's a quiet refuge available to us—the presence of God. Psalm 16:11 beautifully reminds us that in God's presence, we discover not just joy but fullness of joy. It's a joy that surpasses circumstances, a joy that runs deeper than our troubles, and a joy that brings solace to our souls.

Imagine for a moment being in the presence of someone who deeply loves and understands you, who knows your every need and cares for your every concern. That's the essence of being in God's presence. It's a place of refuge where we can find comfort, healing, and the assurance that we're never alone in our journey. It's in this divine presence that we experience the greatest comfort—a comfort that soothes our worries and fills our hearts with unshakable peace.

PRAYER: Heavenly Father, we thank you for the gift of your presence. In times of trial and triumph, help us find solace, joy, and strength in being near you. May your comforting presence guide us through each day, and may we rest in the fullness of your joy. In Jesus' name, we pray. Amen

DAY 142

Healing Through Worship and Praise

SCRIPTURE: *Psalm 103:2 - "Bless the Lord, O my soul, and forget not all his benefits.»*

DEVOTIONAL: Worship and praise are powerful avenues for healing. When we lift our voices in adoration and gratitude to the Lord, it has a profound impact on our souls. Psalm 103 beautifully reminds us to bless the Lord with all that is within us and to remember His countless benefits.

In worship, we acknowledge the One who forgives our sins and heals our afflictions. It is in His presence that we find restoration and renewal. Like a loving Father, God redeems us from the depths, crowns us with His steadfast love, and satisfies our souls with His goodness. Worship and praise draw us near to Him, where we experience His healing touch.

As you enter into a time of worship and praise, remember all the ways the Lord has been faithful in your life. Allow His presence to bring healing to your heart, mind, and body. In worship, you'll discover that your youth is renewed, and you'll find strength and solace for the journey ahead.

PRAYER: Heavenly Father, we come before you in worship and praise, acknowledging your goodness and mercy. Thank you for the healing and renewal you bring to our lives. As we lift our voices to you, may your presence surround us with comfort and peace. In Jesus' name, we pray. Amen.

Embracing God's Abundant Grace

SCRIPTURE: *Ephesians 2:7 - "...so that in the coming ages he might show the immeasurable riches of his grace in kindness toward us in Christ Jesus."*

DEVOTIONAL: God's grace is a boundless treasure, and it is something we can continually embrace as we navigate life's challenges. Ephesians 2:7 reminds us that God's grace is not only for this lifetime but for the ages to come. It's a grace that never runs dry, an unending wellspring of His kindness and favor. In times of grief, we may feel unworthy or burdened by our circumstances. However, God's grace is not earned; it's freely given to us through Christ Jesus. It's a gift that provides solace and strength when we need it most.

As you embrace God's abundant grace, allow it to wash over you like a soothing balm. Let go of any feelings of inadequacy or guilt, knowing that His grace is sufficient for you. In His grace, there is healing, forgiveness, and a future filled with hope.

PRAYER: Heavenly Father, we thank you for your immeasurable grace, which sustains us through every trial. Help us to fully embrace the richness of your kindness and favor. In times of grief, may your grace bring us solace and the assurance of your unwavering love. In Jesus' name, we pray. Amen.

The Unbreakable Bond of God's Love

SCRIPTURE: *Romans 8:38-39 - "For I am sure that neither death nor life, nor angels nor rulers, nor things present nor things to come, nor powers, nor height nor depth, nor anything else in all creation, will be able to separate us from the love of God in Christ Jesus our Lord."*

DEVOTIONAL: In times of grief and uncertainty, one thing remains unshaken—the love of God. Romans 8:38- 39 reminds us of the unbreakable bond we share with God through His love in Christ Jesus. Nothing in this world or beyond it can separate us from this divine and unwavering love.

When the storms of life toss us about, when grief threatens to overwhelm us, we can find solace in the assurance that God's love stands firm. It is a love that endures all things, a love that conquered sin and death on the cross, and a love that continues to hold us close, no matter what we face.

As you navigate the challenges of life, remember that you are held securely in the embrace of God's unchanging love. In times of grief, let this love be your anchor, your source of strength, and your enduring comfort.

PRAYER: Heavenly Father, we are grateful for the unbreakable bond of your love. In moments of grief and uncertainty, help us to find solace and strength in the assurance that nothing can separate us from your love in Christ Jesus. May your love be our anchor and our source of enduring comfort. In Jesus' name, we pray. Amen.

DAY 145

The God of All Comfort and Compassion

SCRIPTURE: *2 Corinthians 1:3-4 - "Blessed be the God... of all comfort, who comforts us in all our affliction...»*

DEVOTIONAL: In the depths of our grief and trials, we encounter the God of all comfort and compassion. 2 Corinthians 1:3-4 reminds us that our Heavenly Father is not distant in our pain but draws near to console us in our affliction.

God's comfort isn't limited by the circumstances or the depth of our suffering; it's boundless and overflowing. He embraces us with His tender mercies, soothing our wounded hearts and offering solace in times of distress.

But His comfort doesn't stop there. As recipients of His divine comfort, we are called to become comforters ourselves, extending the same compassion to others who are hurting. Our experiences of God's comforting touch enable us to bring His healing grace to those around us.

Let us take refuge in the God of all comfort, and as we receive His compassion, let us also become channels of His comfort to a hurting world.

PRAYER: Heavenly Father, we praise You as the God of all comfort and compassion. In our times of affliction, draw near to us, and may we experience the depth of Your mercy. Equip us to comfort others with the comfort we've received from You. In Jesus' name, we pray. Amen.

Healing Through Community and Fellowship

SCRIPTURE: *Hebrews 10:24-25 - "Let us consider how to stir up one another to love and good works, not neglecting to meet together, as is the habit of some, but encouraging one another..."*

DEVOTIONAL: In the tapestry of our lives, community, and fellowship with fellow believers are like vibrant threads that weave through our experiences, providing strength, comfort, and healing. The writer of Hebrews encourages us not to forsake the assembly of believers but to come together to stir up love and good works, just as iron sharpens iron.

Community is a gift from God, a place where we find solace in the midst of life's challenges. It's a haven where we share our joys and sorrows, knowing we are not alone. When we gather with fellow believers, we create a space where encouragement and support flow freely. It's in these moments of togetherness that we discover healing for our wounded hearts, hope for our weary souls, and the strength to persevere in faith.

PRAYER: Heavenly Father, we thank you for the gift of Christian community and fellowship. May we always be eager to gather with our brothers and sisters in faith, offering love, encouragement, and support as we journey together toward healing and wholeness. In Jesus' name, we pray. Amen.

Embracing the Beauty of God's Creation

SCRIPTURE: *Psalm 19:1 - "The heavens declare the glory of God, and the sky above proclaims his handiwork."*

DEVOTIONAL: In the grand tapestry of our lives, God's creation serves as a breathtaking backdrop, a constant reminder of His glory and majesty. When we look to the heavens, we see not just the vast expanse of the universe but also the intricate craftsmanship of the Creator. The mountains, the seas, the forests, and the skies all proclaim His handiwork.

Amid life's challenges and uncertainties, taking a moment to embrace the beauty of God's creation can bring solace and wonder. It's a reminder that the same Creator who painted the skies and sculpted the mountains cares deeply for us. When we find ourselves overwhelmed, we can look to the world around us and find comfort in the knowledge that the One who created it all is with us, guiding us through each season of life.

PRAYER: Heavenly Father, we thank you for the awe-inspiring beauty of your creation. Help us to find solace and inspiration in the world around us, knowing that you, the Creator of all, are always with us. May we steward and protect the beauty of your creation as an act of worship and gratitude. In Jesus' name, we pray. Amen.

DAY 148

The Gift of God's Grace and Salvation

SCRIPTURE: *Ephesians 2:8-9 - "For by grace you have been saved through faith. And this is not your own doing; it is the gift of God, not a result of works, so that no one may boast."*

DEVOTIONAL: In the depths of our souls, we often long for solace, seeking something to fill the void and give meaning to our lives. Ephesians 2:8-9 reminds us of the greatest source of comfort—the unmerited grace of God. We can never earn His love or salvation through our efforts, for they are freely given gifts. It's a comfort to know that our worthiness isn't a prerequisite for His love.

The gift of salvation offers us eternal solace. It's a lifeline in the storms of life, a promise that we are loved and cherished by our Heavenly Father. As we reflect on this precious gift, let us express our gratitude and rest in the comforting embrace of God's grace.

PRAYER: Dear Lord, we thank you for the immeasurable gift of your grace and salvation. In times of turmoil and uncertainty, may we find solace in the assurance of your love, knowing that we are saved not by our works but by your unmerited favor. Grant us the wisdom to share this comforting truth with others. In Jesus' name, we pray. Amen.

The God of Compassion and Comfort

SCRIPTURE: *Psalm 103:13 - "As a father shows compassion to his children, so the Lord shows compassion to those who fear him."*

DEVOTIONAL: In the tapestry of life, moments of grief and sorrow are inevitable. Yet, in the midst of our pain, we find solace in a God who is not distant or indifferent but is compassionate beyond measure. Psalm 103:13 beautifully paints a picture of God's compassion as that of a loving father to his children.

Often, in our moments of weakness and sadness, we struggle to extend the same compassion to ourselves that God freely gives. We harbor regrets, guilt, and self-doubt. But today, remember that the God who comforts is also the God who loves and forgives. Let His compassion flow through you, offering yourself the grace to heal, to grow, and to find solace in His loving embrace.

PRAYER: Heavenly Father, we are grateful for your boundless compassion. Help us, Lord, to not only receive your comfort but to extend it to ourselves. In moments of doubt and self-criticism, remind us of your unwavering love and compassion. May we find solace in your embrace and share that solace with others. In Jesus' name, we pray. Amen.

SEEKING MEANING AMIDST LOSS

Finding Purpose in Pain

SCRIPTURE: *Psalm 34:18 – "The Lord is near to the brokenhearted and saves the crushed in spirit."*

DEVOTIONAL: In times of loss, it's easy to feel adrift in a sea of sorrow. But remember, the Lord is near to the brokenhearted. He draws close to those who are hurting, wrapping His arms of comfort around them. Even in the depths of despair, there is hope because God is with us. He saves the crushed in spirit, offering a lifeline of grace and meaning amidst the pain.

As you navigate the complexities of loss, cling to this truth: God's presence in your life provides a source of profound meaning. Your pain is not meaningless; it's part of a larger story where God's love and comfort prevail. In your brokenness, you find the depth of God's compassion and the assurance that you are never alone. Through Him, you can discover purpose, even amidst the most profound losses.

PRAYER: Heavenly Father, in my moments of loss, help me find solace in Your presence. Let me feel Your nearness and know that even in my brokenness, there is meaning in Your love. Amen.

Wisdom from Suffering

SCRIPTURE: *James 1:2- 4 – "Consider it pure joy... whenever you face trials... the testing of your faith produces perseverance. Let perseverance finish its work so that you may be mature and complete."*

DEVOTIONAL: Suffering is a profound teacher in our journey of seeking meaning amidst loss. James reminds us to consider it joy when we face trials, not because suffering is pleasant, but because it can lead to wisdom and maturity. Just as the rough edges of a stone are smoothed by constant friction, our faith is refined and strengthened through trials.

In our losses, we often grapple with questions like "Why?" and "How could this happen?" While these questions may linger, the wisdom gained through suffering is that we can endure and emerge stronger. Suffering produces perseverance, shaping us into mature and complete individuals. It's in these challenging times that we learn the value of faith, resilience, and, ultimately, the depth of our relationship with God. So, as you navigate loss, trust that even amidst the pain, God is at work, molding you into a wiser and more complete person.

PRAYER: Gracious God, in times of suffering and loss, grant me the wisdom to see the lessons and growth amidst the pain. Help me find meaning in trials, knowing that You are shaping me for a greater purpose. Amen.

DAY 152

Finding Comfort in His Presence

SCRIPTURE: *Psalm 16:8 - "I have set the Lord always before me; because he is at my right hand, I shall not be shaken."*

DEVOTIONAL: In times of loss, the presence of God can be our greatest source of comfort and strength. When grief surrounds us, it's easy to feel shaken and overwhelmed, but the psalmist reminds us of the power of setting the Lord always before us.

Just as a ship relies on the constancy of the North Star to navigate through stormy seas, we can fix our gaze upon God's unwavering presence. He is the anchor in the midst of life's tempests, the steady hand guiding us through the darkest nights. When we intentionally focus on God's presence, we find solace, knowing that we are not alone in our pain.

Today, take a moment to set the Lord before you. Close your eyes, breathe deeply, and invite His presence to fill your heart. In His presence, you'll discover a refuge where your shaken soul can find peace.

PRAYER: Heavenly Father, thank you for your unwavering presence, especially in times of loss and grief. Help me set my gaze upon you so that I may find the comfort and strength needed to navigate life's challenges. In your name, I pray. Amen.

Sharing Burdens, Finding Meaning

SCRIPTURE: *Galatians 6:2 - "Bear one another's burdens, and so fulfill the law of Christ."*

DEVOTIONAL: Grief can be an incredibly heavy burden to carry alone. Yet, in the midst of our pain and sorrow, we are reminded by the Apostle Paul in Galatians 6:2 of the power of sharing our burdens with one another.

When we open up and share our grief, we allow others to come alongside us in our journey of healing. In their support, we often find profound meaning. As we bear one another's burdens, we fulfill the law of Christ, which is rooted in love, compassion, and selflessness.

Today, consider reaching out to someone you trust and share a part of your grief with them. In doing so, you may discover that, amidst loss, there is also a powerful opportunity to strengthen bonds, offer and receive comfort, and find meaning in the love and support of others.

PRAYER: Lord, grant me the courage to share my burdens with others and the wisdom to be a compassionate listener when they do the same. May we fulfill the law of Christ as we bear one another's burdens in love and support. Amen.

Finding Solace of God's Creation

SCRIPTURE: *Psalm 104:24-25 - "O Lord, how manifold are your works! In wisdom have you made them all; the earth is full of your creatures."*

DEVOTIONAL: In times of loss and grief, it's easy to become consumed by sorrow and pain. Yet, even in the midst of our darkest moments, God's creation stands as a testament to His boundless wisdom and creativity.

The psalmist in Psalm 104 reminds us that the earth is full of God's creatures and that His works are manifold. Take a moment to step outside and observe the beauty of nature. Marvel at the intricacies of a blooming flower, the grace of a soaring bird, or the vastness of the starry night sky.

In these moments, we find solace in the fact that the same Creator who fashioned the universe with such precision and wonder cares deeply for us. His creation can serve as a source of comfort, reminding us that, even in our grief, we are part of a vast and awe-inspiring tapestry.

PRAYER: Heavenly Father, I thank You for the beauty of Your creation, which brings solace to my soul. Help me to see Your handiwork and wisdom in every aspect of the natural world. In moments of loss, may I find comfort in knowing that You are the Creator of all things, including my life, and that You hold me in Your loving embrace. Amen.

The Healing Power of Gratitude

SCRIPTURE: *1 Thessalonians 5:18 - "Give thanks in all circumstances; for this is the will of God in Christ Jesus for you."*

DEVOTIONAL: Gratitude has a remarkable way of healing the wounds of our hearts, even in the midst of grief. When we're faced with loss, it's natural to focus on what's been taken away. However, the wisdom of Scripture encourages us to find reasons to be thankful, even in the most challenging circumstances. 1 Thessalonians 5:18 reminds us that giving thanks is not dependent on our circumstances but is a choice we can make in all situations. It's not about denying our pain but about finding a glimmer of hope and healing through gratitude.

When we intentionally count our blessings, even when they seem few, we shift our perspective. We begin to see how God's grace continues to touch our lives. It might be the memory of a loved one, the support of friends, or the simple beauty of a sunrise. In these moments of thanksgiving, we find meaning amidst our grief, and our hearts begin to heal.

PRAYER: Heavenly Father, in times of loss and grief, help me to cultivate a heart of gratitude. Teach me to find reasons to give thanks, even when my heart is heavy. Let the practice of gratitude bring healing, hope, and renewed meaning to my life. Amen.

Embracing Redemption Amidst Loss

SCRIPTURE: *Isaiah 43:19 - "Behold, I am doing a new thing; now it springs forth, do you not perceive it? I will make a way in the wilderness and rivers in the desert."*

DEVOTIONAL: In times of loss, we often carry the weight of past mistakes and regrets. These burdens can make our grief even heavier. Yet, in the midst of our pain, God offers us the gift of redemption and the promise of new beginnings.

Isaiah 43:19 reminds us that God is in the business of doing new things. He can make a way in the wilderness of our despair and bring forth rivers of hope in the deserts of our sorrow. Even when we feel surrounded by loss, His redemptive power can transform our lives.

To embrace this gift of redemption, we must first surrender our past to God. Acknowledge the mistakes, the regrets, and the pain, and release them into His capable hands. As we do, God can begin the process of making all things new. He can take our brokenness and create something beautiful from it.

PRAYER: Gracious God, I come before You with my past mistakes and regrets. I surrender them to You, trusting in Your promise to make all things new. In the midst of my loss, help me to perceive the new thing You are doing in my life. May Your redemption bring healing and hope, even in the darkest of times. Amen.

DAY 157

The Abiding Presence in Loss

SCRIPTURE: *Psalm 139:7 - "Where shall I go from your Spirit? Or where shall I flee from your presence?"*

DEVOTIONAL: In times of loss, we often long for the comforting presence of our loved ones. Their physical absence can create a deep void in our lives. However, we are reminded in Psalm 139:7 that we can never flee from the presence of God.

God's presence is not bound by time or circumstance. He is with us in every moment, including those marked by loss and grief. His abiding presence offers solace when we miss our loved ones the most.

As we cherish memories of those we've lost, we can find comfort in knowing that God is present in those moments, too. He was there during the laughter, the tears, and the shared experiences. In our memories, we can sense His presence, providing us with a source of solace and strength.

PRAYER: Heavenly Father, in times of loss, I find solace in Your unchanging presence. Thank You for being with me in every memory, in every moment of joy and sorrow. May Your abiding presence continue to comfort and sustain me as I navigate the challenges of grief. In Jesus' name, I pray. Amen.

Healing Through Worship and Praise

SCRIPTURE: *Psalm 103:1-5 - "Bless the Lord, O my soul, and all that is within me, bless his holy name."*

DEVOTIONAL: Grief can cast a heavy shadow over our lives, making it difficult to find solace. Yet, in the midst of loss, we can discover a source of healing and renewal through worship and praise.

The words of Psalm 103 remind us to bless the Lord with our entire being, to praise His holy name. When we lift our hearts in worship, even in the depths of grief, we find a sacred space where God's presence can bring comfort and restoration.

Worship and praise connect us with the One who is our ultimate source of healing. In these moments, we can pour out our sorrows, our joys, and our gratitude to God. We may find that as we draw near to Him in worship, He draws near to us, offering the healing and renewal our souls so desperately need.

PRAYER: Gracious God, in the midst of my grief, I turn to You in worship and praise. You are the source of healing and renewal, and I bless Your holy name with all that is within me. May Your presence bring comfort and restoration to my weary soul. In Jesus' name, I pray. Amen.

Seeking Meaning

SCRIPTURE: *Psalm 73:26 - "My flesh and my heart may fail, but God is the strength of my heart and my portion forever."*

DEVOTIONAL: In times of loss, it's natural to search for meaning and purpose in our experiences. We question why we must endure such pain and heartache. It's during these moments of questioning that we can find solace in the knowledge that even when our own strength falters, God remains the unwavering strength of our hearts.

Life's trials may leave us feeling weak and vulnerable, but in our weakness, we discover that God's strength is more than sufficient. He becomes our refuge, our portion, and our hope in the midst of despair. In Him, we find meaning amidst loss, for He offers us comfort, purpose, and the promise of eternal life.

As we navigate the complexities of grief, let us remember that our strength doesn't have to be self-sustained. Instead, we can lean on the eternal strength of God, trusting that He will guide us through the darkest valleys and ultimately lead us to a place of healing, understanding, and meaning.

PRAYER: Heavenly Father, in my moments of grief and loss, I find strength in knowing that You are the anchor of my soul. When my heart is heavy, help me lean on Your enduring strength and find meaning amidst the trials of life. In Jesus' name, I pray. Amen.

Finding Hope

SCRIPTURE: *Romans 15:13 – "May the God of hope fill you with all joy and peace in believing, so that by the power of the Holy Spirit you may abound in hope."*

DEVOTIONAL: In the depths of our grief and loss, it can feel as though we've been enveloped by darkness. But even in the darkest of times, there is a glimmer of hope that shines through. As we trust in the God of hope, He promises to fill us with joy and peace, not in spite of our circumstances but in the midst of them.

This hope isn't a fleeting wish; it's a confident expectation. It's the assurance that God is with us, guiding us through the shadows and into the light. It's the knowledge that even when we can't see the way forward, God's Spirit is at work, bringing comfort, healing, and a renewed sense of purpose.

So, as we navigate the challenging journey of loss, let us hold fast to the hope that transcends our grief. Let us trust in the God who specializes in bringing beauty from ashes and who fills our hearts with hope that overflows, dispelling the darkness and leading us toward brighter days.

PRAYER: Heavenly Father, in times of loss, I cling to the hope that only You can provide. Fill me with Your joy and peace as I trust in You, and may Your Spirit's power bring light to my darkest moments. In Jesus' name, I pray. Amen.

The Comfort of His Rod and Staff

SCRIPTURE: *Psalm 23:4 - "Even though I walk through the valley of the shadow of death, I will fear no evil, for you are with me; your rod and your staff, they comfort me."*

DEVOTIONAL: In the journey of life, there are moments when we walk through valleys, especially in times of loss. These valleys can be dark and filled with sorrow, but the Lord promises His presence and comfort even in the midst of these shadows. The image of God's rod and staff in this verse represents His guidance and protection. Just as a shepherd uses his rod and staff to lead, protect, and comfort his sheep, God does the same for us. When we feel lost, vulnerable, or overwhelmed by grief, He gently guides us with His rod and shields us with His staff. His comforting presence is our assurance that, even in the darkest valleys, we need not fear.

As you navigate the challenges of loss, remember that the Lord is with you, ready to lead you through the shadows. His guidance brings hope, and His protection offers solace. Take comfort in knowing that His unfailing love will sustain you through every valley you encounter.

PRAYER: Heavenly Father, in times of loss and sorrow, I thank You for being my guide and protector. Even when I walk through the darkest valleys, I find comfort in Your presence. Help me trust in Your guidance and feel the reassurance of Your staff. In Jesus' name, I pray. Amen.

The God of Healing and Wholeness

SCRIPTURE: *Jeremiah 30:17 - "For I will restore health to you, and your wounds I will heal, declares the Lord."*

DEVOTIONAL: In the midst of loss and sorrow, we often find ourselves in need of healing, not only for our physical wounds but also for the wounds that reside deep within our hearts. God, in His infinite love and compassion, promises to be the healer of our wounds.

The verse from Jeremiah reminds us that the Lord is the one who brings restoration to our brokenness. Just as He heals physical ailments, He also mends the wounds of our hearts. His healing touch can bring wholeness to the most shattered places of our souls.

As you journey through the difficulties of loss, remember that God is the source of healing and wholeness. In Him, there is the promise of restoration, and He longs to bring health to your heart and soul.

PRAYER: Heavenly Father, I thank You for Your promise to heal and restore. In times of loss, I lean on Your healing touch to mend my brokenness. Please bring health to my heart and soul, and may I find wholeness in You. In Jesus' name, I pray. Amen.

The Peace That Comes from Trusting God's Plan

SCRIPTURE: *Isaiah 55:8-9 - "For my thoughts are not your thoughts, neither are your ways my ways, declares the Lord."*

DEVOTIONAL: Loss can lead us to question and doubt, leaving us in the midst of uncertainty. During such times, we find solace in the profound truth that God's thoughts and ways are higher than our own.

Isaiah reminds us that God's understanding transcends our limited human perspective. His plans, even when we don't fully comprehend them, are filled with wisdom and purpose. Trusting in God's plan, despite our circumstances, allows us to find peace in the midst of uncertainty.

When faced with loss, remember that you serve a God whose ways are beyond your understanding but always rooted in love. Trust in His plan, lean on His wisdom, and you will discover a peace that surpasses all understanding.

PRAYER: Heavenly Father, in moments of loss and uncertainty, help me trust in Your higher ways and perfect plan. Grant me the peace that comes from knowing Your thoughts are higher than mine. In Jesus' name, I pray. Amen.

A Firm Foundation

SCRIPTURE: *Psalm 18:2 - "The Lord is my rock and my fortress and my deliverer, my God, my rock, in whom I take refuge, my shield, and the horn of my salvation, my stronghold."*

DEVOTIONAL: Loss can shake the very ground beneath our feet, leaving us feeling unsteady and vulnerable. In these moments, we can find comfort and strength in God, our firm foundation.

The psalmist beautifully describes God as a rock, fortress, and stronghold. He is our unshakable refuge, our shield in times of trouble. When life's storms rage around us, we can stand firm on the solid foundation of God's unwavering love and strength.

Even in the midst of loss, remember that you are not alone. The Lord is your rock, providing stability, protection, and a refuge of peace. Rest in His unchanging presence.

PRAYER: Gracious Father, in times of loss and uncertainty, I find my refuge and strength in You. Thank you for being my firm foundation. Help me to stand strong and secure in Your love. In Jesus' name, I pray. Amen.

Hope in the Midst of Suffering

SCRIPTURE: *Romans 5:3-4 - "Not only that, but we rejoice in our sufferings, knowing that suffering produces endurance, and endurance produces character, and character produces hope."*

DEVOTIONAL: Suffering, in its various forms, often accompanies loss. It can be a heavy burden to bear, yet even in the midst of suffering, there is hope.

The apostle Paul reminds us that suffering can have a purpose. It produces endurance, like a runner building strength through training. Endurance, in turn, molds our character, shaping us into more compassionate and resilient individuals. And as our character develops, so does hope.

Hope is the beacon that guides us through the darkest nights of grief and suffering. It's the assurance that God can bring beauty from ashes and turn our mourning into dancing. In the crucible of hardship, we discover a deeper, more profound hope—one that is not dependent on circumstances but rooted in our faith in a loving and faithful God.

PRAYER: Heavenly Father, in the midst of suffering and loss, help me to find endurance, build character, and ultimately discover the enduring hope that comes from knowing You. May Your presence be my anchor in troubled times. In Jesus' name, I pray. Amen.

DAY 166

Finding Purpose in God's Kingdom

SCRIPTURE: *Matthew 6:33 - "But seek first the kingdom of God and his righteousness, and all these things will be added to you."*

DEVOTIONAL: In the wake of loss, we may grapple with questions about the meaning and purpose of life. It's in these moments that the words of Jesus in Matthew 6:33 offer profound wisdom. He encourages us to seek first God's kingdom and His righteousness. This seeking isn't merely an external pursuit; it's an internal transformation. It's a shift of focus from our circumstances to aligning our lives with God's divine purposes.

When we seek God's kingdom, we discover that our purpose isn't solely defined by our earthly roles or achievements. It's found in living out God's will, in loving others, and in participating in His work of redemption. This purpose transcends loss, providing a foundation of meaning that can withstand life's storms. As we seek God's kingdom, we find that God Himself becomes our purpose, and in Him, we discover the richness of life's true meaning.

PRAYER: Heavenly Father, help me to seek Your kingdom and Your righteousness above all else. May I find my purpose and meaning in You, even in the midst of loss and uncertainty. In Jesus' name, I pray. Amen.

Healing Through Forgiveness

SCRIPTURE: *Ephesians 4:32 – "Be kind to one another, tenderhearted, forgiving one another, as God in Christ forgave you."*

DEVOTIONAL: Loss can sometimes bring with it feelings of anger, bitterness, and even a desire for retribution. It's in these moments that the wisdom of Ephesians 4:32 becomes a healing balm for our wounded souls. The verse encourages us to be kind, tenderhearted, and forgiving. This isn't just a suggestion; it's a path to healing. Forgiveness doesn't mean that what happened is okay or that we forget. Instead, it means that we release the grip of bitterness and anger on our hearts.

As God has forgiven us through Christ, we, too, are called to extend forgiveness. When we do, we free ourselves from the burden of carrying resentment. Forgiveness is not about condoning wrongs; it's about choosing healing over hatred. In the act of forgiving, we find that our hearts become tender again, allowing the healing process to begin. As we forgive, we open the door to God's grace, which can bring peace and wholeness to even the deepest wounds.

PRAYER: Dear Lord, grant me the strength to forgive as You have forgiven me. Help me release the burden of anger and bitterness, finding healing and peace through forgiveness. In Jesus' name, I pray. Amen.

The Promise of Eternal Life

SCRIPTURE: *John 11:25-26 - "Jesus said to her, 'I am the resurrection and the life. Whoever believes in me, though he die, yet shall he live, and everyone who lives and believes in me shall never die.'"*

DEVOTIONAL: When we face loss, the idea of death can become an unsettling reality. But in the midst of this, Jesus offers us profound reassurance. He proclaims, "I am the resurrection and the life."

These words remind us that our existence doesn't end with physical death. In Christ, we find the promise of eternal life. The pain of loss is real, but it's not the final word. Our faith in Jesus leads us to believe that there is a life beyond this one, a life in His presence where there is no more pain or sorrow.

Through faith in Jesus, we can find hope even in the darkest moments of grief. This eternal perspective can provide solace and meaning in the midst of loss, knowing that those we love, though they may have left this world, have found life eternal with the Savior.

PRAYER: Dear Lord, thank you for the promise of eternal life through faith in Jesus. In times of loss, help us hold onto this hope, finding comfort in the knowledge that death is not the end but the doorway to a life that knows no end. Amen.

Trusting in God's Sovereignty

SCRIPTURE: *Proverbs 16:9 - "The heart of man plans his way, but the Lord establishes his steps."*

DEVOTIONAL: In times of loss, we often grapple with the "whys" and "hows" of our circumstances. We make plans, and sometimes those plans are shattered. Yet, in the midst of life's unpredictable journey, we find solace in knowing that God is sovereign.

Proverbs 16:9 reminds us that while we may make our own plans, ultimately, it is the Lord who establishes our steps. This verse invites us to surrender our need for control and place our trust in the One who sees the bigger picture. Even in the face of loss, we can find meaning in knowing that God's sovereignty is at work.

Though we may not understand everything, we can trust that God's plan is perfect, and His purposes will prevail. This trust offers comfort, knowing that even in the most challenging moments, we are held by the One who guides our steps.

PRAYER: Heavenly Father, in moments of loss and uncertainty, help us to trust in Your sovereignty. Remind us that Your plans are perfect, and Your purposes prevail. Grant us the wisdom to surrender our need for control and find meaning in knowing You are guiding our steps. Amen.

The Comfort of God's Word

SCRIPTURE: *Psalm 119:105 – "Your word is a lamp to my feet and a light to my path."*

DEVOTIONAL: In the midst of loss, when darkness seems to surround us, we find comfort in the radiant light of God's Word. Like a lamp to our feet and a guiding light on our path, the Scriptures offer solace and direction in times of uncertainty.

Psalm 119:105 reminds us that God's Word is not just a book of wisdom but a source of profound comfort. It illuminates our understanding, revealing the way forward even when we feel lost. In our moments of grief, it provides assurance that we are not navigating life's challenges alone.

As we open our hearts to God's Word, we discover the healing power of His promises. His Word breathes life into our weary souls, reminding us of His presence and purpose even in the midst of loss.

PRAYER: Gracious Father, Your Word is a lamp that guides us through the darkest of valleys. We find comfort in its promises and wisdom. May Your Word continue to be a source of solace and light on our journey, especially in times of loss. In Jesus' name, we pray. Amen.

Embracing the Beauty of Creation

SCRIPTURE: *Genesis 1:31 - "And God saw everything that he had made, and behold, it was very good."*

DEVOTIONAL: In times of loss, when the world can seem cold and harsh, we can find solace and wonder in the beauty of God's creation. Reflect on Genesis 1:31, where God, after creating everything, saw that it was "very good."

Despite the pain of loss, the world around us still carries the fingerprints of its Creator. From the majesty of mountains to the delicate petals of a flower, creation reveals the artistry of God. It's a reminder that even in the face of sorrow, there is still beauty and goodness in the world.

Take a moment today to embrace the beauty around you. Allow the wonders of creation to soothe your soul and remind you of the loving Creator who cares for every detail. In these moments, find solace in the knowledge that the same God who crafted the world cares for you and holds your heart through every season of life.

PRAYER: Heavenly Father, we thank You for the beauty of Your creation, which offers solace and wonder even in times of loss. Help us to see Your hand in every detail of the world around us, and may this awareness bring comfort to our hearts. In Jesus' name, we pray. Amen.

Trusting in God's Unfailing Love

SCRIPTURE: *Psalm 136:26 - "Give thanks to the God of heaven, for his steadfast love endures forever."*

DEVOTIONAL: In times of loss, we may question many things, but one thing remains constant - the unfailing love of God. The psalmist reminds us in Psalm 136:26 that His steadfast love endures forever.

Loss can shake our foundations and leave us feeling adrift, but we can anchor our souls in the unchanging love of God. It's a love that has been there from the beginning and will remain with us throughout eternity.

Today, take a moment to reflect on the countless ways God has shown His love in your life, even in the midst of loss. His love is a source of comfort, strength, and meaning. Trust in His enduring love, and let it fill the spaces in your heart that loss has left behind.

PRAYER: Heavenly Father, we thank You for Your unfailing and enduring love. In times of loss, help us to find comfort and meaning in the knowledge that Your love is constant and unwavering. May it fill our hearts and guide us through every season of life. In Jesus' name, we pray. Amen.

DAY 173

The Comfort of God's Shelter

SCRIPTURE: *Psalm 91:1 - "He who dwells in the shelter of the Most High will abide in the shadow of the Almighty."*

DEVOTIONAL: Life often brings storms of uncertainty and loss that leave us feeling vulnerable and exposed. In those moments, Psalm 91:1 offers a beautiful reminder: "He who dwells in the shelter of the Most High will abide in the shadow of the Almighty."

Just as a shelter provides refuge from the elements, God's presence is our sanctuary amidst life's challenges. We can find solace in the assurance that, no matter the loss we face, we are under the protective shadow of the Almighty.

Today, take a moment to dwell in the shelter of God's love and grace. In His presence, you'll find refuge, strength, and the comfort needed to navigate the storms of life.

PRAYER: Heavenly Father, we thank You for being our shelter in times of loss and uncertainty. Help us to find refuge in Your presence, knowing that we are under the shadow of the Almighty. May Your comfort and protection surround us today and always. In Jesus' name, we pray. Amen.

The Healing Power of Gratitude

SCRIPTURE: *Colossians 3:17 - "And whatever you do, in word or deed, do everything in the name of the Lord Jesus, giving thanks to God the Father through him."*

DEVOTIONAL: In the face of loss, gratitude might seem elusive. Yet, Colossians 3:17 reminds us that giving thanks to God can be a source of healing, even in our darkest moments.

When we express gratitude, we shift our focus from what we've lost to what we still have. It's a powerful antidote to grief. Gratitude helps us see the goodness that remains in our lives, drawing us closer to God's comforting presence.

Today, take a moment to thank God for the blessings that persist even amidst loss. In doing so, you'll find a glimmer of hope and healing in your heart.

PRAYER: Heavenly Father, in times of loss, we thank You for being our constant source of comfort and strength. Help us to cultivate a heart of gratitude, even when circumstances are challenging. May our thanksgiving draw us nearer to Your loving embrace. In Jesus' name, we pray. Amen.

Finding Peace in His Presence

SCRIPTURE: *Psalm 16:11 - "You make known to me the path of life; in your presence, there is fullness of joy; at your right hand are pleasures forevermore."*

DEVOTIONAL: During times of loss, we often seek solace and meaning. Psalm 16:11 reminds us that true solace can be found in God's presence.

In the midst of grief, it's easy to feel adrift, as if the path of life has become uncertain. Yet, God promises to guide us, revealing the way to true and everlasting joy. His presence is not only a source of comfort but also a wellspring of joy that transcends our circumstances.

As you navigate the complexities of loss, take time to seek God's presence. In His nearness, you will find the peace that surpasses understanding and a sense of purpose that loss cannot diminish.

PRAYER: Heavenly Father, in Your presence, we find solace, joy, and purpose, even in the midst of loss. Help us seek You diligently, knowing that Your guidance leads us to a life of meaning and fullness. May we find peace in Your nearness. In Jesus' name, we pray. Amen.

DAY 176

The God of Compassion and Comfort

SCRIPTURE: *Psalm 34:18 - "The Lord is near to the brokenhearted and saves the crushed in spirit."*

DEVOTIONAL: Loss often leaves us feeling broken and crushed in spirit. In such times, we find solace in the God of compassion and comfort, as revealed in Psalm 34:18.

God's nearness to the brokenhearted is a profound source of comfort. He doesn't stand aloof from our pain but draws near to us, offering His presence as a balm for our wounds. In His nearness, we discover that we are not alone in our grief.

Furthermore, God doesn't merely sympathize with our suffering; He saves us from despair. His comforting presence restores hope and brings healing to our crushed spirits. As you navigate the challenges of loss, remember that the Lord is near and that His compassion is a wellspring of solace.

PRAYER: Gracious Father, we thank You for being near to us in our times of sorrow. Your compassion and comfort sustain us when we are brokenhearted and crushed in spirit. We find hope and healing in Your presence. In Jesus' name, we pray. Amen.

Embracing God's Promises

SCRIPTURE: *2 Corinthians 1:20 – "For all the promises of God find their Yes in him."*

DEVOTIONAL: In times of loss, it can be challenging to find meaning and hope. However, as believers, we have the assurance that all of God's promises find their "Yes" in Christ.

God's promises are like beacons of light in the darkness of life's struggles and losses. They remind us that we serve a faithful God who keeps His word. When we feel adrift in our grief, we can anchor our souls in the promises found throughout His Word.

Whether it's the promise of His presence, His comfort, His guidance, or the hope of eternal life, these assurances provide a foundation upon which we can build our lives. Embrace God's promises today, for they are the keys to finding hope, meaning, and peace, even amidst the challenges of loss.

PRAYER: Heavenly Father, we thank You for the promises that find their "Yes" in Christ. Help us to anchor our hearts in these assurances, especially in times of loss. May Your promises be a source of hope and meaning in our lives. In Jesus' name, we pray. Amen.

The Blessing of God's Guidance

SCRIPTURE: *Psalm 32:8 – "I will instruct you and teach you in the way you should go; I will counsel you with my eye upon you."*

DEVOTIONAL: During times of loss and uncertainty, we often yearn for guidance. We may wonder which path to take or how to navigate the challenges that lie ahead. In these moments, we can find solace in God's promise to instruct and counsel us.

God knows the way we should go, and He watches over us with His loving eye. He provides guidance through His Word, His Spirit, and sometimes through the wisdom of others. When we seek His counsel, we can be confident that we are on the right path.

Today, if you are facing difficult decisions or feeling lost amidst the trials of life, turn to God. Seek His guidance through prayer and His Word, and trust that He will lead you in the way you should go.

PRAYER: Heavenly Father, we thank You for Your promise to instruct and counsel us. In moments of uncertainty and loss, help us to seek Your guidance and trust in Your loving care. Lead us in the way we should go, and may we find solace in Your presence. In Jesus' name, we pray. Amen.

DAY 179

The Joy of the Lord as Our Strength

SCRIPTURE: *Nehemiah 8:10 - "And do not be grieved, for the joy of the Lord is your strength."*

DEVOTIONAL: In times of loss and sorrow, it's easy to feel weakened and burdened. The weight of grief can make each step feel heavy, and joy may seem distant. However, God's Word reminds us that the joy of the Lord is our strength.

This joy is not dependent on our circumstances but is found in our unshakable relationship with God. It's a deep-rooted gladness that springs from knowing Him and trusting in His unfailing love. This joy empowers us to carry on, to find hope amidst despair, and to be resilient in the face of adversity.

Today, if you're in a season of loss, seek the joy of the Lord. Spend time in His presence, worship Him with a grateful heart, and allow His joy to strengthen you. With His joy as your foundation, you can face even the darkest days with unwavering strength.

PRAYER: Heavenly Father, we thank You for being the source of our joy and strength. In times of loss and hardship, help us to lean on the joy that comes from knowing You. Fill our hearts with Your gladness, and grant us the resilience to press forward with confidence in Your love. In Jesus' name, we pray. Amen.

Restoring Hope Amidst Despair

SCRIPTURE: *Psalm 30:5 (ESV) – "For his anger is but for a moment, and his favor is for a lifetime. Weeping may tarry for the night, but joy comes with the morning."*

DEVOTIONAL: In the darkest of nights, it's easy to lose hope. Grief and despair may cloud our vision, making it challenging to see a way forward. But God's Word reminds us that even in our deepest sorrow, joy comes with the morning.

Just as the night eventually gives way to the dawn, so too can our moments of grief transform into moments of hope and healing. God's favor, His unfailing love, extends far beyond our temporary pain. His promise is one of restoration and renewal.

So, if you find yourself in a night of despair, remember that joy will come in the morning. Trust in God's timing, lean on His promises, and hold onto the hope that His light will pierce the darkness of your grief.

PRAYER: Heavenly Father, we thank You for the promise of joy that comes with the morning. During our times of sorrow and despair, help us to trust in Your unfailing love and restoration. May we find hope in Your promises and look forward to the dawn of joy. In Jesus' name, we pray. Amen.

The Beauty of God's Creation

SCRIPTURE: *Psalm 19:1 - "The heavens declare the glory of God, and the sky above proclaims his handiwork."*

DEVOTIONAL: Amidst the struggles and losses of life, we can find solace in the beauty that surrounds us. Look up at the sky, the stars, and the vastness of creation, and you'll witness God's artistry on full display. The heavens themselves declare His glory.

Even in moments of sorrow, the grandeur of nature can be a source of comfort. The intricate details of a flower, the majesty of a mountain, or the serenity of a sunset remind us of the Creator's loving touch. When we take time to appreciate the world around us, it can ease the burdens we carry.

So, as you navigate the challenges of life, remember to pause and behold the beauty of God's creation. Let it be a reminder that the same Creator who crafted the universe cares for you and is with you in your losses and joys.

PRAYER: Lord, we thank You for the breathtaking beauty of Your creation. In moments of loss and grief, help us find solace in the wonders of nature. May Your handiwork remind us of Your presence and love. In Jesus' name, we pray. Amen.

The Gift of God's Grace and Salvation

SCRIPTURE: *Ephesians 2:8-9 - "For by grace you have been saved through faith. And this is not your own doing; it is the gift of God, not a result of works, so that no one may boast."*

DEVOTIONAL: In times of loss, we may wrestle with feelings of inadequacy or despair, wondering how we can find solace amidst the pain. It's during these moments that we should remember the incredible gift of God's grace and salvation. We are saved not through our own efforts but by the boundless grace of God. This grace is a gift, freely given to us. It reminds us that even when we face the darkest days, God's love shines as a beacon of hope. We don't have to earn it, for it's given out of His immeasurable love.

So, as we navigate the losses in life, let's find solace in this gift of grace and salvation. It's a reminder that God's love is constant, His forgiveness is boundless, and through faith in Him, we can discover meaning and hope even in the most challenging times.

PRAYER: Heavenly Father, we thank You for the incredible gift of Your grace and salvation. During times of loss, help us remember that Your love is steadfast and Your grace is sufficient. May we find solace in Your unmerited favor, knowing that through faith in Christ, we have eternal hope. In Jesus' name, we pray. Amen.

More Compassion and Comfort

SCRIPTURE: *Psalm 103:13 - "As a father shows compassion to his children, so the Lord shows compassion to those who fear him."*

DEVOTIONAL: Loss can often lead us to a place of self-criticism, where we blame ourselves or question our worthiness of comfort and compassion. However, in times of hardship, it's essential to remember that our Heavenly Father, the God of compassion, is always ready to embrace us with His love.

God's compassion is not conditional; it's as natural as a loving parent comforting a hurting child. Even when we struggle to extend compassion to ourselves, God's arms are wide open, waiting to provide solace and reassurance.

In the face of loss, let's learn to accept God's compassion, trusting in His loving care. Allow His comforting presence to heal your wounds, for His compassion is boundless, and it extends to you, just as you are.

PRAYER: Loving Father, we thank You for the compassion and comfort You offer us, especially in our times of loss. Help us to accept Your love and grace, even when we find it difficult to extend compassion to ourselves. May Your boundless love bring solace and healing to our wounded hearts. In Jesus' name, we pray. Amen.

DAY 184

Surrender

SCRIPTURE: *Zephaniah 3:17 - "The Lord your God is in your midst, a mighty one who will save; he will rejoice over you with gladness; he will quiet you by his love; he will exult over you with loud singing."*

DEVOTIONAL: In times of loss, when we feel the weight of our own limitations, it can be challenging to imagine finding strength in surrender. However, there's a profound truth hidden in surrender - the assurance that the Lord, our mighty Savior, is with us.

Zephaniah 3:17 reminds us that God is not a distant observer but is right in our midst. He delights in us, quiets our fears with His love, and even celebrates us with joyful singing. Surrendering to His presence and love brings strength beyond our comprehension. Today, as you navigate the difficulties of loss, surrender to the Lord's reassuring presence. In that surrender, you'll discover a strength that only His love can provide.

PRAYER: Heavenly Father, thank You for being our mighty Savior who rejoices over us with love. Help us find strength in surrendering to Your presence, especially during times of loss. In Your comforting embrace, may we discover the peace and strength we need. In Jesus' name, we pray. Amen.

Releasing the Grip of Bitterness

SCRIPTURE: *Ephesians 4:32 – "Be kind to one another, tenderhearted, forgiving one another, as God in Christ forgave you."*

DEVOTIONAL: In the journey through loss, the weight of pain and grief can become almost unbearable. In these moments, it's vital to remember the healing power of forgiveness. Ephesians 4:32 encourages us to be kind, tenderhearted, and forgiving, just as God forgave us through Christ. Forgiveness is a balm for the wounded soul. It doesn't erase the pain, but it can release the grip of bitterness and resentment. By forgiving those who may have caused or contributed to our loss, we unburden ourselves from the heavy load of anger and hurt.

Moreover, forgiveness doesn't just apply to others but to ourselves as well. Often, we carry guilt or regret over things we couldn't change or prevent. Just as God forgives us, we must learn to forgive ourselves.

Today, reflect on the healing power of forgiveness. Allow God's grace to flow through you, forgiving others and forgiving yourself. It's a step toward healing amidst loss, one that can bring freedom and peace.

PRAYER: Heavenly Father, thank You for Your incredible forgiveness through Christ. Help us to extend that same forgiveness to others and to ourselves, especially in times of loss. May forgiveness be a source of healing and peace in our lives. In Jesus' name, we pray. Amen.

Embracing the Beauty of God's Creation

SCRIPTURE: *Job 12:7-9 7 - "But ask the beasts, and they will teach you; the birds of the heavens, and they will tell you; or the bushes of the earth, and they will teach you, and the fish of the sea will declare to you. Who among all these does not know that the hand of the Lord has done this?"*

DEVOTIONAL: In the midst of loss and grief, we can often find solace and beauty in the world around us. Job 12:7-9 reminds us to embrace the wisdom of God's creation. Look at the animals, the birds, the plants, and the fish. They all declare the hand of the Lord in creating this magnificent world.

Nature has a way of revealing the Creator's artistry, offering a sense of peace and wonder. Take a moment today to step outside, breathe in the fresh air, and observe the beauty that surrounds you. Even in the face of loss, the intricate design of creation can bring comfort and remind us of the enduring presence of the Creator.

As you ponder the simplicity and complexity of the natural world, let it be a source of inspiration and healing. God's handiwork is all around us, and it speaks of His love and care, even in our times of sorrow.

PRAYER: Creator God, we thank You for the beauty of Your creation, which speaks of Your wisdom and love. In moments of loss, help us to find solace and inspiration in the world You've made. May the beauty of nature remind us of Your presence and bring comfort to our hearts. Amen.

Hidden Treasures of God's Comfort

SCRIPTURE: *2 Corinthians 1:7 - "Our hope for you is unshaken, for we know that as you share in our sufferings, you will also share in our comfort."*

DEVOTIONAL: In times of loss and sorrow, we often search for comfort in familiar places. But just as a treasure hunter seeks hidden gems, we can discover a unique kind of treasure in the comforting words of 2 Corinthians 1:7.

Paul, the author of this letter, reminds us that our hope in God's comfort is unshaken. As we share in the sufferings of life, we also have the privilege of sharing in the deep well of comfort that God provides. It's a comfort unlike any other, one that understands our pain intimately and offers solace beyond measure.

PRAYER: Dear Lord, we thank you for being our source of comfort in times of loss and grief. Help us, Lord, to recognize the treasure of your presence, which brings solace beyond measure. As we share in the sufferings of life, may we also share in the profound comfort that only you can provide. In the name of Jesus, our ultimate Comforter, we pray. Amen.

The Renewed in Christ

SCRIPTURE: *2 Corinthians 5:17 - "Therefore, if anyone is in Christ, he is a new creation. The old has passed away; behold, the new has come."*

DEVOTIONAL: Loss and grief can often leave us feeling like a part of us has been taken away, leaving a void. Yet, in 2 Corinthians 5:17, we find a glimmer of hope amidst this pain. It reminds us that when we are in Christ, we become new creations. The old, marked by sorrow and loss, passes away, making room for the new.

In Christ, we discover a source of renewal and transformation that transcends our worldly understanding. He brings healing to our broken hearts and renews our spirits. This renewal is not just a fresh start; it's a beautiful metamorphosis that begins to take shape even in the midst of our deepest losses.

PRAYER: Heavenly Father, we are grateful for the promise of renewal in Christ. In times of loss, when we feel broken and empty, help us remember that in you, we are made new. May this renewal fill us with hope and strength as we navigate the challenges of life. In Jesus' name, we pray. Amen.

DAY 189

Embracing God's Spirit of Power, Love, and Self-Control

SCRIPTURE: *2 Timothy 1:7 - "For God gave us a spirit not of fear but of power and love and self-control."*

DEVOTIONAL: In times of loss, fear can become a formidable adversary, robbing us of peace and hope. However, 2 Timothy 1:7 reminds us that as children of God, we have been gifted with a different spirit—a spirit characterized by power, love, and self-control.

God's Spirit empowers us to face our fears and the challenges of loss with courage. His love envelops us, offering solace and comfort even in our deepest sorrow. His gift of self-control helps us navigate the tumultuous seas of grief, finding strength in restraint.

Today, if you find yourself overwhelmed by fear due to loss, remember that God's Spirit resides in you, offering power, love, and self-control. Embrace this divine gift, and let it guide you through the darkest of days.

PRAYER: Heavenly Father, we thank you for the gift of your Spirit—a spirit of power, love, and self-control. When we are gripped by fear in the face of loss, help us to lean on Your strength, be comforted by Your love, and exercise self-control over our emotions. In your name, we pray. Amen.

The Promise of Christ's Return

SCRIPTURE: *Acts 1:11 - "Men of Galilee, why do you stand looking into heaven? This Jesus, who was taken up from you into heaven, will come in the same way as you saw him go into heaven."*

DEVOTIONAL: Loss can leave us longing for restoration, for things to be made right once more. Acts 1:11 reminds us of the promise of Christ's return. Just as the disciples saw Jesus ascend into heaven, they were assured that He would return in the same way.

In times of loss and despair, we find hope in the certainty of Christ's second coming. His return will bring ultimate restoration, when tears will be wiped away, and all pain will cease. As we long for this day, let us also find comfort in knowing that Jesus is with us in our present grief, offering solace and strength.

Today, as you face loss and yearn for restoration, hold fast to the promise of Christ's return. His coming will bring eternal joy and healing beyond measure.

PRAYER: Lord Jesus, we eagerly anticipate your return. In moments of loss, remind us of the hope we have in your promise to come again. Be our comfort and strength as we navigate the challenges of today, knowing that you are with us. Amen.

Redemption Through Christ

SCRIPTURE: *Acts 10:43 - "To him all the prophets bear witness that everyone who believes in him receives forgiveness of sins through his name."*

DEVOTIONAL: In times of loss and despair, it can be easy to feel burdened by our sins and shortcomings. Acts 10:43 reminds us that through faith in Jesus Christ, we can find redemption and forgiveness. All the prophets of old testified to this truth: in Christ's name, sins are forgiven, and we are reconciled with God.

Loss may make us acutely aware of our human frailty and imperfections. However, it is precisely in these moments that we can turn to Christ for solace and renewal. Through faith in Him, we receive the incredible gift of forgiveness, allowing us to move forward with hope and a sense of purpose.

Today, if you are weighed down by the weight of past mistakes, remember Acts 10:43 and the assurance of forgiveness through faith in Jesus Christ. Embrace this gift and find healing for your soul.

PRAYER: Heavenly Father, we thank you for the forgiveness and redemption we find in your Son, Jesus Christ. In moments of loss, help us remember that through His name, we are forgiven and made whole. Grant us the strength to live in the freedom of this forgiveness and share it with others. In Jesus' name, we pray. Amen.

Assurance Through Faith

SCRIPTURE: *Acts 16:31 – "And they said, 'Believe in the Lord Jesus, and you will be saved, you and your household.'"*

DEVOTIONAL: Loss can shake the foundations of our lives, leaving us searching for something solid to hold onto. Acts 16:31 offers a steadfast promise in times of uncertainty. The message is clear: believe in the Lord Jesus, and you will be saved.

It's a simple yet profound truth. Through faith in Jesus Christ, salvation is offered not only to us but to our households as well. In the face of loss, this promise provides assurance and a source of enduring hope.

When the storms of life rage, we can find refuge in the unwavering promise of salvation through faith in Jesus. It is a lifeline that can sustain us through even the darkest of times. Today, take hold of this promise, believing in the Lord Jesus for your salvation and the well-being of your loved ones.

PRAYER: Heavenly Father, we place our faith in the Lord Jesus for our salvation and the salvation of our households. In times of loss and uncertainty, may this promise be a source of unshakable assurance. Help us to rest in the security of our faith and share this hope with others. In Jesus' name, we pray. Amen.

Serving the Lord

SCRIPTURE: *Colossians 3:24 – "Knowing that from the Lord you will receive the inheritance as your reward. You are serving the Lord Christ."*

DEVOTIONAL: In times of loss, it can be challenging to see the purpose in our pain. Colossians 3:24 reminds us that even our most trying moments can be turned into acts of service to the Lord.

When we serve with a heart focused on Christ, our efforts become more than just tasks; they become offerings. Every act of kindness, every word of comfort, and every gesture of love becomes a service to the Lord Himself.

So, if you find yourself amidst loss and wondering about the meaning of it all, remember that you can find purpose in serving the Lord Christ. Your actions, motivated by faith and love, become part of a grander design orchestrated by a loving God.

PRAYER: Dear Lord, help us to serve You faithfully, even in the midst of loss and uncertainty. May we find purpose and meaning in serving You with all our hearts. Let our actions be a reflection of Your love and grace. In Jesus' name, we pray. Amen.

DAY 194

Our Life Hidden in Christ

SCRIPTURE: *Colossians 3:4 – "When Christ who is your life appears, then you also will appear with him in glory."*

DEVOTIONAL: In times of loss, we can feel as though a part of us is missing. But Colossians 3:4 offers a profound reminder: our lives are hidden in Christ.

Loss can take many forms—loss of a loved one, a job, health, or dreams. But no matter the type of loss, when we have Christ, we possess an unchanging and eternal source of life. He is our constant, our refuge, and our hope.

When we anchor our lives in Christ, we can face loss with a different perspective. Our true life isn't defined by our circumstances but by our relationship with Him. And when He appears in His glory, we will also share in that glory.

In your moments of loss, remember that your life is hidden in Christ. Find solace in the eternal hope He provides.

PRAYER: Dear Lord, help us to remember that our lives are hidden in You. When loss surrounds us, may we find comfort in knowing that our true life is found in You and that one day, we will share in Your glory. In Jesus' name, we pray. Amen.

Compassion Amidst Sorrow

SCRIPTURE: *Daniel 9:9 – "To the Lord our God belong mercy and forgiveness, for we have rebelled against him."*

DEVOTIONAL: In the depths of sorrow, it's easy to feel isolated and burdened by guilt or regret. Yet, in Daniel 9:9, we find a beautiful truth: God's nature is characterized by mercy and forgiveness.

Loss often brings with it a flood of emotions and questions. We may question our choices or actions. But the Lord's mercy knows no bounds, and His forgiveness is ever-present. He doesn't turn away from us when we've rebelled or made mistakes; instead, He offers us compassion.

As you navigate the sea of sorrow, remember that God's arms are open wide. He offers the solace of His mercy and the grace of His forgiveness, providing a path to healing amidst loss.

PRAYER: Dear Lord, in our moments of sorrow and loss, remind us of Your boundless mercy and forgiveness. Help us find solace in the compassion You offer, knowing that even in our weaknesses, Your grace prevails. In Jesus' name, we pray. Amen.

The God of Miracles

SCRIPTURE: *Deuteronomy 10:21 – "He is your praise. He is your God, who has done for you these great and terrifying things that your eyes have seen."*

DEVOTIONAL: In times of loss, it can be easy to lose sight of the miracles that God has performed in our lives. We may become overwhelmed by grief, forgetting the moments when God's power and grace were undeniably evident.

Deuteronomy 10:21 serves as a powerful reminder that God is the source of our praise. He is the One who has done great and awe-inspiring things in our lives, things that our own eyes have witnessed. These moments of God's intervention, no matter how big or small, should not be forgotten.

As you journey through the challenges of loss, take time to reflect on the miracles God has already performed in your life. Let them serve as a source of hope and encouragement, knowing that the same God who acted then is with you now.

PRAYER: Heavenly Father, in times of loss, help us remember the great and wondrous things You have done in our lives. May these reminders of Your power and grace be a source of comfort and hope as we navigate the path ahead. In Jesus' name, we pray. Amen.

DAY 197

The Lord, Your Deliverer

SCRIPTURE: *Deuteronomy 20:4 – "For the Lord your God is he who goes with you to fight for you against your enemies, to give you the victory."*

DEVOTIONAL: In times of loss and adversity, it's easy to feel overwhelmed and as if you're fighting battles on multiple fronts. Yet, in Deuteronomy 20:4, we are reminded that we don't face these struggles alone. The Lord, our God, is not only with us but goes before us into the battles we encounter.

Imagine the assurance of having the Almighty God fighting on your behalf, ensuring victory over your adversaries. This promise extends beyond earthly conflicts; it encompasses the spiritual and emotional battles that often accompany loss.

So, when you face challenges, remember that the Lord, your Deliverer, is by your side. In Him, you can find the strength and confidence needed to overcome life's obstacles.

PRAYER: Heavenly Father, thank you for being our Deliverer in times of trouble. Help us trust in Your presence and find victory through You, no matter the battles we face. In Your name, we pray. Amen.

Finding Meaning in Serving Others

SCRIPTURE: *Galatians 5:13 - "For you were called to freedom, brothers. Only do not use your freedom as an opportunity for the flesh, but through love serve one another."*

DEVOTIONAL: In times of loss, it's common to turn inward, consumed by our own pain and grief. However, Galatians 5:13 reminds us that we are called to something greater – serving one another in love. When we focus on helping and serving others, we often find profound meaning and healing.

Serving isn't just about helping those in need; it's about rediscovering our purpose. It shifts our perspective from our own struggles to the needs of others. By reaching out to others with compassion, we not only extend God's love but also experience the transformative power of love in our own lives.

As you navigate loss, consider how you can serve others in love. Whether through acts of kindness, lending a listening ear, or offering support, you'll discover that in serving, you find meaning, healing, and a deeper connection to your faith.

PRAYER: Dear Lord, help us embrace the calling to serve one another in love. Grant us the strength and wisdom to extend a helping hand to those in need, even in our own times of loss. May our acts of service be a source of healing and meaning in our lives. In Your name, we pray. Amen.

The Comfort of God's Promises

SCRIPTURE: *2 Peter 1:4 - "By which he has granted to us his precious and very great promises, so that through them you may become partakers of the divine nature, having escaped from the corruption that is in the world because of sinful desire."*

DEVOTIONAL: Loss can leave us feeling adrift in a sea of uncertainty and sorrow. Yet, in these challenging moments, we find solace in God's precious promises. 2 Peter 1:4 reminds us that God has granted us His great and precious promises. These promises are like anchors for our souls, grounding us in His unchanging love and purpose.

When we hold onto God's promises, we are reminded of His faithfulness and the hope He provides. His promises assure us that we can become partakers of His divine nature, transcending the brokenness of this world. In our grief, we find meaning and healing by trusting in His word.

Take time to reflect on the promises of God as you navigate loss. Let His assurances become a source of comfort and strength, knowing that His promises are true and enduring.

PRAYER: Heavenly Father, we thank you for the precious promises you've given us. In times of loss and uncertainty, help us cling to your word as an anchor for our souls. May your promises provide us with comfort, healing, and a renewed sense of purpose. In Jesus' name, we pray. Amen.

The Courage to Face Tomorrow

SCRIPTURE: *Deuteronomy 31:6 – "Be strong and courageous. Do not fear or be in dread of them, for it is the Lord your God who goes with you. He will not leave you or forsake you."*

DEVOTIONAL: As we journey through life, especially during seasons of loss, we may feel apprehensive about the unknown future. It's in these moments that we find strength and courage in God's reassuring words. Deuteronomy 31:6 reminds us that we should be strong and courageous, not living in fear or dread of what lies ahead. Why? Because the Lord our God goes with us. He promises never to leave us or forsake us.

In the face of loss, we can hold on to this promise with unwavering trust. God's presence is a constant source of comfort and guidance. He walks with us through the valleys of grief and uncertainty, providing the courage we need to face each new day.

Today, let this verse be a reminder that you are not alone. God is with you, offering His strength, His courage, and His unwavering love to carry you through.

PRAYER: Heavenly Father, we thank you for your promise to always be with us. In times of loss and uncertainty, grant us the strength and courage to face each new day. Help us trust in your unfailing presence. In Jesus' name, we pray. Amen.

Embracing the Comfort of the Holy Spirit

SCRIPTURE: *Romans 8:26 – "Likewise, the Spirit helps us in our weakness. For we do not know what to pray for as we ought, but the Spirit himself intercedes for us with groanings too deep for words."*

DEVOTIONAL: In times of loss and grief, when our hearts ache, and words seem inadequate, the Holy Spirit steps in as our Comforter. Romans 8:26 beautifully illustrates this truth. When we are at our weakest and unable to express the depths of our sorrow, the Spirit intercedes for us. He communicates our pain, our longings, and our unspoken prayers to God.

This verse reminds us that in our moments of vulnerability, we are not alone. The Holy Spirit is there to provide solace, bringing our brokenness before the throne of grace. When we don't know what to pray, when words fail us, the Spirit bridges the gap, ensuring that our cries are heard.

Today, take comfort in the presence of the Holy Spirit. Embrace His soothing presence, knowing that even in your weakness, He intercedes on your behalf, offering solace and hope.

PRAYER: Holy Spirit, our Comforter, we thank you for your presence in our times of weakness and grief. Help us feel your nearness and find solace in your intercession when words escape us. In Jesus' name, we pray. Amen.

Trusting in God's Assurance

SCRIPTURE: *Deuteronomy 31:8 - "The Lord himself goes before you and will be with you; he will never leave you nor forsake you. Do not be afraid; do not be discouraged."*

DEVOTIONAL: In the face of loss, we may often feel abandoned and fearful, but Deuteronomy 31:8 reminds us of God's unwavering presence and faithfulness. This verse reassures us that the Lord not only goes before us but remains with us through all life's trials and tribulations.

During times of loss, it's easy to become discouraged and fearful of what lies ahead. Yet, God's promise is clear: He will never leave nor forsake us. Our Heavenly Father is a constant source of comfort and strength, even when we may feel the most alone.

Today, take solace in the assurance that God is walking beside you in your journey through grief. Trust in His unfailing presence, and do not be afraid or discouraged, for He is your refuge and strength in times of need.

PRAYER: Heavenly Father, we thank you for your unchanging presence in our lives. In our moments of loss, help us find comfort in your unwavering faithfulness and the assurance that you are always with us. In Jesus' name, we pray. Amen.

DAY 203

The Eternal Arms of God

SCRIPTURE: *Deuteronomy 33:27 - "The eternal God is your refuge, and underneath are the everlasting arms. He will drive out your enemies before you, saying, 'Destroy them!'"*

DEVOTIONAL: In seasons of loss, when we feel most vulnerable, Deuteronomy 33:27 reminds us that we have an eternal refuge in God. This verse paints a powerful image of the Almighty as our refuge, with His everlasting arms beneath us, supporting and carrying us through life's challenges.

Like a loving parent embracing their child, God's arms are our shelter, a place of safety and comfort. Even when faced with difficulties, His presence never wavers. In fact, this verse tells us that He goes before us, fighting our battles on our behalf.

During times of loss, we may be confronted with overwhelming circumstances. However, remember that you are cradled in the everlasting arms of the eternal God. He is your refuge and strength, guiding you through every trial.

PRAYER: Eternal God, we take comfort in knowing that you are our refuge and strength. Thank you for your everlasting arms that support and protect us, especially in times of loss. May we find solace in your unwavering presence. In Jesus' name, we pray. Amen.

DAY 204

Seeking God with All Your Heart

SCRIPTURE: *Deuteronomy 4:29 - "But if from there you seek the Lord your God, you will find him if you seek him with all your heart and with all your soul."*

DEVOTIONAL: In the midst of loss, we often find ourselves searching for meaning, comfort, and answers. Deuteronomy 4:29 reassures us that when we seek the Lord with all our heart and soul, we will find Him.

This verse invites us to turn to God in our times of need, to earnestly seek His presence and guidance. It's a reminder that even in our pain and confusion, God is near, ready to offer us solace and direction.

Grief can be a lonely journey, but the promise of this verse is that God is waiting for us to seek Him. He longs to walk with us through the darkest valleys, to bring us comfort and healing. Let us approach Him with all our heart and soul, confident that He is faithful to respond to our cries.

PRAYER: Heavenly Father, in our moments of loss and confusion, we seek you with all our heart and soul. Thank you for the promise that when we search for you, we will find you. Be our comfort and guide through every trial. In Jesus' name, we pray. Amen.

Blessings Beyond Measure

SCRIPTURE: *Deuteronomy 8:18 – "You shall remember the Lord your God, for it is he who gives you power to get wealth, that he may confirm his covenant that he swore to your fathers, as it is this day."*

DEVOTIONAL: Loss can sometimes make us feel as though we have been stripped of everything. In these moments, it's crucial to remember that our blessings go beyond material possessions. Deuteronomy 8:18 reminds us to remember the Lord our God, for He provides us with the power to attain wealth and prosperity.

It's not just about financial wealth but about the richness of life in God's love, grace, and promises. Even in the face of loss, we can find blessings in the form of strength, resilience, and the support of loved ones.

This verse encourages us to recognize that God's faithfulness extends to us in various ways. While we may face challenges and losses, we can trust that He will always be there, guiding us and confirming His covenant of love with us.

PRAYER: Dear Lord, help us remember that your blessings are not limited to material wealth. In times of loss, help us find solace in the abundance of your love and grace. Thank you for your faithfulness. In Jesus' name, we pray. Amen.

Learning Through Discipline

SCRIPTURE: *Deuteronomy 8:5 - "Know then in your heart that, as a man disciplines his son, the Lord your God disciplines you."*

DEVOTIONAL: Loss often comes with pain and hardship, and in those moments, it can be difficult to see any purpose or meaning. However, Deuteronomy 8:5 reminds us that even in difficult times, there is an opportunity for growth and learning. Just as a loving parent disciplines their child to teach them and help them grow, the Lord sometimes allows challenges and losses in our lives to discipline and shape us. These experiences can teach us valuable lessons, build character, and deepen our dependence on God.

While it may not be easy to understand why we face certain losses, we can find comfort in knowing that God is using these moments to mold us into better versions of ourselves. Embracing this perspective can help us find meaning even in the midst of pain.

PRAYER: Heavenly Father, in times of loss and hardship, help us to recognize the opportunities for growth and learning that you provide. Grant us the strength to endure and the wisdom to understand your purpose in our lives. In Jesus' name, we pray. Amen.

The Riches of His Glorious Inheritance

SCRIPTURE: *Ephesians 1:18-19 - "I pray that the eyes of your heart may be enlightened, so that you will know what is the hope of His calling, what are the riches of the glory of His inheritance in the saints, 19 and what is the surpassing greatness of His power toward us who believe."*

DEVOTIONAL: In times of loss and uncertainty, it's easy to lose sight of the hope and inheritance that God has promised to those who believe. Ephesians 1:18-19 reminds us of the incredible spiritual blessings available to us. The hope of God's calling is an anchor that steadies us when life's storms threaten to overwhelm us. It's a reminder that our lives have purpose and meaning in Christ.

Additionally, as God's children, we share in the glorious inheritance of His saints. This inheritance is rich beyond measure, filled with the abundance of His grace and love.

Lastly, the verse speaks of the surpassing greatness of God's power toward us. Even in times of loss, God's power is at work within us, giving us strength, resilience, and the ability to find meaning and purpose amidst our trials. Today, let us take comfort in these promises and remember that our hope, inheritance, and the power of God are ever-present, even in the face of loss.

PRAYER: Heavenly Father, open the eyes of our hearts to fully grasp the hope, inheritance, and power that You provide. In moments of loss and uncertainty, help us to stand firm in the knowledge of Your blessings. May we find meaning and purpose in Your promises. In Jesus' name, we pray. Amen.

Redemption Through His Blood

SCRIPTURE: *Ephesians 1:7 – "In him, we have redemption through his blood, the forgiveness of our trespasses, according to the riches of his grace."*

DEVOTIONAL: In times of loss and difficulty, it's easy to be weighed down by regret or guilt. We may question our decisions or wonder if we could have done things differently. Yet, Ephesians 1:7 reminds us of a powerful truth: in Christ, we have redemption through His blood.

Through the sacrifice of Jesus, our sins are forgiven. His grace is so abundant that it covers every mistake and trespass we've made. In Him, we find freedom from the burdens of guilt and regret. This redemption is not something we can earn but is a gift from God, given out of His incredible love for us.

As we navigate the challenges of life and the losses we encounter, let's hold onto the assurance of forgiveness and redemption. In Christ, we can find healing and restoration, knowing that His grace is more than sufficient to carry us through any trial.

PRAYER: Dear Lord, thank you for the redemption and forgiveness that we find in Christ. In moments of loss and struggle, help us remember that we are covered by Your grace. Grant us the strength to accept this gift and find healing and restoration in You. In Jesus' name, we pray. Amen.

Finding Peace in Unity

SCRIPTURE: *Ephesians 2:14 – "For he himself is our peace, who has made us both one and has broken down in his flesh the dividing wall of hostility."*

DEVOTIONAL: In times of loss and grief, divisions among people can exacerbate our pain and suffering. Yet, Ephesians 2:14 reminds us that in Christ, we find our ultimate source of peace, and He has the power to break down the walls of hostility that separate us.

The unity that Christ brings extends beyond race, nationality, or any other factor that may divide us. Through His sacrifice, He reconciles us to God and to one another. As we face the challenges of loss, we can seek unity and peace in our relationships. Instead of letting differences drive us apart, let's allow the love and grace of Christ to bring us together, supporting one another in our times of need.

In Christ, we find the strength to build bridges of understanding and compassion, which can provide solace and healing, not only for ourselves but also for those around us.

PRAYER: Lord Jesus, thank you for being our ultimate source of peace and for breaking down the walls of hostility that divide us. Help us to seek unity and reconciliation in times of loss, extending your love and grace to those around us. In your name, we pray. Amen.

Finding Purpose Amidst Loss

SCRIPTURE: *Ephesians 2:10 – "For we are his workmanship, created in Christ Jesus for good works, which God prepared beforehand, that we should walk in them."*

DEVOTIONAL: In the midst of loss and grief, it's easy to wonder about the purpose of our lives. Why do we go through these difficult moments? Ephesians 2:10 reminds us that we are God's workmanship, created with intention and purpose. Even in our pain, there are good works that God has prepared for us to walk in.

Loss can be a catalyst for discovering and fulfilling our God-given purpose. It can lead us to reach out to others who are hurting, to advocate for change, or to deepen our compassion for those in need. When we seek God's guidance and trust His plan, even amidst loss, we can find meaning in the roles we play in His greater story.

So, when you're grappling with the pain of loss, remember that you are not without purpose. God has uniquely designed you for good works, and these works can bring light and hope into a world that desperately needs it.

PRAYER: Heavenly Father, in moments of loss and grief, help us remember that we are your workmanship, created with purpose. Guide us in discovering and fulfilling the good works you have prepared for us, even in our times of pain. In Jesus' name, we pray. Amen.

DAY 211

Confidence in God's Presence

SCRIPTURE: *Ephesians 3:12 - "In whom we have boldness and access with confidence through our faith in him."*

DEVOTIONAL: In times of loss and uncertainty, we may feel alone and helpless. Yet, Ephesians 3:12 reminds us of the incredible privilege we have as believers. We can approach God with boldness and confidence because of our faith in Him.

Even in our moments of grief, we are not isolated from God's presence. We have uninterrupted access to His comfort, guidance, and love. In the face of loss, our faith in Christ becomes a source of strength, allowing us to draw near to God without fear.

So, when you encounter loss, remember that you can approach God confidently, knowing that He is with you, ready to provide the peace and solace that only He can offer.

PRAYER: Dear Heavenly Father, thank you for the assurance that we can come to you with boldness and confidence through our faith in Christ. In moments of loss, help us remember that we are never separated from your comforting presence. Strengthen our faith, Lord, and grant us the peace that surpasses all understanding. In Jesus' name, we pray. Amen.

The Depths of God's Love

SCRIPTURE: *Ephesians 3:19 - "And to know the love of Christ that surpasses knowledge, that you may be filled with all the fullness of God."*

DEVOTIONAL: The love of Christ is beyond our comprehension. Ephesians 3:19 reminds us that it surpasses knowledge itself. In times of loss and grief, it's this unfathomable love that can bring profound healing and meaning to our lives.

As we seek to understand this love, we find that it fills us with the fullness of God. It comforts us in our pain, provides meaning in our suffering, and grants hope amidst despair. In embracing the depths of God's love, we discover a wellspring of solace that can carry us through the most challenging moments of loss.

So, in your times of sorrow, meditate on the love of Christ. Allow it to surround you, fill you, and give you the strength to find purpose and healing amidst your loss.

PRAYER: Heavenly Father, we acknowledge that your love surpasses all knowledge. In our moments of loss, help us to grasp the depth of your love for us. Fill us with your fullness, Lord, and grant us comfort, meaning, and hope. In Jesus' name, we pray. Amen.

Walking in the Light

SCRIPTURE: *Ephesians 5:8 - "For at one time you were darkness, but now you are light in the Lord. Walk as children of light."*

DEVOTIONAL: Ephesians 5:8 reminds us that, in Christ, we transition from darkness to light. This transition is significant, especially when we are grappling with loss and seeking meaning in the midst of it.

When we walk as children of light, we choose to live in the truth, embracing God's guidance and wisdom. In this light, we find clarity and purpose even when we've experienced loss. It allows us to see life from a heavenly perspective, understanding that God's love and grace are with us, even in difficult times.

So, in the face of loss, let us walk as children of light. Let us find meaning and solace in God's eternal promises and the knowledge that, in Him, we have a purpose that transcends the temporal challenges we encounter.

PRAYER: Heavenly Father, thank you for calling us out of darkness into your marvelous light. In moments of loss, help us walk as children of light, finding meaning and purpose in your eternal truth. May your guidance be our comfort. In Jesus' name, we pray. Amen.

DAY 214

Chosen in Him

SCRIPTURE: *Ephesians 1:4 – "Even as he chose us in him before the foundation of the world, that we should be holy and blameless before him. In love."*

DEVOTIONAL: Ephesians 1:4 beautifully reminds us that God has chosen us in Christ before the foundation of the world. This profound truth holds immense significance, especially when we're navigating the challenges of loss and seeking meaning within them.

In moments of sorrow and uncertainty, remember that you are not alone. You are chosen by God, wrapped in His love and purpose. This choice was made before time began, and it stands firm through all the trials and tribulations of life.

As you reflect on this truth, find solace in the knowledge that you are holy and blameless in God's eyes through Christ. You have a divine purpose, even amidst loss, and your life holds eternal significance.

PRAYER: Heavenly Father, we thank you for choosing us in Christ. In moments of loss and confusion, help us remember that we are holy and blameless in your sight. May we find meaning and purpose in your eternal plan. In Jesus' name, we pray. Amen.

Love Like Christ Loved

SCRIPTURE: *Ephesians 5:25 – "Husbands, love your wives, as Christ loved the church and gave himself up for her."*

DEVOTIONAL: Ephesians 5:25 is a reminder of Christ's sacrificial love for the church, which serves as a profound example for all of us, whether we're navigating loss or seeking meaning in our daily lives.

In times of hardship and grief, love can be a healing balm. Just as Christ gave Himself up for the church, we are called to love one another sacrificially. This love extends not only to our spouses but to our family, friends, and neighbors.

Through Christ's example, we find that love, compassion, and selflessness have the power to bring meaning and healing, even in the most challenging circumstances. As you reflect on this verse, consider how you can love others with the same selflessness and sacrificial love that Christ demonstrated.

PRAYER: Lord Jesus, thank you for your example of sacrificial love. Help us to love one another in the same way, especially in times of loss and difficulty. May our love be a source of healing and meaning in our lives and the lives of those around us. In your precious name, we pray. Amen.

Stand Firm in God's Deliverance

SCRIPTURE: *Exodus 14:13 – "And Moses said to the people, 'Fear not, stand firm, and see the salvation of the Lord, which he will work for you today. For the Egyptians whom you see today, you shall never see again.'"*

DEVOTIONAL: In Exodus 14:13, Moses encourages the Israelites as they stand on the shores of the Red Sea, with the Egyptian army pursuing them. It's a moment of great fear and uncertainty, much like the moments of loss and adversity we face in our lives.

Moses' words, "Fear not, stand firm," are a powerful reminder for us. In times of distress and loss, when we feel pursued by challenges, we can find meaning in standing firm in our faith and trust in God. Just as the Israelites witnessed God's salvation that day, we, too, can experience His deliverance when we put our trust in Him.

No matter the difficulties we face, we can be assured that God is with us, working for our good. In your own moments of uncertainty and loss, remember these words and stand firm, for the Lord is your deliverer.

PRAYER: Heavenly Father, in moments of fear and loss, help us to stand firm in our faith, knowing that you are our deliverer. We trust in your salvation, even when circumstances seem impossible. Grant us the strength and courage to face each day with confidence in your presence. In Jesus' name, we pray. Amen.

DAY 217

The Strength of the Lord

SCRIPTURE: *Exodus 15:13 – "You have led in your steadfast love the people whom you have redeemed; you have guided them by your strength to your holy abode."*

DEVOTIONAL: In Exodus 15:13, we witness a beautiful acknowledgment of God's strength and guidance. As the Israelites sang this song of praise after their miraculous deliverance from the pursuing Egyptian army at the Red Sea, they recognized that it was God's steadfast love and strength that had brought them through. Loss and trials can often leave us feeling weak and vulnerable. Yet, in our weakness, we can find strength by turning to the Lord. He leads us with His steadfast love and guides us with His unwavering strength. Just as He guided the Israelites to safety, He can guide us through the challenges we face.

Today, find solace in knowing that the same God who delivered the Israelites is with you, offering His strength and guidance. Lean on His steadfast love as you navigate the trials of life.

PRAYER: Gracious God, we thank you for your steadfast love and unwavering strength. In moments of weakness and loss, help us to turn to you, knowing that you guide us to safety. May we find comfort in your presence and draw strength from your love. In Jesus' name, we pray. Amen.

A Kingdom of Priests

SCRIPTURE: *Exodus 19:6 – "And you shall be to me a kingdom of priests and a holy nation. These are the words that you shall speak to the people of Israel."*

DEVOTIONAL: In Exodus 19:6, God declares His intention for the people of Israel to be a "kingdom of priests" and a "holy nation." This profound statement reflects His desire for them to have a unique and sacred role in His plan.

Loss and trials can sometimes make us feel distant from God's purposes, but they don't diminish our significance in His eyes. Just as Israel was called to be a kingdom of priests, we, too, are chosen to be His ambassadors in the world, reflecting His love and grace.

Even amidst life's challenges, remember that you are part of God's holy nation, called to a special purpose. Embrace this role and find meaning in your journey, knowing that you are a representative of the Most High God.

PRAYER: Heavenly Father, thank you for choosing us to be part of your holy nation and a kingdom of priests. Help us to understand our unique role and to find meaning in our lives, even amidst trials and loss. May we reflect your love and grace to the world. In Jesus' name, we pray. Amen.

DAY 219

Abundant Blessings from God

SCRIPTURE: *Exodus 34:24 – "For I will cast out nations before you and enlarge your borders; no one shall covet your land, when you go up to appear before the Lord your God three times in the year."*

DEVOTIONAL: In Exodus 34:24, God promises to cast out nations before His people and enlarge their borders. This assurance of protection and provision reflects His faithfulness to those who seek Him.

During seasons of loss and uncertainty, it's easy to feel like we're in a state of diminishment. However, God's promise to enlarge borders reminds us that He is in control and can bring abundance out of scarcity.

Remember that God's blessings can come unexpectedly, even in the midst of trials. Continue to seek Him, and you'll discover that His provision exceeds your expectations.

PRAYER: Gracious God, thank you for your promises of provision and protection. Help us to trust in your faithfulness, especially in times of loss and uncertainty. May we find abundance in your presence and experience the joy of your blessings. In Jesus' name, we pray. Amen.

DAY 220

God's Showers of Blessing

SCRIPTURE: *Ezekiel 34:26 - "And I will make them and the places all around my hill a blessing, and I will send down the showers in their season; they shall be showers of blessing."*

DEVOTIONAL: In Ezekiel 34:26, God promises to send showers of blessing. Just as rain refreshes the earth, God's blessings renew and nourish our lives. During times of loss, we may feel spiritually dry, but God assures us that He will provide the refreshing rains of His blessings.

As we walk through the valleys of life's challenges, let's remember that God's blessings are not only for our benefit but also for those around us. His blessings can flow through us, touching the lives of others.

Let's open our hearts to receive God's showers of blessing and share them with those we encounter, becoming channels of His grace and love.

PRAYER: Heavenly Father, thank you for your promise of showers of blessing. Help us recognize your blessings, even in difficult times. Use us to share your grace and love with those around us. In Jesus' name, we pray. Amen.

Our God of Compassion

SCRIPTURE: *Ezekiel 34:31 – "And you are my sheep, human sheep of my pasture, and I am your God, declares the Lord God."*

DEVOTIONAL: In Ezekiel 34:31, the Lord speaks of His compassionate relationship with His people. He refers to us as His sheep, emphasizing His role as our Shepherd and our identity as those under His loving care.

During seasons of loss, it's comforting to know that we have a Shepherd who cares for us deeply. Our Shepherd, God, knows each of us intimately, and He tenderly guides us through life's challenges.

May we find solace and strength in knowing that we are His, and He is ours. Even in times of grief, His compassion is our anchor, providing us with hope and comfort.

PRAYER: Dear Lord, thank you for being our Shepherd and for your deep compassion. In times of loss, help us remember that we are yours, and you are ours. May your loving care bring us peace and hope. In Jesus' name, we pray. Amen.

A Renewed Heart

SCRIPTURE: *Ezekiel 36:26 – "And I will give you a new heart, and a new spirit I will put within you. And I will remove the heart of stone from your flesh and give you a heart of flesh."*

DEVOTIONAL: In Ezekiel 36:26, God promises to give us new hearts and renew our spirits. This transformation is a beautiful reminder that even in times of loss, God is at work in our lives, bringing renewal and restoration.

Grief can weigh heavily on our hearts, but God offers us the gift of a heart of flesh, soft and responsive to His love and comfort. He replaces the hardness of a stone heart, which can be cold and unfeeling, with one that can heal, love, and find meaning even in the midst of sorrow.

May we trust in God's promise to renew our hearts, finding solace and hope in His transformative love.

PRAYER: Heavenly Father, thank you for the promise of a new heart and spirit. During times of loss, help us lean on your renewal, finding meaning and comfort in your love. In Jesus' name, we pray. Amen.

DAY 223

Abundant Blessings Restored

SCRIPTURE: *Ezekiel 36:9 - "For behold, I am for you, and I will turn to you, and you shall be tilled and sown."*

DEVOTIONAL: In times of loss, it can feel like the world has turned against us, leaving us desolate. But Ezekiel 36:9 brings a message of hope. It reminds us that God is for us, and He is the ultimate Restorer.

God promises to turn to us, to nurture and cultivate our lives once more, just as a field is tilled and sown with the promise of an abundant harvest. In our darkest moments, God's hand is still at work, preparing us for a season of blessings.

As you navigate through loss, remember that God's plans for you are plans for good, to give you a hopeful future. Trust in His promise to restore and bless your life.

PRAYER: Heavenly Father, thank you for being the ultimate Restorer in our lives. In times of loss, help us to cling to your promise that you are for us and that you will turn our desolation into a season of abundance. Grant us the faith to trust in your plans and timing. In Jesus' name, we pray. Amen.

Children of God Through Faith

SCRIPTURE: *Galatians 3:26 – "For in Christ Jesus, you are all sons of God, through faith."*

DEVOTIONAL: Loss can sometimes make us feel adrift, questioning our identity and purpose. But Galatians 3:26 reminds us of a profound truth – in Christ Jesus, we are all children of God through faith.

Regardless of the losses we've experienced or the struggles we face, our identity as children of God remains unshaken. Our faith in Christ solidifies this relationship, connecting us to the Creator of the universe.

When the storms of life rage, remember that you are a beloved child of God. Your heavenly Father watches over you, guiding you through each trial. Through faith in Christ, you have an unbreakable bond with your Creator, a bond that brings comfort and assurance even in times of loss.

PRAYER: Heavenly Father, thank you for adopting us as your children through faith in Christ. In moments of loss, help us to find solace in our identity as your beloved sons and daughters. Grant us the strength to trust in your guidance and provision. In Jesus' name, we pray. Amen.

Blessing to Others

SCRIPTURE: *Genesis 12:3 – "I will bless those who bless you, and him who dishonors you I will curse, and in you, all the families of the earth shall be blessed."*

DEVOTIONAL: In the face of loss, we often seek meaning and purpose. Genesis 12:3 reminds us that God's blessings extend not only to us but also through us to others.

God promised Abraham that in him, all the families of the earth would be blessed. This profound statement reminds us that even in our losses, we can be a source of blessing to those around us. Our struggles and trials can be transformed into opportunities to bring God's light and love to others.

As we navigate our own losses, let us remember that we are called to be instruments of blessing to those we encounter. In doing so, we discover a deeper sense of purpose and meaning, even amidst life's challenges.

PRAYER: Heavenly Father, thank you for the promise of blessing through us to others. May we find purpose and fulfillment in being channels of your love and grace, especially in times of loss. Help us to honor you by being a source of blessing to those around us. In Jesus' name, we pray. Amen.

DAY 226

God's Promised Land

SCRIPTURE: *Genesis 12:7 - "Then the Lord appeared to Abram and said, 'To your offspring, I will give this land.' So he built there an altar to the Lord, who had appeared to him."*

DEVOTIONAL: Loss often leaves us feeling like we are in a wilderness, searching for a place of belonging and purpose. In Genesis 12:7, God's promise to Abram (later known as Abraham) reminds us that God guides us to our own "promised land" even in the midst of uncertainty and loss.

Just as God led Abraham to a land of promise, He led us toward His divine purpose for our lives. It might not always be a physical place but rather a state of being where we discover our true identity and purpose in Him.

During times of loss, let's build our "altars" of gratitude and trust in God, recognizing that He is still guiding us to the places and purposes He has ordained for us.

PRAYER: Dear Lord, even in times of loss and uncertainty, we trust that you are guiding us toward our own "promised land" of purpose and fulfillment. Help us to build altars of gratitude and trust in you, acknowledging your faithful presence in our lives. In Jesus' name, we pray. Amen.

God's Everlasting Covenant

SCRIPTURE: *Genesis 17:7 - "And I will establish my covenant between me and you and your offspring after you throughout their generations for an everlasting covenant, to be God to you and to your offspring after you."*

DEVOTIONAL: In moments of loss, we might question the constancy of things. Yet, God's covenant with Abraham, found in Genesis 17:7, reminds us of His unwavering faithfulness.

God's promise to be with us and our descendants for all generations serves as an enduring beacon of hope. He remains our God, even when circumstances suggest otherwise. As we navigate loss and change, remember that God's covenant extends to us, promising His presence, guidance, and love.

In your moments of uncertainty, cling to the assurance of God's everlasting covenant. It's a reminder that His faithfulness endures, providing strength and solace during times of loss.

PRAYER: Gracious God, thank you for your everlasting covenant, assuring us of your unchanging love and presence, even in times of loss. Help us hold onto this promise and find comfort in your unwavering faithfulness. In Jesus' name, we pray. Amen.

The Healing Touch of Jesus

SCRIPTURE: *Matthew 9:35 - "And Jesus went throughout all the cities and villages, teaching in their synagogues and proclaiming the gospel of the kingdom and healing every disease and every affliction."*

DEVOTIONAL: In our moments of profound loss, we may feel broken, afflicted, and in need of healing—physically, emotionally, and spiritually. Yet, we find solace and hope in the actions of Jesus, as described in Matthew 9:35.

His ministry was marked by teaching, proclaiming the gospel, and bringing healing to all forms of affliction. It reminds us that in our deepest moments of suffering and grief, Jesus is not distant. He is the healer of our wounds, the mender of our brokenness, and the source of our ultimate solace.

As you grapple with personal loss, turn to Jesus, who offers the promise of healing through faith. Just as He healed the sick and afflicted, He can bring restoration and comfort to your hurting heart.

PRAYER: Heavenly Father, we thank you for the healing touch of Jesus, who brings solace and restoration in our times of loss. Help us to have faith in His power to heal and mend our wounded spirits. In Jesus' name, we pray. Amen.

DAY 229

The God Who Comforts

SCRIPTURE: *2 Corinthians 7:6 – "But God, who comforts the downcast, comforted us by the coming of Titus."*

DEVOTIONAL: In seasons of loss and grief, when our hearts are heavy and our spirits downcast, we find solace in the comforting presence of God. The verse from 2 Corinthians 7:6 reminds us that God is not distant from our pain; He is the very source of our comfort.

Just as God sent Titus to comfort the Corinthians in their distress, God sends His presence, His Word, and His peace to comfort us in our times of sorrow. His comfort is like a gentle balm for our wounded souls, bringing a sense of calm amidst life's storms.

As you navigate the challenges of loss, turn to the God who comforts you. Seek His presence through prayer, His wisdom through His Word, and His peace through His promises. He is the ultimate source of solace in the midst of pain.

PRAYER: Heavenly Father, we thank you for being the God who comforts the downcast. In times of loss, we seek your presence and your peace. Wrap us in your loving embrace and bring us the comfort only you can provide. In Jesus' name, we pray. Amen.

The God Who Stands by Us

SCRIPTURE: *Genesis 28:15 - "Behold, I am with you and will keep you wherever you go, and will bring you back to this land. For I will not leave you until I have done what I have promised you."*

DEVOTIONAL: In times of loss and uncertainty, it can feel as though we are adrift in a vast sea of emotions and challenges. However, the promise in Genesis 28:15 serves as a reassuring anchor for our souls. God's words to Jacob echo through the ages, reminding us that He is with us, guiding our steps and protecting us wherever we go.

No matter how turbulent the seas of life may become, God remains faithfully by our side. He keeps His promises, providing comfort and assurance as we navigate through the storms of grief and loss. Just as God promised to bring Jacob back to the land, He promises to bring us through our trials, ultimately fulfilling His purpose for our lives.

Take solace in the unchanging presence of God. As you journey through loss, trust that He is with you every step of the way, faithfully keeping His promises.

PRAYER: Heavenly Father, we find peace in knowing that You are with us, just as You were with Jacob. In times of loss and uncertainty, help us to cling to Your promises and trust in Your guiding hand. We thank You for Your unwavering presence. In Jesus' name, we pray. Amen.

Treading on High Places

SCRIPTURE: *Habakkuk 3:19 - "God, the Lord, is my strength; he makes my feet like the deer's; he makes me tread on my high places."*

DEVOTIONAL: In the midst of loss and life's challenges, it's easy to feel weak and weary. But Habakkuk 3:19 reminds us that our strength doesn't come from our circumstances or our own abilities; it comes from the Lord.

Like a deer gracefully navigating the rugged terrain, the Lord enables us to tread on the high places of adversity with courage and endurance. He empowers us to rise above our circumstances, finding strength and resilience in His presence.

As you face the trials of life, remember that God is your strength. In Him, you can overcome any obstacle or loss that comes your way. Lean on His unwavering support and find the courage to journey through difficult times.

PRAYER: Lord, we thank You for being our strength, especially when we face loss and adversity. Help us to rely on Your power to overcome life's challenges and to find hope in Your presence. In Jesus' name, we pray. Amen.

Take Courage

SCRIPTURE: *Haggai 2:4 - "Yet now be strong, O Zerubbabel, declares the Lord. Be strong, O Joshua, son of Jehozadak, the high priest. Be strong, all you people of the land, declares the Lord. Work, for I am with you, declares the Lord of hosts."*

DEVOTIONAL: Loss and difficult times can leave us feeling weak and discouraged. But in Haggai 2:4, the Lord calls us to take courage and be strong. This message was given to Zerubbabel, Joshua, and all the people of the land, reminding them that God is with them in their work and challenges.

Just as these ancient leaders and people were encouraged to press on, so were we. God's presence and strength are with us as we navigate our own hardships. In Him, we find the courage to face each day, knowing that we are not alone.

Today, let these words inspire you to take courage. God is with you, enabling you to work through whatever loss or difficulty you're experiencing. Trust in His presence and strength to guide you forward.

PRAYER: Heavenly Father, we thank You for being our source of strength and courage in times of loss and hardship. Help us to trust in Your presence and find the determination to keep moving forward. In Your name, we pray. Amen.

Patient Endurance

SCRIPTURE: *Hebrews 10:36 – "For you have need of endurance, so that when you have done the will of God you may receive what is promised."*

DEVOTIONAL: In seasons of loss and waiting, it's often difficult to find the patience to endure. But Hebrews 10:36 reminds us that endurance is crucial. The passage emphasizes the need for patient endurance in doing the will of God, for in doing so, we receive what is promised.

Loss can test our patience and faith, but this verse encourages us to keep moving forward, trusting that God's promises will be fulfilled. God's timing is perfect, and as we endure, we grow in character and faith.

So, during times of waiting and loss, remember that God is working out His plans for you. Keep enduring with patience, and in due time, you will receive what is promised.

PRAYER: Lord, grant us the patience and endurance to navigate the challenges of loss and waiting. Help us to trust in Your perfect timing and remain steadfast in doing Your will. In Jesus' name, we pray. Amen.

A Crown of Beauty Instead of Ashes

SCRIPTURE: *Isaiah 61:3 - "...to grant to those who mourn in Zion— to give them a beautiful headdress instead of ashes, the oil of gladness instead of mourning, the garment of praise instead of a faint spirit; that they may be called oaks of righteousness, the planting of the Lord, that he may be glorified."*

DEVOTIONAL: In seasons of loss, our hearts can often feel heavy, covered in ashes of grief and mourning. Yet, Isaiah 61:3 reveals God's incredible promise: He offers us a crown of beauty instead of ashes, the oil of gladness instead of mourning, and the garment of praise instead of a faint spirit.

This promise reminds us that, even in the depths of sorrow, God is working to transform our pain into something beautiful. He replaces our grief with joy, our despair with praise, and our weakness with strength. As we allow God to work in our lives, we become like oaks of righteousness, firmly rooted in His grace.

So, during times of loss, hold on to the promise of beauty from ashes. Trust that God is at work, and in due time, He will bring forth new growth and renewal in your life.

PRAYER: Heavenly Father, we thank You for Your promise to exchange our mourning for gladness and our ashes for beauty. In times of loss, help us hold onto this promise and find strength in Your transformative grace. May our lives bring glory to You. In Jesus' name, we pray. Amen.

The Refining Hand of God

SCRIPTURE: *Hebrews 12:10 - "For they disciplined us for a short time as it seemed best to them, but he disciplines us for our good, that we may share his holiness."*

DEVOTIONAL: During times of loss and hardship, we may wonder why we're experiencing such challenges. Hebrews 12:10 reminds us that just as parents discipline their children for their benefit, God also disciplines us for our good. His purpose is to shape us and refine us so that we may share in His holiness.

It's often in the furnace of adversity that our character is forged, our faith deepened, and our relationship with God strengthened. While the process may be difficult, the outcome is a life more closely aligned with His will and filled with His holiness. So, when faced with adversity, remember that God's refining hand is at work in your life. Embrace the process, trust His wisdom, and know that the hardships you endure are ultimately for your good and His glory.

PRAYER: Heavenly Father, help us to understand that Your discipline and refining in our lives are for our good and Your glory. Grant us the strength and patience to endure difficulties, knowing that they are shaping us to be more like You. In Jesus' name, we pray. Amen.

Contentment in God's Presence

SCRIPTURE: *Hebrews 13:5 – "Keep your life free from love of money, and be content with what you have, for he has said, "I will never leave you nor forsake you."*

DEVOTIONAL: In a world often filled with desires for more, Hebrews 13:5 encourages us to find contentment in God's presence. It reminds us to keep our hearts free from the love of money and to be content with what we have because of God's promise: "I will never leave you nor forsake you."

Loss, whether it's of material possessions or something dear to our hearts, can make us yearn for what we've lost. But God's presence is a constant source of comfort and assurance. It's in His company that we find true contentment, for nothing in this world can compare to the abiding love and faithfulness of our Creator.

In times of loss, we can hold fast to the promise that God will never leave us. He remains our constant companion, offering solace and a sense of completeness that the world cannot provide. So, let us find contentment in His presence and trust that He will see us through every loss we face.

PRAYER: Heavenly Father, we thank You for Your unwavering presence in our lives. Help us to find contentment in You, especially during times of loss and longing. May Your promise to never leave us bring us peace and reassurance. In Jesus' name, we pray. Amen.

Unshaken Confidence in God

SCRIPTURE: *Hebrews 13:6 - "So we can confidently say, "The Lord is my helper; I will not fear; what can man do to me?"*

DEVOTIONAL: In moments of loss and uncertainty, it's natural to feel fear and anxiety. However, Hebrews 13:6 reminds us that we can confidently declare, "The Lord is my helper; I will not fear; what can man do to me?"

This powerful statement is a testament to our unshaken confidence in God. When we face trials and adversity, we are not alone. God is our ever-present helper, offering His guidance, strength, and comfort. No matter what challenges we encounter, His unwavering support is our source of confidence.

Loss can sometimes make us vulnerable, but our trust in God empowers us to stand firm. We need not fear the actions of others or the uncertainties of life because the Creator of the universe is on our side. Our confidence in God's help enables us to navigate the trials of life with courage and resilience.

PRAYER: Dear Heavenly Father, we thank You for being our ever-present helper. In times of loss and fear, help us to remember that You are with us, and with You by our side, we need not be afraid. Strengthen our confidence in Your love and support. In Jesus' name, we pray. Amen.

God Remembers Your Work

SCRIPTURE: *Hebrews 6:10 – "For God is not unjust so as to overlook your work and the love that you have shown for his name in serving the saints, as you still do."*

DEVOTIONAL: In times of loss and hardship, it's easy to feel overlooked and forgotten. But take heart in the assurance of Hebrews 6:10, which tells us that God is not unjust; He does not overlook your work and the love you have shown in serving others.

Even when it seems that your efforts go unnoticed by the world, God sees and remembers. He recognizes the love you've poured into serving others in His name. Your acts of kindness, your sacrifices, and your love for His people are all known to Him. Loss may dim your earthly recognition, but it cannot diminish the value of your service in God's eyes. Your faithfulness, even through difficult times, is precious to Him. Your work matters, and it's a testament to your love for Him and His people.

So, take comfort in knowing that God sees, remembers, and values your labor of love. Your service in His name is never in vain, and He is just and faithful in all things.

PRAYER: Heavenly Father, thank You for the assurance that You see and remember our work and love for Your name's sake. Help us to serve faithfully, even in challenging times, knowing that our efforts are valued by You. In Jesus' name, we pray. Amen.

The Intercession of Christ

SCRIPTURE: *Hebrews 7:25 – "Consequently, he is able to save to the uttermost those who draw near to God through him, since he always lives to make intercession for them."*

DEVOTIONAL: In times of loss and struggle, we may wonder if anyone truly understands our pain and suffering. Yet, Hebrews 7:25 reminds us of the incredible truth: Jesus Christ not only understands but also intercedes on our behalf. Christ's work goes beyond the cross; He continues to intercede for us, advocating for our needs and ensuring that we are saved to the utmost. His eternal presence before God's throne means that there is never a moment when He is not standing up for us.

When life becomes overwhelming, remember that Jesus is there, making intercession for you. He knows your pain, your struggles, and your heartache, and He brings them before the Father on your behalf. You are not alone in your suffering; you have a Savior who actively works for your good. So, draw near to God through Jesus, knowing that He always lives to make intercession for you. Find comfort and strength in His advocacy, even in times of loss and difficulty.

PRAYER: Dear Lord, thank You for the incredible promise that Jesus intercedes for us. In times of loss and hardship, help us draw near to You through Him, finding solace in the knowledge that we are never alone. In Jesus' name, we pray. Amen.

The Promise of Christ's Return

SCRIPTURE: *Hebrews 9:28 - "…so Christ, having been offered once to bear the sins of many, will appear a second time, not to deal with sin but to save those who are eagerly waiting for him."*

DEVOTIONAL: Amidst the challenges and losses of life, there's a promise that shines brightly in Hebrews 9:28. It reminds us that while Christ bore our sins in His first coming, He will return a second time. However, this time, He won't deal with sin but will come to save those who eagerly await Him. The return of Christ is not merely a theological concept; it's a source of hope and meaning for every believer. When we face loss, uncertainty, or the hardships of life, the assurance of Christ's return provides us with a deep sense of purpose. It means that our suffering is not in vain, and our hope is not misplaced.

As we eagerly await His return, we find strength to persevere through life's trials. The promise of His coming gives us the motivation to live with faith, love, and righteousness. It's a beacon of hope that illuminates even our darkest days. So, in the midst of life's challenges, keep your eyes fixed on the promise of Christ's return. Let it be a source of inspiration, reminding you that there is a glorious future beyond the present trials.

PRAYER: Heavenly Father, we eagerly await the return of Your Son, Jesus Christ. In times of loss and suffering, help us find hope and meaning in this promise. Let the assurance of His coming inspire us to live faithfully and with great anticipation. In Jesus' name, we pray. Amen.

The Promise of Resurrection

SCRIPTURE: *Hosea 13:14 - "I shall ransom them from the power of Sheol; I shall redeem them from Death. O Death, where are your plagues? O Sheol, where is your sting? Compassion is hidden from my eyes."*

DEVOTIONAL: In Hosea 13:14, we find a promise of God's triumph over death and the grave. It declares that God will ransom us from the power of death and Sheol, the realm of the dead.

This promise is the essence of our hope in the face of loss. It reminds us that even death cannot thwart God's compassion and power. Through Christ's resurrection, we witness the fulfillment of this promise.

As we navigate life's losses and challenges, let's cling to the assurance of resurrection. It's a beacon of hope that infuses our lives with profound meaning. In Christ, we are redeemed, and death's grip on us is broken.

PRAYER: Gracious God, we thank You for the promise of resurrection through Jesus Christ. In times of loss and in the face of death, help us remember Your redemptive power and find hope in the assurance of eternal life. May this promise bring comfort and meaning to our lives. In Jesus' name, we pray. Amen.

DAY 242

Seeking God's Presence

SCRIPTURE: *Hosea 6:3 - "Let us know; let us press on to know the Lord; his going out is sure as the dawn; he will come to us as the showers, as the spring rains that water the earth."*

DEVOTIONAL: In Hosea 6:3, we're encouraged to press on in seeking the presence of the Lord. This verse reminds us that just as surely as the dawn breaks and the rains come to refresh the earth, God's faithfulness is unwavering.

During times of loss, it's easy to feel adrift or alone. Yet, when we press on in our pursuit of God's presence, we find solace and meaning. His presence is like the refreshing rain that nourishes our spirits and renews our strength.

As we journey through life's challenges, let's commit to knowing the Lord more deeply. In His presence, we discover comfort, guidance, and a profound sense of purpose that transcends any loss we may experience.

PRAYER: Heavenly Father, help us press on in our pursuit of Your presence. May we find comfort and meaning in the assurance of Your unwavering faithfulness, especially in times of loss. In Jesus' name, we pray. Amen.

The Hope of Transformation

SCRIPTURE: *1 Corinthians 15:51 – "Behold! I tell you a mystery. We shall not all sleep, but we shall all be changed,"*

DEVOTIONAL: In 1 Corinthians 15:51, the apostle Paul shares a profound mystery: a future transformation awaits us. While earthly losses and struggles can weigh us down, this verse reminds us that a day is coming when we will experience a glorious change.

When we face the pain of loss, whether of loved ones or dreams, this promise offers profound hope. It assures us that our suffering is temporary and a glorious transformation awaits. We shall not remain in the depths of grief forever; change is coming.

Today, let's find solace and meaning in this hope of transformation. It reminds us that God is working in the midst of our losses, preparing something beautiful and eternal.

PRAYER: Heavenly Father, thank you for the hope of transformation offered in 1 Corinthians 15:51. May this hope sustain us in times of loss and remind us of the glorious future you have prepared for us. In Jesus' name, we pray. Amen.

Co-Workers with God

SCRIPTURE: *1 Corinthians 3:9 - "For we are God's fellow workers. You are God's field, God's building."*

DEVOTIONAL: In 1 Corinthians 3:9, Paul reminds us that we are co-workers with God. Even in seasons of loss, we are part of God's grand design. Our lives are His field, and our experiences, including loss, are the building blocks of His greater purpose.

During times of grief, it's easy to feel isolated or adrift. But this verse invites us to see our lives as interconnected with God's divine plan. Our losses, struggles, and victories all play a role in God's redemptive work.

As we navigate the complexities of life, let's find comfort and meaning in the truth that we are co-workers with God, contributing to a beautiful tapestry of His design.

PRAYER: Dear Lord, help us embrace the role of co-workers in Your divine plan, finding meaning even in our losses. May our lives be a testimony to Your redemptive work. In Jesus' name, we pray. Amen.

RESTORING HOPE
AND RENEWAL

The Judge of Hearts

SCRIPTURE: *1 Corinthians 4:3 - But with me, it is a very small thing that I should be judged by you or by any human court. In fact, I do not even judge myself."*

DEVOTIONAL: In 1 Corinthians 4:3, the apostle Paul reminds us of a profound truth: the ultimate judge of our hearts is not people or even ourselves but God alone. This is a liberating concept, especially when we're grappling with losses, failures, or judgments from others. When we experience loss, we often encounter various opinions and judgments from those around us. Some may question our choices, actions, or responses. At times, we might even harshly criticize ourselves, dwelling on what we could have done differently.

As we navigate the challenges of loss, let's find solace in the fact that God, who understands us intimately, is the final and most compassionate judge. His grace and understanding surpass any human critique, allowing us to heal and find meaning in His unwavering love.

PRAYER: Dear Heavenly Father, we thank You for being the ultimate judge of our hearts. Help us release the weight of human judgment and find comfort in Your understanding and grace, especially in times of loss. In Jesus' name, we pray. Amen.

Cleansed and Renewed

SCRIPTURE: *1 Corinthians 6:11 - And such were some of you. But you were washed, you were sanctified, you were justified in the name of the Lord Jesus Christ and by the Spirit of our God."*

DEVOTIONAL: In 1 Corinthians 6:11, the apostle Paul reminds us of the transformative power of God's grace. This verse serves as a beacon of hope, especially when we're navigating seasons of loss, regret, or guilt. Loss often brings with it a range of emotions and experiences, and sometimes, it can lead us to reflect on past mistakes or regrets. We might carry the weight of our own wrongdoings or feel a sense of unworthiness.

In times of loss and reflection, remember that your identity is not defined by your past mistakes or regrets. You are a new creation in Christ, cleansed and renewed by His grace. This truth can bring solace, healing, and a profound sense of purpose as you move forward.

PRAYER: Heavenly Father, we thank You for the cleansing and renewing power of Your grace through Jesus Christ. Help us to let go of past regrets and find solace and purpose in the newness of life that You provide. In Jesus' name, we pray. Amen.

Confession of Sins

SCRIPTURE: *1 John 1:9 - If we confess our sins, he is faithful and just to forgive us our sins and to cleanse us from all unrighteousness."*

DEVOTIONAL: In our journey of faith, we sometimes stumble and fall into sin. These moments can leave us burdened with guilt, regret, and a heavy heart. During seasons of loss, this burden can feel even more profound. But God's Word, found in 1 John 1:9, offers us a message of profound hope and healing. It reminds us that when we confess our sins to God, He is both faithful and just. Faithful to His promise of forgiveness and just because Jesus paid the price for our sins on the cross.

During times of loss, when our souls are weighed down by sorrow and regret, it's essential to remember that God offers a path to cleansing and renewal. He invites us to come before Him, confess our sins, and experience His loving forgiveness. In His mercy, He not only forgives us but also cleanses us from all unrighteousness, making us pure and whole again. Embracing forgiveness is a powerful step toward finding healing and meaning amidst loss. It allows us to release the burden of guilt and shame, knowing that God's grace is greater than our failures.

PRAYER: Heavenly Father, we thank You for Your faithfulness and justice in forgiving our sins. During times of loss, help us to come to You with contrite hearts, confess our wrongdoings, and experience the cleansing and renewal that Your forgiveness brings. In Jesus' name, we pray. Amen.

DAY 248

The Profound Gift of Abiding in Christ

SCRIPTURE: *1 John 2:23 - "No one who denies the Son has the Father. Whoever confesses the Son has the Father also."*

DEVOTIONAL: In times of loss, we often seek solace and meaning in various ways. Yet, amidst our search for answers and comfort, it's crucial to recognize the profound gift of abiding in Christ. 1 John 2:23 reminds us that confessing the Son, Jesus Christ, not only connects us to Him but also to the Father. This truth highlights the essential nature of our relationship with Jesus in our pursuit of meaning and healing. When we confess Jesus as Lord and Savior, we are acknowledging our dependence on Him as the source of life, hope, and purpose.

As we abide in Him, we are drawn closer to the Father's heart, finding solace and meaning in His presence. Let us, therefore, cling to this profound gift: the assurance that through Christ, we not only have hope for today but also the promise of eternal life with our Heavenly Father.

PRAYER: Lord Jesus, we confess You as our Savior and Lord. In times of loss, help us to draw nearer to You and, in doing so, find a deeper connection with our Heavenly Father. May we continually abide in Your love, finding meaning and comfort in the assurance of eternal life through You. Amen.

Embracing the Promise of Transformation

SCRIPTURE: *1 John 3:2 – "Beloved, we are God's children now, and what we will be has not yet appeared; but we know that when he appears, we shall be like him because we shall see him as he is."*

DEVOTIONAL: In our journey of seeking meaning amidst loss, the promise of transformation holds profound significance. As 1 John 3:2 reminds us, we are God's children, and while we may not fully grasp what our future holds, we have a glimpse of the beautiful truth that awaits us. Loss often leaves us with a sense of incompleteness and a yearning for something more. Yet, this verse assures us that when Christ appears, we will be transformed to be like Him. This transformation is not just about our physical state but our spiritual and emotional selves as well.

This verse invites us to look beyond the here and now to fix our eyes on the promise of becoming more like Jesus. Embracing this promise can bring deep meaning to our journey of loss. It reminds us that our suffering is not in vain, and as we walk with Christ, we are being molded into His image. We can find solace in the hope of a glorious transformation that awaits us in His presence. As you navigate through your season of loss, may you hold onto this promise and find comfort in the assurance that you are becoming more like your loving Saviour.

PRAYER: Heavenly Father, thank you for the promise of transformation through your Son, Jesus Christ. In times of loss and uncertainty, help us fix our eyes on this hope, finding meaning in the knowledge that we are becoming more like Him. Strengthen our faith, Lord, and remind us of the glorious future you have prepared for us. In Jesus' name, we pray. Amen.

Overcoming Sin by His Seed

SCRIPTURE: *1 John 3:9 - "No one born of God makes a practice of sinning, for God's seed abides in him; and he cannot keep on sinning because he has been born of God."*

DEVOTIONAL: In our journey through life's challenges and losses, we often confront the struggle against sin, both in our actions and in our hearts. Yet, 1 John 3:9 offers us a powerful reminder that, as children of God, we possess a divine seed within us. This divine seed is God's presence in our lives, the Holy Spirit. It transforms our hearts, guiding us away from a lifestyle of sin. As we face grief and loss, this verse encourages us to rely on this inner transformation. It reminds us that we have been born of God, and His Spirit empowers us to overcome the temptations that can lead us astray during difficult times.

As we journey onward, let us remember that God's seed empowers us to overcome, strive for holiness, and discover purpose in our pursuit of Him.

PRAYER: Heavenly Father, we are grateful for the divine seed of your presence within us. As we face challenges and losses, help us rely on your Spirit to overcome sin and draw nearer to you. May our lives be a testament to the transformation your seed brings. In Jesus' name, we pray. Amen.

Eternal Life Through Christ

SCRIPTURE: *1 John 5:11 - "And this is the testimony, that God gave us eternal life, and this life is in his Son."*

DEVOTIONAL: In the midst of life's trials and tribulations, we often find ourselves seeking something enduring, something that transcends the temporal nature of our existence. 1 John 5:11 reminds us that this eternal life is found in Christ, God's precious gift to humanity. As we navigate loss and the challenges it brings, we can take solace in knowing that the trials of this world do not have the final say. Instead, we have the promise of eternal life through our faith in Jesus Christ. This eternal life is not merely an extension of our earthly existence; it is a quality of life characterized by the presence of God, filled with His love, joy, and peace.

Embracing this truth provides a profound sense of meaning amidst life's uncertainties. It anchors us when we feel adrift, reminding us that we are partakers in a divine story that stretches beyond the confines of time. It's a story of redemption, of transformation, and ultimately, of eternal life. In the face of loss, remember that this life is a precious gift from God, and our faith in Christ ensures that it endures into eternity. Even in the midst of trials, we can find meaning and purpose in living for the One who offers us life everlasting.

PRAYER: Dear Lord, we thank you for the gift of eternal life through your Son, Jesus Christ. In times of loss and uncertainty, help us hold onto this precious promise, finding meaning in our journey towards eternity with you. In Jesus' name, we pray. Amen.

Confidence in Prayer

SCRIPTURE: *1 John 5:14 – "And this is the confidence that we have toward him, that if we ask anything according to his will, he hears us."*

DEVOTIONAL: In our journey through life, especially in times of loss and grief, prayer becomes a lifeline to God, a means of pouring out our hearts and seeking His guidance and comfort. 1 John 5:14 reminds us of the incredible confidence we can have in prayer when we align our requests with God's will. It's natural to wonder if our prayers are heard, especially when we face situations that seem insurmountable. Remember that prayer is your direct line to the One who holds the universe in His hands. Approach Him with confidence, knowing that He not only hears your prayers but also answers them according to His perfect will. In this divine interaction, you can discover profound meaning and a sense of purpose, even in the midst of trials.

PRAYER: Heavenly Father, we thank you for the gift of prayer and for the confidence it gives us in times of need. Help us to align our desires with your will and to find solace and meaning in the knowledge that you hear us. In Jesus' name, we pray. Amen.

The Protection of God's Children

SCRIPTURE: *1 John 5:18 – "We know that everyone who has been born of God does not keep on sinning, but he who was born of God protects him, and the evil one does not touch him."*

DEVOTIONAL: In times of loss and adversity, it's natural to feel vulnerable and exposed. We may wonder if we have the strength to withstand life's challenges. But 1 John 5:18 offers us a comforting assurance: as children of God, we have divine protection. This verse reminds us that those who are born of God, who have placed their faith in Him, are under His watchful care. He is our protector, our shield against the attacks of the evil one. Even in the face of loss, grief, and trials, we can find solace in the knowledge that God is our defender.

As we navigate the complexities of life, including the losses we encounter, take refuge in the protective love of your Heavenly Father. Remember that you are His child, and He is committed to safeguarding you from harm. This knowledge can bring profound meaning and peace, knowing that you are never alone and that God is your ultimate protector.

PRAYER: Heavenly Father, thank you for being our protector and defender. In times of loss and vulnerability, help us to trust in your loving care and find comfort in your presence. Shield us from the attacks of the evil one and guide us on the path of righteousness. In Jesus' name, we pray. Amen.

The Living Hope in Christ

SCRIPTURE: *1 Peter 1:3 - "Blessed be the God and Father of our Lord Jesus Christ! According to his great mercy, he has caused us to be born again to a living hope through the resurrection of Jesus Christ from the dead."*

DEVOTIONAL: In seasons of loss and uncertainty, where can we find hope? 1 Peter 1:3 reminds us that as believers in Jesus Christ, we are born again to a living hope. This hope is unlike any other, for it is not based on circumstances or worldly assurances; it is anchored in the resurrection of Jesus from the dead. The world may offer temporary solutions to our grief and struggles, but true and lasting hope can only be found in Christ. The resurrection of Jesus is the bedrock of our faith. It signifies victory over death, sin, and despair. Through His triumph, we have been granted a living hope that transcends the trials and losses of this world.

This living hope assures us that God's mercy is abundant and His promises are unwavering. No matter what losses we may face, we have a future filled with hope because of Jesus. It is a hope that sustains us, uplifts us, and points us to the eternal glory that awaits those who trust in Him.

PRAYER: Heavenly Father, we thank you for the living hope we have through the resurrection of Jesus Christ. In times of loss and difficulty, help us to hold onto this hope, knowing that it is a source of strength, comfort, and assurance. May it shine brightly in our lives, drawing others to you. In Jesus' name, we pray. Amen.

Spiritual Growth through God's Word

SCRIPTURE: *1 Peter 2:2 – "Like newborn infants, long for the pure spiritual milk, that by it you may grow up into salvation."*

DEVOTIONAL: Have you ever observed a newborn baby? They possess an incredible instinct: the longing for milk. Just as a baby yearns for nourishment, 1 Peter 2:2 encourages us to long for the pure spiritual milk of God's Word. Just as milk is essential for the growth and development of a newborn, the Word of God is vital for our spiritual growth. It provides us with the sustenance needed to mature in our faith and walk with Christ.

This verse also implies an ongoing process of growth. As we continually feed on God's Word, we mature in our salvation. It's not about instant transformation but a lifelong journey of becoming more like Christ. During seasons of loss, take extra time to immerse yourself in the Scriptures. Read, meditate, and reflect on God's promises and teachings. Just as a baby grows steadily with nourishment, so will your faith and resilience grow through the spiritual nourishment found in God's Word.

PRAYER: Heavenly Father, we thank you for the nourishment and guidance we receive through your Word. Help us to long for it as newborns long for milk, and may we find strength and growth in our faith, even in times of loss. In Jesus' name, we pray. Amen.

Chosen and Set Apart for God's Purpose

SCRIPTURE: *1 Peter 2:9 – "But you are a chosen race, a royal priesthood, a holy nation, a people for his own possession, that you may proclaim the excellencies of him who called you out of darkness into his marvelous light."*

DEVOTIONAL: As believers, we are not simply ordinary people going through life's trials. We are a chosen race, selected by God Himself. We are a royal priesthood, called to serve Him in a special way. We are part of a holy nation, set apart for His purposes. We are a people that God treasures as His very own possession. What a remarkable identity! Even in the midst of loss and suffering, we can find purpose and meaning in knowing that we are chosen and set apart by God. Our lives have a divine calling – to proclaim the excellencies of the One who rescued us from darkness and brought us into His marvelous light.

During seasons of loss, remember that God has a plan and purpose for your life. You are not alone, and your suffering is not in vain. You are part of a chosen people with a mission to declare God's goodness and grace to the world.

PRAYER: Heavenly Father, we thank you for choosing us and setting us apart for your purpose. In times of loss and hardship, help us remember our identity in Christ and the calling to proclaim Your excellencies to the world. May we find strength and purpose in you. In Jesus' name, we pray. Amen.

Seeking Peace and Pursuing It

SCRIPTURE: *1 Peter 3:11 - "Let him turn away from evil and do good; let him seek peace and pursue it."*

DEVOTIONAL: The verse reminds us that true peace is found when we align our lives with goodness and righteousness. It's easy to become disheartened or tempted to react with negativity. However, by choosing the path of righteousness and avoiding evil, we lay the foundation for lasting peace. The second part of the verse emphasizes seeking and pursuing peace actively. Peace is not a passive state but something we actively strive for. We might be tempted to dwell on our grief or become entangled in conflicts. Yet, this verse encourages us to actively seek reconciliation, understanding, and harmony with others.

As we seek peace, we can find it not only in our relationships with others but also in our relationship with God. Turning to Him in times of loss can provide a deep sense of peace, knowing that He is our refuge and source of comfort. So, as you navigate the challenges of life, especially in moments of loss, remember 1 Peter 3:11. Turn away from evil, do good, and actively seek peace in your relationships and in your connection with God. In this pursuit, you'll discover a peace that transcends circumstances and brings solace to your soul.

PRAYER: Dear Lord, in a world often filled with conflict and unrest, help us to turn away from evil and do good. Teach us to actively seek and pursue peace, both in our relationships with others and in our connection with You. Grant us the peace that surpasses understanding, especially in times of loss. In Jesus' name, we pray. Amen.

The Eyes of the Lord

SCRIPTURE: *1 Peter 3:12 - "For the eyes of the Lord are on the righteous, and his ears are open to their prayer. But the face of the Lord is against those who do evil."*

DEVOTIONAL: These words remind us that God is not distant or detached from our suffering. His gaze is upon the righteous, those who seek Him and strive to live in accordance with His will. When it feels like the world is against us, we can take solace in the fact that the Lord's eyes are fixed on us. He sees our struggles, our grief, and our tears. The latter part of the verse provides a sobering contrast: "But the face of the Lord is against those who do evil." While the righteous find comfort in God's presence and attention, those who persist in wrongdoing face His opposition. Remember that you are not alone. The eyes of the Lord are upon you, and His ears are open to your prayers. Seek His presence, pour out your heart to Him, and find solace in the assurance that He is with you in every trial.

PRAYER: Heavenly Father, thank you for the reassurance that your eyes are on the righteous and your ears are open to our prayers. In times of loss and adversity, help us to seek your presence and find comfort in knowing that you are with us. We commit our burdens and pains to you, trusting in your unfailing love. In Jesus' name, we pray. Amen.

Restoration and Strength

SCRIPTURE: *1 Peter 5:10 - "And after you have suffered a little while, the God of all grace, who has called you to his eternal glory in Christ, will himself restore, confirm, strengthen, and establish you."*

DEVOTIONAL: This verse reminds us that our suffering, though real and painful, is temporary. It is but "a little while" when measured against the eternal backdrop of God's glory. Our Heavenly Father, the "God of all grace," is not distant or indifferent to our suffering. He has called us to share in His eternal glory through Christ. What a beautiful promise follows: He will Himself restore, confirm, strengthen, and establish us. In times of loss, when we feel broken and uncertain, God steps in as our Restorer. He mends our wounded hearts, confirming His love and presence. He strengthens us when we are weak, providing the resilience needed to endure.

As we navigate the hardships and losses of life, may we hold fast to this promise. Remember that the suffering is temporary, but God's grace is eternal. He will not only see you through but also lead you to a place of restoration, confirmation, strength, and establishment in Him.

PRAYER: Gracious Father, we thank you for your promise of restoration, confirmation, strength, and establishment in our lives. In times of suffering and loss, help us cling to the hope of your eternal glory and grace. May we find strength and resilience through Christ, knowing that you are with us every step of the way. In His name, we pray. Amen.

The Crown of Glory

SCRIPTURE: *1 Peter 5:4 - "And when the chief Shepherd appears, you will receive the unfading crown of glory."*

DEVOTIONAL: This verse speaks of a time when the "chief Shepherd" appears. This is a reference to Jesus Christ, who is not only our Shepherd but also our Saviour and King. When He returns, we are assured of receiving the "unfading crown of glory." This crown is not like the temporary accolades and honors of this world; it is eternal, unchanging, and filled with the radiant glory of God Himself. For those who have faithfully followed Christ, endured trials, and remained steadfast, this promise is a source of great encouragement. It reminds us that our earthly struggles are but a fleeting moment compared to the glorious eternity that awaits us in the presence of our Shepherd and Saviour.

As you face the challenges and losses of life, remember that your faithful service to the Lord is seen and valued by the One who promises an unfading crown of glory. Let this assurance fill you with hope and perseverance, knowing that your ultimate reward is beyond compare.

PRAYER: Heavenly Father, we thank you for the promise of the unfading crown of glory that awaits us in Christ. Help us to remain steadfast in our faith, even in the face of challenges and losses. May we find hope and encouragement in the assurance of our eternal reward in your presence. In Jesus' name, we pray. Amen.

Victory Through Faith

SCRIPTURE: *1 Samuel 17:47 -"...for the battle is the Lord's, and he will give you into our hand."*

DEVOTIONAL: The story of David and Goliath is one of the most famous accounts of victory against all odds in the Bible. David, a young shepherd, faced the giant warrior Goliath, armed only with faith and a slingshot. When he stood before Goliath, David proclaimed, "For the battle is the Lord's, and he will give you into our hand." David's words hold a profound truth that can bring us comfort and strength during times of loss and adversity. Often, life's challenges can seem like insurmountable giants, overwhelming us with fear and uncertainty. Yet, just as David placed his trust in the Lord, we, too, can find courage in our faith.

As you journey through life, facing your own battles and losses, cling to the faith that sustained David. Recognize that victory comes not by our own might but by entrusting our battles to the Almighty God. With Him on our side, we can conquer the giants in our lives and emerge victorious.

PRAYER: Heavenly Father, we thank you for being our ultimate source of strength and victory. Help us to trust in you, especially during times of loss and adversity. May we remember that the battle is yours, and with you by our side, we can face any challenge with confidence. In Jesus' name, we pray. Amen.

God's Lifting Hand

SCRIPTURE: *1 Samuel 2:8 - "He raises up the poor from the dust; he lifts the needy from the ash heap to make them sit with princes and inherit a seat of honor. For the pillars of the earth are the Lord's, and on them, he has set the world."*

DEVOTIONAL: Hannah's prayer in 1 Samuel 2:8 beautifully captures the essence of God's compassion and His ability to transform our circumstances. Hannah, who had experienced the pain of barrenness, sang of a God who lifts the poor from the dust and exalts the needy to places of honor. Our Heavenly Father cares for us deeply, and His love extends to every corner of our lives, especially during moments of loss. He is the lifter of our heads when we are bowed down, the comforter of our hearts when we are grieving, and the source of hope when all seems lost.

As you face the challenges and losses of life, remember that the God who raised the poor from the dust is the same God who can lift you from any circumstance. Trust in His faithfulness, and allow Him to bring you from the ashes to a place of honor.

PRAYER: Gracious God, we thank you for your promise to lift us from the dust and set us in places of honor. In our moments of loss and despair, help us to trust in your loving care. May we find hope in your unfailing love and the assurance that you are working all things for our good. In Jesus' name, we pray. Amen.

Hope in the Face of Grief

SCRIPTURE: *1 Thessalonians 4:13 - "But we do not want you to be uninformed, brothers, about those who are asleep, that you may not grieve as others do who have no hope."*

DEVOTIONAL: Grief is a universal experience. At some point in our lives, we all encounter loss, and it can be a profoundly challenging and painful journey. In moments of grief, the weight of sorrow can feel overwhelming, leaving us with a sense of despair. As followers of Christ, we possess a unique and profound hope. It's a hope that extends beyond the boundaries of this earthly life. It's the hope that in Christ, death is not the end but a transition into eternity with God. This hope doesn't eliminate our grief, but it transforms it.

In our moments of loss and mourning, we can cling to the hope of resurrection and reunion. We can find solace in the promise that one day, we will be reunited with our loved ones who have gone before us. This hope, rooted in Christ's victory over death, sustains us through the darkest times. So, when you face grief, remember that you are not without hope. As you mourn, lean into the hope that Jesus provides—a hope that transcends the sorrow of this world. Your grief is real, but your hope is even more profound.

PRAYER: Dear Lord, in times of grief and loss, we find solace in the hope you've given us through your Son, Jesus Christ. Help us navigate the difficult journey of mourning with the assurance that one day, we will be reunited with our loved ones in your eternal presence. May this hope sustain us and bring comfort to our grieving hearts. In Jesus' name, we pray. Amen.

Living a Life Pleasing to God

SCRIPTURE: *1 Thessalonians 4:3 – "For this is the will of God, your sanctification."*

DEVOTIONAL: Understanding God's will for our lives can sometimes feel like searching for hidden treasure. We long to know what choices will lead us to please Him. Fortunately, the Bible provides clear guidance on this matter. It's about aligning our hearts and minds with God's standards and principles. As we strive to live lives pleasing to God, let us remember that sanctification is not about perfection but progress.

It's a journey of growth and transformation, and it requires God's grace and our willingness to yield to His guidance. Today, reflect on areas in your life where you can grow in sanctification. Seek God's help and wisdom to live in a manner that pleases Him, remembering that His grace is sufficient for every step of the journey.

PRAYER: Heavenly Father, we acknowledge that your will for us is sanctification and purity. Help us to live lives that please you, and to continually grow in holiness. Grant us the strength and wisdom to align our hearts with your desires, and may our lives be a pleasing offering to you. In Jesus' name, we pray. Amen.

Remaining Steadfast in Tribulations

SCRIPTURE: *1 Thessalonians 3:3 - "that no one be moved by these afflictions. For you yourselves know that we are destined for this."*

DEVOTIONAL: In 1 Thessalonians 3:3, the apostle Paul addresses the believers in Thessalonica and reminds them that afflictions and tribulations are not unexpected in the life of a Christian. He speaks of the inevitability of facing such challenges. Paul knew that these believers would encounter various forms of opposition and adversity in their journey of faith.

Today, if you find yourself facing afflictions, take comfort in knowing that you are not alone. Remember that God is with you, and He will help you stand firm. Trust in His unwavering love and the strength He provides to remain steadfast in the face of tribulations.

PRAYER: Heavenly Father, we acknowledge that afflictions and tribulations are a part of our journey as believers. Give us the strength and endurance to stand firm in our faith when faced with difficulties. Help us trust in your unwavering love and find comfort in your presence during challenging times. In Jesus' name, we pray. Amen.

The Promise of Christ's Return

SCRIPTURE: *1 Thessalonians 4:16 - "For the Lord himself will descend from heaven with a cry of command, with the voice of an archangel, and with the sound of the trumpet of God. And the dead in Christ will rise first."*

DEVOTIONAL: This passage is a source of great comfort and anticipation for believers. It assures us that Christ will return, and when He does, something incredible will happen—the dead in Christ will rise first. Those who have gone before us in faith will be resurrected to eternal life. This is a moment of triumphant victory over death and the promise of a glorious future.

The promise of Christ's return serves as a reminder of our ultimate hope as Christians. It encourages us to live in readiness, to be watchful, and to eagerly anticipate His coming. While we do not know the exact time or day of His return, we can live with the assurance that He will return, and we will be united with Him forever. In times of uncertainty or difficulty, the promise of Christ's return brings solace and encouragement. It reminds us that our current struggles are temporary, and a day is coming when all things will be made new. Let this truth anchor your faith and fill you with hope as you face the challenges of each day.

PRAYER: Lord Jesus, we eagerly await your glorious return. Help us to live with anticipation and readiness, knowing that our ultimate hope rests in you. May the promise of your coming bring comfort and encouragement to our hearts, especially in times of difficulty. In your precious name, we pray. Amen.

DAY 267

A Call to Humble Prayer

SCRIPTURE: *2 Chronicles 7:14 – "If my people who are called by my name humble themselves, and pray and seek my face and turn from their wicked ways, then I will hear from heaven and will forgive their sin and heal their land."*

DEVOTIONAL: The verse outlines a series of actions that God's people are called to take: humbling themselves, praying, seeking God's face, and turning from wicked ways. These actions reflect a posture of repentance and dependency on God. It's a call to acknowledge our need for His intervention and healing in our lives and our land. This is a timeless call to prayer and repentance. When we humble ourselves, acknowledge our dependence on Him, and seek His face, we position ourselves to receive His forgiveness and healing. 2 Chronicles 7:14 is a beacon of hope. It reminds us that God's response to sincere, humble prayer is to hear, forgive, and heal. Let us heed this call to humble prayer, seeking God's face with contrite hearts. In doing so, we can expect God to move, bringing forgiveness, healing, and transformation to our lives and our world.

PRAYER: Heavenly Father, we come before you in humility, acknowledging our need for your intervention and healing. We pray for forgiveness for our sins and the sins of our land. May our prayers be pleasing to you, and may you hear, forgive, and heal as you have promised. In Jesus' name, we pray. Amen.

Transformed into His Image

SCRIPTURE: *2 Corinthians 3:18 - "And we all, with unveiled face, beholding the glory of the Lord, are being transformed into the same image from one degree of glory to another. For this comes from the Lord who is the Spirit."*

DEVOTIONAL: The verse begins with "And we all, with unveiled face," reminding us that, through Christ, we have direct access to God's glory. In the Old Testament, Moses veiled his face after encountering God's glory on Mount Sinai. But in Christ, there is no need for veils or barriers. We can approach God with unveiled faces, boldly and without hindrance.

Crucially, this transformation doesn't rely on our efforts alone. The verse makes it clear: "For this comes from the Lord who is the Spirit." The Holy Spirit is the One who empowers and guides us in this process of becoming like Christ. It's a partnership between our willingness to fix our gaze on Jesus and the Spirit's work within us. Today, let us embrace this transformative journey. Fix your eyes on Jesus, seek His glory, and allow the Holy Spirit to shape you into His image. Rejoice in the assurance that, step by step, degree by degree, you are becoming more like your Saviour.

PRAYER: Lord, we thank you for the incredible privilege of being transformed into the likeness of your Son, Jesus Christ. Help us fix our gaze on Him daily, and may the Holy Spirit continue His work in us. We long to reflect your glory more and more in our lives. In Jesus' name, we pray. Amen.

The Assurance of Resurrection Hope

SCRIPTURE: *2 Corinthians 4:14 – "knowing that he who raised the Lord Jesus will raise us also with Jesus and bring us with you into his presence."*

DEVOTIONAL: The verse begins with "knowing," emphasizing the certainty of this hope. It's not a wishful thinking kind of hope but a confident assurance based on the historical reality of Jesus' resurrection. Just as God raised the Lord Jesus from the dead, so too will He raise us with Jesus. This truth is the core of our Christian faith—the promise of eternal life through faith in Christ.

Our hope in the resurrection reminds us that death does not have the final say. Just as Jesus conquered death and rose again, so will we. This hope offers comfort in times of grief, strength in times of weakness, and purpose in the midst of life's challenges. Let this assurance of resurrection hope fill your heart today. No matter what you face, remember that you are destined for eternal glory in God's presence. Live with the confidence that, just as God raised Jesus, He will raise you, too.

PRAYER: Heavenly Father, we thank you for the incredible hope we have in the resurrection of Jesus Christ. In times of trial and loss, help us to hold fast to this hope, knowing that you will raise us with Jesus into your presence. May this hope sustain us and inspire us to live for your glory. In Jesus' name, we pray. Amen.

Clothed in Christ's Righteousness

SCRIPTURE: *2 Corinthians 5:21 – "For our sake, he made him to be sin who knew no sin, so that in him we might become the righteousness of God."*

DEVOTIONAL: As believers, our righteousness is not achieved through our own efforts but is a gift from God through faith in Christ. This truth is especially comforting in times of loss or struggle. We don't have to rely on our own flawed righteousness to find favor with God; instead, we rest in the perfect righteousness of Jesus. This exchange transforms our relationship with God. Instead of living under the weight of guilt and condemnation, we are embraced by God's grace and love. In times of loss, when we might be tempted to question our worth or God's love, we can find solace in knowing that we are seen through the lens of Christ's righteousness.

Today, let's embrace the reality that we stand before God clothed in Christ's righteousness. In times of grief or loss, remember that your worth and acceptance before God are secure in Jesus. His righteousness covers you completely, offering comfort, hope, and assurance.

PRAYER: Heavenly Father, we thank you for the gift of Christ's righteousness that covers us. In times of loss or hardship, remind us of our standing in Jesus. May we find comfort and hope in knowing that we are made righteous through faith in Him. In His name, we pray. Amen.

Embracing Our Identity as Children of God

SCRIPTURE: *2 Corinthians 6:18 - "And I will be a father to you, and you shall be sons and daughters to me, says the Lord Almighty."*

DEVOTIONAL: During seasons of loss or uncertainty, we may question our identity and purpose. It's easy to define ourselves by our roles, achievements, or the opinions of others. However, this verse reminds us that our primary identity is as children of God. As His children, we have the privilege of drawing near to our Heavenly Father. In times of sorrow, we can find solace in His comforting embrace. When life's challenges weigh us down, we have a loving Father to turn to for guidance and strength.

Knowing that we are sons and daughters of the Lord Almighty provides a deep sense of security and belonging. We are not alone in our struggles or losses. Our Father walks with us through every season, offering His unwavering love and support. Today, as you reflect on your identity, remember that you are a beloved child of God. Embrace the comfort and security that comes from being a part of His family. In Him, you find your purpose and significance, even in the midst of life's trials.

PRAYER: Heavenly Father, we are grateful for the privilege of being called Your sons and daughters. In times of loss or uncertainty, help us to hold onto our identity in You. May we find comfort and purpose in the knowledge that we belong to the Lord Almighty. In Jesus' name, we pray. Amen.

Abundance Through God's Provision

SCRIPTURE: *2 Corinthians 9:10 - "He who supplies seed to the sower and bread for food will supply and multiply your seed for sowing and increase the harvest of your righteousness."*

DEVOTIONAL: Consider your life as a field. God provides the seeds, representing the resources, talents, and abilities He's given you. He also provides the daily bread, meeting your immediate needs. But here's the remarkable promise: as you faithfully sow the seeds He's given you—whether it's love, kindness, time, or resources—God multiplies them, increasing the harvest of your righteousness.

Even in times of loss, God's provision continues. Your acts of kindness, your words of encouragement, your willingness to help others—all of these are seeds sown in His name. Trust that God will multiply the impact of your righteous deeds, blessing both you and those you touch. In seasons of scarcity, let us remember that God's provision goes beyond our immediate needs. He is a generous God who multiplies our efforts and ensures that we lack nothing as we continue to serve Him and sow seeds of goodness.

PRAYER: Gracious Provider, we thank You for Your abundant provision. Help us to trust that even in times of loss, You multiply our efforts for Your glory. May we faithfully sow seeds of righteousness, knowing that You will increase the harvest. In Jesus' name, we pray. Amen.

Deliverance From Trials

SCRIPTURE: *2 Corinthians 1:10 - "He delivered us from such a deadly peril, and he will deliver us. On him, we have set our hope that he will deliver us again."*

DEVOTIONAL: Paul's testimony is not just about past deliverance; it's a declaration of unwavering hope. He sets his hope on God, the One who has rescued him time and time again. This hope is not grounded in wishful thinking but in the unchanging character of God. In times of loss and hardship, we can follow Paul's example. We can look back on the times God has delivered us, both big and small, and find assurance that He remains our ever-present help. We can set our hope in Him, knowing that His faithfulness endures.

Let this verse be a source of strength for you. When trials come your way, remember that God is your Deliverer. He has delivered you before, and He will do it again. Your hope is not in your own strength but in the unwavering faithfulness of your Heavenly Father.

PRAYER: Faithful Deliverer, we place our hope in You. Just as You have delivered us in the past, we trust that You will continue to rescue us from life's trials. Strengthen our faith, and help us find comfort in Your unchanging character. In Jesus' name, we pray. Amen.

DAY 274

God's Abundant Grace

SCRIPTURE: *2 Corinthians 9:8 - "And God is able to make all grace abound to you so that having all sufficiency in all things at all times, you may abound in every good work."*

DEVOTIONAL: God's grace is boundless, extending far beyond what we can comprehend. It's not just a trickle or a stream; it's an overflowing river of love, mercy, and provision. This abundant grace isn't just for our own benefit. It equips us to "abound in every good work." It empowers us to be a blessing to others, to serve our communities, and to make a positive impact in the world.

In times of loss or need, we can take refuge in the abundance of God's grace. When our own resources fall short, His grace is more than enough. When we face challenges and uncertainties, we can rely on His grace to sustain us and enable us to bless others. Today, let's open our hearts to the incredible abundance of God's grace. Trust that He is not just able but willing to pour it out upon you. Embrace His grace, and let it flow through you to bring hope, healing, and goodness to those around you.

PRAYER: Heavenly Father, thank You for Your abundant grace that sustains us in every season of life. Help us to fully receive and embrace this grace, and may it overflow from our lives to bless others. In Jesus' name, we pray. Amen.

God's Precious Promises

SCRIPTURE: *2 Peter 1:3 - "His divine power has granted to us all things that pertain to life and godliness, through the knowledge of him who called us to his own glory and excellence."*

DEVOTIONAL: Imagine the vastness of this promise. All things that pertain to life—whether it's guidance in our decisions, strength in our weaknesses, or comfort in our sorrows—are available through God's divine power. Not only does God grant us what we need for life, but He also provides for our godliness. He equips us to live in a way that reflects His glory and excellence. This divine enablement comes through knowing Him deeply and intimately.

When we face loss or difficulties, we can rest in the assurance that God's precious promises remain steadfast. His power, glory, and excellence are available to us. In Him, we find everything we need to navigate life's challenges and to live in a way that honors Him. Today, take time to deepen your knowledge of God. Seek Him in prayer, study His Word, and allow His divine power to equip you for whatever life may bring. His promises are your firm foundation.

PRAYER: Heavenly Father, thank You for Your precious promises and the assurance that in You, we have everything we need for life and godliness. Help us to draw nearer to You each day, so we may reflect Your glory and excellence in all we do. In Jesus' name, we pray. Amen.

God's Heart of Compassion

SCRIPTURE: *2 Samuel 14:14 - "We must all die; we are like water spilled on the ground, which cannot be gathered up again. But God will not take away life, and he devises means so that the banished one will not remain an outcast."*

DEVOTIONAL: This verse speaks of God's relentless pursuit of reconciliation and restoration. It reminds us that, despite our mistakes and failures, God's heart yearns for our return. He seeks to bring the banished back into His presence, to mend the broken, and to offer hope to the outcast. In times of loss, when we may feel separated from God or cast out by circumstances, remember this: God's compassion knows no bounds. His desire is to redeem, to heal, and to restore. Just as He worked through the complexities of David's life, He can work through yours.

Today, let this truth resonate in your heart. You are not beyond the reach of God's compassion. He has devised means for your restoration. Seek Him, and you will find a compassionate and loving Father who longs to welcome you back into His arms.

PRAYER: Gracious Father, thank You for Your unwavering compassion and Your heart for restoration. In moments of loss and distance, help us remember that You are tirelessly working to bring us back to You. May we experience the fullness of Your love and grace. In Jesus' name, we pray. Amen.

DAY 277

Our Refuge and Saviour

SCRIPTURE: *2 Samuel 22:4 - "I call upon the Lord, who is worthy to be praised, and I am saved from my enemies."*

DEVOTIONAL: In our lives, we may face our own set of enemies—be they external challenges, personal struggles, or adversities that threaten to overwhelm us. But like David, we have the privilege of calling upon the Lord. He is not only worthy to be praised but also mighty to save. When we turn to Him in faith, we find our refuge and strength.

Consider this verse a reminder that God is your fortress, your shield, and your deliverer. In times of trouble, when the storms of life rage, remember to call upon the Lord. He is ready and willing to save you from your enemies, to bring you through challenges, and to lead you to a place of safety and peace.

PRAYER: Heavenly Father, we call upon You, our worthy and gracious Saviour. In times of trouble, help us to remember that You are our refuge and strength. Thank You for being our deliverer and our fortress. We trust in Your unwavering love and protection. In Jesus' name, we pray. Amen.

God's Righteous Judgment

SCRIPTURE: *2 Thessalonians 1:6 – "Since indeed God considers it just to repay with affliction those who afflict you."*

DEVOTIONAL: For many who have experienced injustices, this verse provides solace and hope. It reassures us that God is not indifferent to our suffering, and He will ultimately set things right. However, it's essential to remember that God's justice is not vindictive but rather corrective. As we navigate through life's challenges, we can find comfort in knowing that God is our ultimate defender. When we face unfair treatment or hardship, we can trust that God is watching over us. In His perfect timing and wisdom, He will bring justice and healing.

Additionally, this verse reminds us of the importance of responding to adversity with grace and forgiveness, leaving room for God's righteous judgment. It encourages us to focus on living a life aligned with God's principles, knowing that, ultimately, He is our protector and vindicator.

In our prayers, let us bring our concerns and grievances before the Lord, trusting in His promise of justice. And as we do so, let us also strive to extend the grace and forgiveness we have received from Him to those who may have wronged us.

PRAYER: Heavenly Father, we thank you for your promise of righteous judgment. Help us to trust in your timing and your wisdom as we face difficulties and injustices. Grant us the grace to forgive as we have been forgiven and to live in a way that honors you. In Jesus' name, we pray. Amen.

The Crown of Righteousness Awaits

SCRIPTURE: *2 Timothy 4:8 - "Henceforth there is laid up for me the crown of righteousness, which the Lord, the righteous judge, will award to me on that day, and not only to me but also to all who have loved his appearing."*

DEVOTIONAL: Grief is a deep and complex emotion. It often accompanies the loss of a loved one or the experience of a significant life change. In times of grief, we may wrestle with questions, doubts, and a sense of longing for what was lost. Paul's words remind us that our current sufferings and losses are temporary. Just as he eagerly anticipated his reward, we, too, can find hope in the promise of a future filled with God's righteousness and glory. This verse tells us that the Lord's righteousness will ultimately prevail, and we will be partakers of that righteousness.

During times of grief, it's natural to focus on our earthly losses, but this scripture encourages us to look ahead to a greater, eternal reward. As believers, we can find solace in the assurance that one day, we will stand in the presence of our Lord and receive the crown of righteousness that He has prepared for us. So, as we journey through the grieving process, let us hold onto this promise of a future filled with God's righteousness and love. It's a reminder that our pain and suffering on this earth will one day give way to eternal joy and peace in His presence.

PRAYER: Heavenly Father, during times of grief, we turn to you for comfort and hope. Help us remember the promise of the crown of righteousness that awaits us in your presence. May this hope sustain us as we navigate the challenges of life and loss. In Jesus' name, we pray. Amen.

Unshakable Confidence in God

SCRIPTURE: *2 Timothy 1:12 – "Which is why I suffer as I do. But I am not ashamed, for I know whom I have believed, and I am convinced that he is able to guard until that day what has been entrusted to me."*

DEVOTIONAL: In times of grief, suffering, and uncertainty, our faith can waver. The weight of life's challenges can sometimes make us question if God is still with us or if He's in control. Yet, as we meditate on 2 Timothy 1:12, we find a profound declaration of unshakable confidence in God. During seasons of grief or when facing trials, we, too, can find comfort in Paul's unwavering faith. We can confidently declare, "I know whom I have believed." Our faith may be tested, but our God remains steadfast. He is the same yesterday, today, and forever.

Are you facing grief, uncertainty, or challenges that have tested your faith? Remember that the God you believe in is faithful and able to guard what you've entrusted to Him. Hold fast to your confidence in Him, knowing that He is with you, even in the darkest of times.

PRAYER: Dear Lord, in moments of grief and uncertainty, help us find unshakable confidence in You. Strengthen our faith and remind us that we know whom we have believed. May we trust in Your faithfulness to guard and guide us through every trial we face. In Jesus' name, we pray. Amen.

The Unwavering Faithfulness of God

SCRIPTURE: *2 Timothy 2:13 - "...if we are faithless, he remains faithful—for he cannot deny himself."*

DEVOTIONAL: Think back to moments when your faith faltered. Perhaps you've felt distant from God, struggled with doubt, or even questioned His presence during difficult times. In those moments, remember that God's faithfulness remains unwavering. The apostle Paul wrote these words to Timothy as a source of encouragement and a reminder that their work for the Kingdom of God was not in vain. Paul had experienced hardship and persecution, yet he held fast to the assurance that God's faithfulness transcended his own weaknesses.

In your journey of faith, cling to the unchanging character of God. Rest in the assurance that His faithfulness is steadfast, regardless of your circumstances. You can find strength and hope in His enduring love. As you face uncertainties or moments of doubt, repeat this verse as a declaration of faith: "If we are faithless, he remains faithful." Your faith may falter, but His faithfulness remains constant.

PRAYER: Heavenly Father, we thank You for Your unwavering faithfulness, even when we falter in our faith. Help us trust in Your unchanging character and find peace in the knowledge that You are always faithful. In times of doubt, draw us nearer to You. In Jesus' name, we pray. Amen.

Cleansed by Grace

SCRIPTURE: *Isaiah 1:18 – "Come now, let us reason together, says the Lord: though your sins are like scarlet, they shall be as white as snow; though they are red like crimson, they shall become like wool."*

DEVOTIONAL: Imagine your sins as scarlet or crimson stains, vivid and deeply ingrained. These stains represent our mistakes, regrets, and imperfections—things we may carry as heavy burdens. This promise is not based on our worthiness or ability to earn forgiveness; it's a testament to God's love and mercy. When we approach Him with humility and repentance, acknowledging our sins, He responds with open arms and offers us cleansing through the redemptive work of Jesus Christ.

It's a grace that doesn't keep a record of our wrongs but forgives and restores. It's a grace that calls us to a new beginning, free from the weight of guilt and shame. As you reflect on this verse, consider areas in your life where you might be carrying the burden of sin. Remember that God's grace is available to cleanse, renew, and restore. Approach Him with a repentant heart, and allow His grace to wash you clean, making you as white as snow.

PRAYER: Dear Heavenly Father, we thank You for Your boundless grace and the promise of forgiveness offered through Jesus Christ. Help us come before You with humility, laying down our sins and receiving the cleansing only You can provide. May we live in the freedom and purity of Your grace. In Jesus' name, we pray. Amen.

Justice and Righteousness

SCRIPTURE: *Isaiah 11:4 - "...but with righteousness, he shall judge the poor, and decide with equity for the meek of the earth; and he shall strike the earth with the rod of his mouth, and with the breath of his lips, he shall kill the wicked."*

DEVOTIONAL: For us today, this verse offers hope and a challenge. We may not have the power to bring about perfect justice in the world, but we can strive to reflect God's justice and righteousness in our own lives. We can advocate for the poor and meek, stand up against injustice, and speak truth in love.

As followers of Christ, we look forward to the day when His perfect justice will reign supreme. Until then, let us be instruments of His righteousness, working to bring a taste of His justice to a world in need.

PRAYER: Dear Heavenly Father, we long for the day when Your justice will reign supreme. Help us to live out Your righteousness in our own lives, advocating for those who need justice and speaking truth in love. May we be reflections of Your character in a world hungry for justice. In Jesus' name, we pray. Amen.

Finding Comfort in Grief

SCRIPTURE: *Isaiah 12:2 - "Behold, God is my salvation; I will trust, and will not be afraid; for the Lord God is my strength and my song, and he has become my salvation."*

DEVOTIONAL: Grief is a heavy burden that we all bear at some point in our lives. It can come in many forms—the loss of a loved one, the end of a relationship, or even the loss of a job or dream. In those moments, it's easy to feel overwhelmed and afraid, to doubt whether we can carry the weight of our sorrow. But Isaiah 12:2 offers us a ray of hope. In the midst of grief and pain, we can find comfort in the truth that God is our salvation. This verse reminds us that He is not only our deliverer from sin and eternal separation but also our salvation from the depths of despair. When we trust in Him, we need not be afraid, for He is our strength and our song.

God doesn't promise that grief won't touch our lives, but He assures us that He will walk through it with us. He becomes our strength when we feel weak, our song when our hearts are heavy, and our salvation when we're drowning in sorrow. He is the source of hope that pulls us out of the darkest depths. As we journey through grief, let's lean into our trust in God. Even when our hearts ache, we can find solace in knowing that He is with us, providing the strength to carry our burdens and the melody to soothe our souls. In Him, we can find the comfort and assurance we need to navigate the difficult path of grief.

PRAYER: Dear Lord, in moments of grief, we cling to the truth that You are our salvation, strength, and song. Please comfort us in our sorrow and help us find peace in Your presence. Remind us that You are with us through every trial and that Your love sustains us. In Jesus' name, we pray. Amen.

The Promise of No More Tears

SCRIPTURE: *Isaiah 25:8 - "He will swallow up death forever; and the Lord God will wipe away tears from all faces, and the reproach of his people he will take away from all the earth, for the Lord has spoken."*

DEVOTIONAL: The image of God wiping away tears from all faces is a tender reminder of His intimate care. He knows our sorrows, and He promises to personally remove the tears from our eyes. No more pain, no more sadness, no more grief. Furthermore, the reproach and suffering of His people will be taken away from the earth. All injustice, discrimination, and oppression will be eradicated, and God's righteousness will reign. What a glorious day that will be!

As we grapple with grief today, let us hold tightly to the promise of Isaiah 25:8. It is a beacon of hope, a glimpse of the beautiful future God has prepared for His children. We can trust in His faithfulness, knowing that a day will come when tears will be no more, and joy will reign eternally.

PRAYER: Heavenly Father, in our grief, we cling to the promise of a future without tears, knowing that You are faithful to fulfill Your Word. Comfort us, wipe away our tears, and help us to hold onto the hope of a glorious tomorrow when all sorrow will be replaced with everlasting joy. In Jesus' name, we pray. Amen.

The Promise of Resurrection Hope

SCRIPTURE: *Isaiah 26:19 - "Your dead shall live; their bodies shall rise. You who dwell in the dust, awake and sing for joy! For your dew is a dew of light, and the earth will give birth to the dead."*

DEVOTIONAL: "Your dead shall live; their bodies shall rise." Just as He breathed life into the first human, He has the authority to resurrect the dead. The promise of resurrection reassures us that separation from our loved ones is not the end of the story; it is but a temporary pause. "Awake and sing for joy!" Grief will one day give way to exuberant joy as we are reunited with those we've lost. The grave will not have the final say; resurrection will.

"For your dew is a dew of light." This image speaks of the gentle refreshment of God's grace and the radiant transformation He brings to those who have passed away. "The earth will give birth to the dead." This profound statement reminds us that even the earth, which has witnessed countless burials, will one day yield its captives to the triumphant power of God. Death cannot hold us captive forever. As we navigate the depths of grief, let us find comfort in Isaiah 26:19. It calls us to embrace the hope of resurrection, to believe in a future where life conquers death, and to anticipate the joyous reunion awaiting us in God's presence.

PRAYER: Heavenly Father, we thank You for the promise of resurrection hope found in Isaiah 26:19. In times of grief, help us hold on to this profound truth – that death does not have the final word, but rather, through Your power, life will triumph. May this hope bring comfort and peace to our grieving hearts. In Jesus' name, we pray. Amen.

Finding Rest in Quietness and Trust

SCRIPTURE: *Isaiah 30:15 - "For thus said the Lord God, the Holy One of Israel, 'In returning and rest you shall be saved; in quietness and in trust shall be your strength.' But you were unwilling."*

DEVOTIONAL: "In returning and rest, you shall be saved." God beckons us to return to Him, to seek refuge in His unwavering love and infinite wisdom. It is in His presence that we find true salvation, not just from the trials of life but also from the turmoil within our hearts. When we return to God in our moments of grief, we open ourselves to His healing touch. "In quietness and in trust shall be your strength." Quietness here doesn't merely mean the absence of noise but a stillness of the soul – a tranquil trust in God's plan, even when life seems tumultuous. In these moments, we find our strength. It's not a strength born of our own efforts, but a strength that emanates from our trust in a sovereign God.

"But you were unwilling." Sometimes, we let our grief and pain hinder us from returning to God. Our stubbornness can make us rely on our own understanding and strength. Yet, God's invitation remains open, regardless of our reluctance. He patiently waits for us to turn to Him, to find rest and strength in His presence. In times of loss, when our hearts ache with sorrow, let us remember Isaiah 30:15. It invites us to return to God, rest in His loving arms, and find the strength that comes from trusting in Him. God longs to offer solace, but it requires our willingness to seek it in Him.

PRAYER: Heavenly Father, in moments of grief and loss, we often struggle to return to You and find rest in Your presence. Please help us overcome our reluctance and trust in Your plan. May we find strength in the quietness of Your love and in unwavering trust in Your sovereignty. In Jesus' name, we pray. Amen.

The Lord, Our Judge, Lawgiver, and King

SCRIPTURE: *Isaiah 33:22 - "For the Lord is our judge; the Lord is our lawgiver; the Lord is our king; he will save us."*

DEVOTIONAL: When we experience loss, it's natural to question why it happened or to wonder if we could have done something differently. In those moments, we find comfort in knowing that God is our ultimate Judge. His judgments are righteous and just. He understands our suffering and grief more deeply than anyone else. We can trust that He will judge our hearts with compassion and mercy.

"He will save us." These words are a source of profound hope. In times of loss, we may feel helpless, but God assures us that He is our Saviour. He can save us from despair, from hopelessness, and from the depths of grief. Through faith in Him, we find salvation that extends beyond this life into the promise of eternity.

PRAYER: Heavenly Father, thank You for being our Judge, Lawgiver, and King. In times of loss, we find comfort and hope in Your roles. Help us trust in Your wisdom and guidance, knowing that You are our Saviour and will lead us through every trial. In Jesus' name, we pray. Amen.

The Stability of God's Times

SCRIPTURE: *Isaiah 33:6 - "And he will be the stability of your times, abundance of salvation, wisdom, and knowledge; the fear of the Lord is Zion's treasure."*

DEVOTIONAL: Life is marked by seasons of change. Some seasons bring joy and abundance, while others bring loss, trials, and uncertainty. In the midst of these fluctuations, we often yearn for stability and security. Isaiah 33:6 reminds us that true stability, the kind that transcends circumstances, is found in God alone. When we anchor our lives in God, we find a steadfast foundation. He is unchanging, faithful, and reliable. In times of loss, when the ground beneath us feels shaky, God remains our constant source of strength and stability. We can trust Him to uphold us and provide a firm footing, even when everything else seems uncertain.

Today, as you may still be grappling with the impact of loss, remember Isaiah 33:6. Let it be a reminder that God offers you stability in the midst of change, abundant blessings in times of need, and the priceless treasure of a reverent relationship with Him. His faithfulness is your refuge and strength.

PRAYER: Heavenly Father, You are the stability of our times, our abundant salvation, and the source of true wisdom and knowledge. We treasure our reverence for You. In seasons of loss and change, help us find our stability and hope in You alone. May we continue to grow in awe of Your greatness. In Jesus' name, we pray. Amen.

DAY 290

Everlasting Joy on Our Journey

SCRIPTURE: *Isaiah 35:10 – "And the ransomed of the Lord shall return and come to Zion with singing; everlasting joy shall be upon their heads; they shall obtain gladness and joy, and sorrow and sighing shall flee away."*

DEVOTIONAL: Life's journey can be filled with twists and turns, some leading to mountaintop moments while others traverse valleys of sorrow and loss. In Isaiah 35:10, we glimpse a beautiful promise of what awaits those who follow the Lord faithfully. In the presence of everlasting joy, sorrow and sighing will have no place. The wounds of loss and grief will be healed, and every tear will be wiped away by the loving hand of God. The pains of this world will give way to a perfect and eternal reality.

As you journey through life, especially in times of loss, hold onto the promise of Isaiah 35:10. It's a reminder that your ultimate destination is a place of singing, joy, and complete restoration. The losses you've experienced here will be overshadowed by the eternal blessings God has prepared for those who love Him.

PRAYER: Heavenly Father, we long for the day when everlasting joy will replace our sorrow and sighing. Help us to trust in Your promises and hold onto the hope of the glorious destination You have prepared for us. In times of loss, remind us that our ultimate joy is found in You alone. In Jesus' name, we pray. Amen.

Strength for the Weary Soul

SCRIPTURE: *Isaiah 35:4 - "Say to those who have an anxious heart, 'Be strong; fear not! Behold, your God will come with vengeance, with the recompense of God. He will come and save you.'"*

DEVOTIONAL: In the midst of life's trials and losses, our hearts can become burdened with anxiety and fear. The weight of grief and hardship can leave us feeling weak and vulnerable. But in Isaiah 35:4, God offers words of encouragement and hope to those with anxious hearts. These words are a call to courage, a divine reminder that even in our weakest moments, we can find strength in God. He doesn't want us to be consumed by fear or anxiety. Instead, He invites us to place our trust in Him, knowing that His power and presence can conquer every adversity.

If you find yourself in a season of loss, anxiety, or fear, take these words from Isaiah 35:4 to heart. God calls you to be strong, to trust Him, and to know that He will come to save you. He is your refuge and your strength, even in the midst of life's most challenging moments.

PRAYER: Heavenly Father, we thank You for being our source of strength and our deliverer. In times of loss and anxiety, help us to trust in Your promises. Remind us that You are near to save and that Your justice will prevail. May we find courage and hope in You. In Jesus' name, we pray. Amen.

The Song of Thanksgiving

SCRIPTURE: *Isaiah 38:20 - "The Lord will save me, and we will play my music on stringed instruments all the days of our lives, at the house of the Lord."*

DEVOTIONAL: What a beautiful reminder of the power of thanksgiving and worship! When we experience God's deliverance and grace in our lives, our response should be one of gratitude. Just as Hezekiah found solace and joy in worshiping the Lord, we can also find comfort and renewal in offering our praises to God.

In your moments of loss or difficulty, remember the example of Hezekiah. Let gratitude flow from your heart as you reflect on God's saving grace. Whether through music, prayer, or simply a heart overflowing with thanksgiving, may your response to God's goodness be a source of solace and healing.

PRAYER: Dear Heavenly Father, we thank You for Your saving power and the countless blessings You bestow upon us. Help us cultivate hearts of gratitude and worship, even in times of loss or hardship. May our lives be a melody of thanksgiving to You, our gracious Savior. In Jesus' name, we pray. Amen.

DAY 293

The Gentle Shepherd

SCRIPTURE: *Isaiah 40:11 - "He will tend his flock like a shepherd; he will gather the lambs in his arms; he will carry them in his bosom, and gently lead those that are with young."*

DEVOTIONAL: Imagine the tender scene described in this verse: God tending His flock, gathering the lambs close to His heart, and gently leading those who are with young. It portrays a God who not only guides us but also carries us in His loving arms. In times of loss or difficulty, when we feel like vulnerable lambs, we can find comfort in knowing that God is our Shepherd. He watches over us, knows our needs, and provides the care and guidance we require. He doesn't rush or force us; instead, He gently leads, understanding our individual circumstances and weaknesses.

Let this image of God as a gentle Shepherd bring solace to your heart. Trust in His guidance and care, even when life is uncertain, and losses weigh heavily on you. He knows the way, and He will lead you with love and compassion.

PRAYER: Dear Lord, our gentle Shepherd, thank You for your loving care and guidance. In times of loss and uncertainty, help us to trust in Your tender leadership. Gather us close to Your heart and guide us with Your wisdom. We place our trust in You. In Jesus' name, we pray. Amen.

The Eternal God

SCRIPTURE: *Isaiah 40:28 – "Have you not known? Have you not heard? The Lord is the everlasting God, the Creator of the ends of the earth. He does not faint or grow weary; his understanding is unsearchable."*

DEVOTIONAL: In times of loss and hardship, when we feel weak and weary, it's comforting to remember that our God is the everlasting God. Isaiah 40:28 reminds us that He is the Creator of the entire world, and His power and understanding are beyond measure. Have you not known? Have you not heard? These questions serve as a reminder that our God's strength and wisdom are unmatched. While we may grow tired and discouraged, He never does. He doesn't faint or become weary, no matter the challenges we face.

This verse invites us to find solace in the unchanging nature of our God. When life's burdens weigh us down, when losses threaten to overwhelm us, we can lean on the One who is eternal and unchanging. His understanding is beyond our comprehension, and His love for us is unending. Take a moment to reflect on the vastness of God's power and wisdom. Entrust your cares and burdens to Him, knowing that He can handle them. Let the knowledge of His eternal nature bring you peace and strength today.

PRAYER: Heavenly Father, the everlasting God, we find comfort in Your unchanging nature. When we grow weary, remind us of Your boundless strength and wisdom. Help us to trust in Your unfailing love, especially in times of loss. In Jesus' name, we pray. Amen.

God's Power

SCRIPTURE: *Isaiah 40:29 - "He gives power to the faint, and to him who has no might, he increases strength."*

DEVOTIONAL: In our journey through life, we often face moments of weariness, where our strength seems to wane, and our spirits grow faint. It's precisely in these times that we can turn to Isaiah 40:29 for solace and encouragement. This verse reminds us that God provides power to those who feel weak and strength to those who believe they have none left. When we are at our lowest point, when loss and hardship leave us feeling powerless, God steps in to lift us up.

God's power is not limited by our limitations. He specializes in taking our weaknesses and transforming them into opportunities for His strength to shine through. When we rely on Him, we tap into a source of strength that is boundless and unwavering. Whatever challenges you may be facing today, whether it's the loss of a loved one, a difficult circumstance, or a heavy burden, know that you can find strength in God's power. Lean on Him, trust in His promises, and let His strength renew your spirit.

PRAYER: Heavenly Father, we thank You for being our source of strength when we feel weak. In moments of loss and hardship, remind us of Your promise to provide power to the faint. Help us trust in Your unwavering strength. In Jesus' name, we pray. Amen.

Fear Not, For God Is with You

SCRIPTURE: *Isaiah 41:13 – "For I, the LORD your God, hold your right hand; it is I who say to you, 'Fear not, I am the one who helps you.'"*

DEVOTIONAL: Fear is a powerful emotion, and in times of loss and uncertainty, it can grip our hearts with a relentless grip. But in Isaiah 41:13, we find a comforting and reassuring promise from the Lord. God reminds us that He is not a distant, uncaring deity. Instead, He is intimately involved in our lives. He says, "I, the LORD your God, hold your right hand." This imagery illustrates God's closeness and His willingness to guide and support us through our trials.

In moments when we're tempted to fear, God's message to us is clear: "Fear not, for I am the one who helps you." It's a reminder that we are not alone in our struggles. God is with us, holding our hands and walking alongside us every step of the way.

Whatever fears or anxieties you may be facing due to loss or other challenges, know that God is there to provide comfort and strength. He is the source of our courage and the assurance that we need not be afraid, for He is our Helper and our Guide.

PRAYER: Heavenly Father, in times of fear and loss, we cling to Your promise that You hold our right hand and help us. Thank You for Your constant presence and guidance. Help us to trust in Your unwavering love. In Jesus' name, we pray. Amen.

Quenching the Thirst of the Soul

SCRIPTURE: *Isaiah 41:17 - "When the poor and needy seek water, and there is none, and their tongue is parched with thirst, I the Lord will answer them; I the God of Israel will not forsake them."*

DEVOTIONAL: The imagery here is profound. Just as physical thirst can be agonizing, our souls can ache for comfort and meaning in the midst of loss. God promises that when we, the poor and needy, seek Him, He will answer. He is the living water that flows, never running dry, and He will not forsake us.

When we feel spiritually parched due to the challenges of life, we can turn to the Lord. He alone can provide the refreshment and sustenance our souls crave. His presence and His Word are like a cool drink for our weary hearts, bringing comfort, hope, and renewal. No matter how dry or desolate the circumstances of loss may seem, remember that God is the wellspring of living water, ready to answer your soul's deepest thirst. Seek Him, and you will find the refreshment you need.

PRAYER: Gracious Lord, we thank You for being the source of living water for our thirsty souls. In times of loss and need, help us turn to You, knowing that You will never forsake us. Quench our spiritual thirst and fill us with Your peace and presence. In Jesus' name, we pray. Amen.

Guided Through the Darkness

SCRIPTURE: *Isaiah 42:16 - "And I will lead the blind in a way that they do not know, in paths that they have not known I will guide them. I will turn the darkness before them into light, the rough places into level ground. These are the things I do, and I do not forsake them."*

DEVOTIONAL: Loss can often make us feel as though we are stumbling in darkness, unsure of which way to turn. Yet, in Isaiah 42:16, God promises to guide us even in the most unfamiliar and challenging terrain of life. When we are spiritually blind, unable to see a clear path forward, God steps in as our divine guide. He leads us along uncharted paths, unveiling a way we may never have known existed. He turns the darkness before us into radiant light, replacing the rough and uneven places with level ground.

These words assure us that God's guidance doesn't depend on our own understanding or familiarity with the terrain. Instead, it depends on His unwavering faithfulness. He doesn't forsake us in our darkest hours but walks with us every step of the way. In times of loss, when everything seems uncertain, remember that God is the ultimate Guide who turns darkness into light and rough places into level ground. Trust Him to lead you through the challenges, and He will never forsake you.

PRAYER: Heavenly Father, we thank You for Your guidance through the darkest moments of our lives. Help us trust Your leading even when we cannot see the way. Illuminate our paths, make our rough places smooth, and lead us with Your unwavering love. In Jesus' name, we pray. Amen.

God's Unshakable Love

SCRIPTURE: *Isaiah 54:10 - "For the mountains may depart and the hills be removed, but my steadfast love shall not depart from you, and my covenant of peace shall not be removed," says the Lord, who has compassion on you.*

DEVOTIONAL: Loss often feels like the removal of familiar landmarks in our lives, leaving us in a state of disarray. Yet, in Isaiah 54:10, God's promise shines as brightly as ever: His love and peace will never depart from us, no matter how much our circumstances change. The imagery of mountains and hills departing speaks of the most stable and enduring elements in our physical world being shaken. But God's love is unshakable. His covenant of peace remains steadfast, a bond that nothing can sever.

In the midst of loss, when everything around us seems to crumble, God remains a constant. His love is unwavering, His peace is unbreakable, and His compassion is unending. We can find solace in the knowledge that His presence and promises remain with us, even in the face of life's most challenging losses.

PRAYER: Gracious God, thank You for Your unshakable love and enduring peace. When our lives are shaken by loss, remind us of Your unwavering presence and steadfast promises. Help us trust in Your unchanging nature. In Jesus' name, we pray. Amen.

Prayers Heard and Answered

SCRIPTURE: *Isaiah 65:24 - "Before they call I will answer; while they are yet speaking I will hear."*

DEVOTIONAL: As we reach this significant milestone in our journey of seeking solace and meaning amidst loss, let us reflect on the beautiful assurance found in Isaiah 65:24. It's a promise that reminds us of the incredible intimacy and attentiveness of our Heavenly Father.

God's love for us is so deep that He not only hears our spoken prayers but responds even before we utter them. He knows the desires of our hearts, the silent cries of our souls, and the unspoken burdens we carry. Before we call, He answers. While we are yet speaking, He hears.

In times of loss, when words often fail us, when grief leaves us speechless, we can take solace in this divine truth. God knows our needs, understands our pain, and is actively working for our good, often in ways we cannot fathom. His tender care and perfect timing bring comfort to our hearts.

Today, let us rest in the knowledge that our God is not only a God who hears but a God who responds with love and grace, especially in our moments of loss.

PRAYER: Heavenly Father, we are grateful that You not only hear our prayers but also answer them before we ask. Help us trust in Your perfect timing and unwavering love, especially in times of loss. In Jesus' name, we pray. Amen.

Blessings for Perseverance

SCRIPTURE: *James 1:12 – "Blessed is the man who remains steadfast under trial, for when he has stood the test, he will receive the crown of life, which God has promised to those who love him."*

DEVOTIONAL: Life's journey is often marked by trials and tribulations, moments of joy and sorrow. In these challenging times, it can be difficult to find solace and meaning. Yet, in James 1:12, we discover a profound promise for those who persevere through life's trials. Blessed is the one who remains steadfast under trial. This blessing is not merely a reward at the end of our journey but a daily source of strength and solace. It is a reminder that our faith, tested and refined through trials, is precious in God's eyes.

The crown of life that God promises is not a fading laurel but an eternal reward, a symbol of our victory over trials and tribulations. It's a reminder that our struggles have a purpose, that our perseverance brings glory to God, and that our love for Him sustains us through it all. In times of loss and sorrow, remember that your steadfastness, rooted in your love for God, is building a legacy of faith that will one day be crowned with the gift of eternal life. Take solace in the fact that your trials are not in vain, for God is with you, and the promise of a heavenly crown awaits those who endure.

PRAYER: Dear Lord, grant us the strength to remain steadfast in our faith, even in the face of trials and loss. Help us remember that our perseverance has a purpose and that the crown of life You promise is our eternal reward. In Jesus' name, we pray. Amen.

Every Good Gift

SCRIPTURE: *James 1:17 - "Every good gift and every perfect gift is from above, coming down from the Father of lights, with whom there is no variation or shadow due to change."*

DEVOTIONAL: Consider the beauty of creation—the breathtaking landscapes, the intricate details of a flower, or the gentle melody of a bird's song. All these are good gifts from the Father of lights, who does not change like shifting shadows. In moments of loss, these glimpses of God's creation can offer solace and remind us of His unwavering love.

Moreover, God's greatest gift is His unchanging love and the promise of eternal life through His Son, Jesus Christ. In the face of loss, we can find comfort in knowing that God's love and salvation remain constant, an everlasting source of hope. As you navigate through seasons of loss, remember to look for the good gifts that surround you, both in the beauty of creation and in the love and promises of your heavenly Father.

PRAYER: Heavenly Father, thank You for being the source of every good and perfect gift. In times of loss, help us find solace in Your unwavering love and the beauty of Your creation. May we always recognize Your blessings and remain steadfast in our faith. In Jesus' name, we pray. Amen.

Wisdom in Times of Loss

SCRIPTURE: *James 1:5 - "If any of you lacks wisdom, let him ask God, who gives generously to all without reproach, and it will be given him."*

DEVOTIONAL: Loss often brings with it a flood of emotions and questions. We wonder why it happened, what it means, and how we can move forward. In the midst of such uncertainty, James 1:5 offers us a beacon of hope. God invites us to seek wisdom from Him. He doesn't reproach us for asking; instead, He generously gives wisdom to all who seek it. This wisdom isn't merely about acquiring knowledge but gaining a deeper understanding of life's trials and tribulations.

When we face loss, we can ask God for the wisdom to navigate through the pain, make sound decisions, and find meaning in our experiences. God's wisdom can guide us toward healing, help us support others who are hurting, and provide clarity in the midst of confusion. So, in the face of loss, turn to God in prayer, asking for His wisdom to light your path. Trust that He will generously answer your request, guiding you through the difficult journey ahead.

PRAYER: Heavenly Father, in times of loss, we seek Your wisdom to understand, heal, and move forward. Thank You for the promise of wisdom when we ask. Grant us discernment and clarity as we navigate life's challenges. In Jesus' name, we pray. Amen.

DAY 304

Finding Comfort in Humility

SCRIPTURE: *James 4:10 - "Humble yourselves before the Lord, and he will exalt you."*

DEVOTIONAL: Loss has a way of humbling us. It reminds us of our vulnerability, our limitations, and our need for support. In James 4:10, we are encouraged to embrace humility in our relationship with God. During times of loss, we may be tempted to ask, "Why me?" or to wrestle with feelings of injustice. While it's natural to have these emotions, humility allows us to surrender control and acknowledge that we are not all-knowing or all-powerful. It reminds us that we need the guidance and strength that only God can provide.

As we humble ourselves before the Lord, we find comfort in knowing that He is there to lift us up. God is the source of our ultimate exaltation, not through worldly success, but through the peace, strength, and wisdom He imparts during life's trials.

So, in the midst of loss, let humility be a guiding light. Trust that as you surrender to God, He will bring you comfort and, in due time, lift you up with His loving and healing presence.

PRAYER: Dear Lord, in moments of loss and vulnerability, we humble ourselves before You. We recognize our need for Your guidance and comfort. Please exalt us with Your presence, peace, and wisdom. In Jesus' name, we pray. Amen.

Drawing Near to God in Grief

SCRIPTURE: *James 4:8 – "Draw near to God, and he will draw near to you."*

DEVOTIONAL: In times of loss and grief, the pain and emptiness we feel can seem overwhelming. It's easy to question where God is in these moments and doubt His presence. But James 4:8 offers us a comforting promise: when we draw near to God, He draws near to us. Grief can create a sense of distance from God, but it's precisely during these times that we need Him the most. Drawing near to God doesn't require elaborate rituals or perfect words; it simply means seeking Him with an open heart.

In your grief, you can find solace by spending time in prayer, reading His Word, or simply sitting quietly in His presence. When you take the step to draw near to God, you will discover that He has been there all along, ready to embrace you with His love, comfort, and healing. Though the pain of loss may linger, know that you are never alone. God is with you, offering His presence and peace as you draw near to Him.

PRAYER: Heavenly Father, in my grief and loss, I draw near to You, seeking Your presence and comfort. Thank You for the promise that as I draw near to You, You draw near to me. May Your presence fill the emptiness in my heart. In Jesus' name, I pray. Amen.

Finding Purpose in Pain

SCRIPTURE: *Jeremiah 15:19 – "Therefore thus says the Lord: 'If you return, I will restore you, and you shall stand before me. If you utter what is precious and not what is worthless, you shall be as my mouth. They shall turn to you, but you shall not turn to them.'"*

DEVOTIONAL: In times of grief and loss, we might wonder why we must endure such pain. Jeremiah's experience teaches us that our trials and suffering can be transformed into something precious when we turn to God. When we allow Him to work in our lives, our pain can become a source of compassion, comfort, and purpose for others.

Consider the possibility that your experiences of loss and grief can be used by God to bring hope and healing to those around you. As you turn to Him, allowing Him to restore and heal your heart, you may find a new-found purpose in sharing your story and comforting others who are going through similar trials. Remember, God can turn our pain into something precious, and our suffering can become a source of strength and hope for others. Lean on Him as you navigate your journey through grief and loss.

PRAYER: Heavenly Father, in my moments of grief and pain, help me turn to You for restoration and purpose. Use my experiences to bring hope and healing to others who are hurting. Thank You for the promise that You can turn my suffering into something precious. In Jesus' name, I pray. Amen.

The Promise of God's Presence

SCRIPTURE: *Jeremiah 15:20 - "And I will make you to this people a fortified wall of bronze; they will fight against you, but they shall not prevail over you, for I am with you to save you and deliver you, declares the Lord."*

DEVOTIONAL: Jeremiah faced opposition and hostility as he faithfully delivered God's messages to the people of Israel. Yet, in the midst of his trials, God provided him with a powerful promise: "I am with you to save you and deliver you." This promise reminds us of God's unwavering presence in our lives, especially in times of adversity and loss. When we experience grief and loss, it can feel as if we are surrounded by darkness and uncertainty. However, just as God assured Jeremiah of His presence, He offered us the same assurance. In our weakest moments, God is our fortress, a solid wall of bronze that shields us from the assaults of despair and hopelessness.

We may face battles—emotional, spiritual, or even physical—in the wake of loss, but we do not face them alone. God stands with us, offering salvation and deliverance from the depths of our pain. His presence is our greatest comfort, and His promise of deliverance reminds us that there is hope even in our darkest moments. Lean on the promise of Jeremiah 15:20 today. Trust that God is with you, and His presence is your strength and refuge in times of loss.

PRAYER: Heavenly Father, I am grateful for Your promise to be with me, especially in times of grief and loss. Help me remember that Your presence is my fortress and strength. In moments of despair, may I find comfort in knowing that You are with me, offering salvation and deliverance. In Jesus' name, I pray. Amen.

The Searchlight of God's Examination

SCRIPTURE: *Jeremiah 17:10 - "I the Lord search the heart and test the mind, to give every man according to his ways, according to the fruit of his deeds."*

DEVOTIONAL: When we face loss, God sees our pain, our questions, and our struggles. He understands the depths of our grief and offers comfort and healing. As we navigate these difficult seasons, we can trust that God's examination of our hearts is not meant to condemn but to bring us closer to Him and reveal His love and purpose in our lives.

Let us approach God with open hearts, allowing His divine searchlight to illuminate our path through grief. May we find comfort in His presence and trust in His righteous ways, knowing that He will give according to His perfect plan.

PRAYER: Heavenly Father, You are the One who searches our hearts and minds. In times of grief and loss, help us find solace in Your loving examination. Guide us through the valleys of life, and may we trust in Your righteous ways, knowing that You bring purpose and healing even in our pain. In Jesus' name, we pray. Amen.

DAY 309

Restoration Beyond Loss

SCRIPTURE: *Jeremiah 33:6 – "Behold, I will bring to it health and healing, and I will heal them and reveal to them abundance of prosperity and security."*

DEVOTIONAL: Jeremiah 33:6 is a promise of restoration and healing from God. It reminds us that even in times of great loss and despair, God's plan is to bring health, healing, prosperity, and security. In our grief and loss, it's crucial to remember that God's restoration goes beyond what we can imagine. He not only heals our wounds but blesses us with abundance and security. His grace knows no bounds, and His love for us is unceasing.

During seasons of loss, we can hold onto this promise of restoration. It may not happen overnight, but as we trust in God's plan and His timing, we can find comfort and hope knowing that He is working for our good. Let us pray for healing and restoration, not only for ourselves but for all who are experiencing loss. May God's promise of health, healing, prosperity, and security shine brightly in our lives.

PRAYER: Heavenly Father, in times of loss and despair, we look to You for healing and restoration. Your promise of health, prosperity, and security brings us hope and comfort. May Your grace abound in our lives and in the lives of those who are hurting. In Jesus' name, we pray. Amen.

Our Redeemer Lives

SCRIPTURE: *Job 19:25 - "For I know that my Redeemer lives, and at the last he will stand upon the earth."*

DEVOTIONAL: In the depths of suffering and loss, Job's words resonate with a profound truth: "For I know that my Redeemer lives." These words hold a promise of hope, a declaration of faith that transcends the most challenging of circumstances. Loss can shake us to our core, leaving us questioning our purpose and the very foundations of our faith. But like Job, we have a Redeemer who lives. We have a Savior who understands our pain, our doubts, and our grief. In times of loss, we can rest in the knowledge that our Redeemer is not distant or indifferent but intimately involved in our lives.

This verse invites us to look beyond our present circumstances and to fix our eyes on the living Redeemer, who brings redemption, restoration, and new life. It is a reminder that even in the darkest moments of our lives, there is hope and assurance in the God who holds the future. As we navigate loss, may we, too, declare with confidence, "For I know that my Redeemer lives." Let this declaration be a source of strength, comfort, and unwavering faith.

PRAYER: Heavenly Father, in times of loss and uncertainty, help us hold fast to the truth that our Redeemer lives. Grant us the faith to trust in Your plans, even when we cannot see the way forward. May Your presence and promise bring comfort and hope to our hearts. In Jesus' name, we pray. Amen.

The Outpouring of God's Spirit

SCRIPTURE: *Joel 2:29 – "Even on the male and female servants in those days I will pour out my Spirit."*

DEVOTIONAL: The prophet Joel speaks of a profound promise from God: the outpouring of His Spirit upon all people, without distinction. This promise isn't limited to a select few; it encompasses all who are willing to receive it. God's Spirit is not partial; it is poured out on both male and female, young and old, rich and poor, servant and free. In times of loss and grief, we may find ourselves longing for the comfort and guidance that only God's Spirit can provide. The Holy Spirit is our counselor, our advocate, and our source of strength. He walks with us through the darkest valleys, bringing the light of God's presence and the assurance of His love.

The beauty of this promise is that it extends to everyone, regardless of our circumstances. In moments of sorrow and uncertainty, we can turn to God and ask for the outpouring of His Spirit. His Spirit brings healing, renewal, and direction. It empowers us to navigate the challenges of life with faith and resilience. As you face the complexities of loss, remember that God's Spirit is available to you. He is the One who comforts, guides, and empowers you. Open your heart to Him, and allow His Spirit to pour into your life, bringing the hope and peace that only God can provide.

PRAYER: Heavenly Father, we thank You for the promise of Your Spirit, poured out on all who seek You. In times of loss, we ask for the outpouring of Your Holy Spirit to comfort us, guide us, and renew our spirits. May Your presence be a source of strength and hope in our lives. In Jesus' name, we pray. Amen.

The Lord Roars from Zion

SCRIPTURE: *Joel 3:16 -"The Lord roars from Zion, and utters his voice from Jerusalem, and the heavens and the earthquake. But the Lord is a refuge to his people, a stronghold to the people of Israel."*

DEVOTIONAL: The prophet Joel reminds us that even when everything around us seems to be trembling, the Lord remains steadfast and unshaken. His voice, like a mighty roar from Zion, reassures us of His presence. He is not distant or indifferent to our struggles; He is deeply concerned for His people. In the midst of life's storms, we find our refuge in the Lord. He is our safe haven, our stronghold in times of trouble. When we face loss, grief, or uncertainty, we can run to Him for shelter. He provides the peace that surpasses understanding, the strength to endure, and the hope to carry on.

Today, as you navigate the challenges of life, remember that the Lord is your refuge. In the midst of the chaos, His voice speaks peace to your soul. His embrace offers comfort, and His strength empowers you to stand firm. Trust in the unshakable refuge that is found in Him.

PRAYER: Heavenly Father, in the midst of life's storms, we find our refuge in You. Your unwavering presence brings us comfort and strength. When our world trembles, help us to anchor our souls in You, knowing that You are our safe haven. In Jesus' name, we pray. Amen

Children of God Through Faith

SCRIPTURE: *John 1:12 - "But to all who did receive him, who believed in his name, he gave the right to become children of God."*

DEVOTIONAL: John 1:12 reminds us of a beautiful truth: through faith in Jesus Christ, we become children of God. This incredible gift transforms our identity and redefines our purpose. We are no longer adrift in the sea of life's challenges but welcomed into the family of God.

As children of God, we find solace in the embrace of our Heavenly Father. His love becomes our anchor in the storms of life. Even in the face of loss, we are never alone, for we belong to a family that extends beyond the boundaries of time and space. Today, if you find yourself grappling with loss or searching for purpose, remember your identity as a child of God. Through faith in Jesus, you have been granted the right to be part of His family. Take comfort in the loving arms of your Heavenly Father, knowing that you are cherished, valued, and never alone.

PRAYER: Heavenly Father, thank You for the incredible privilege of becoming Your children through faith in Jesus Christ. In times of loss and uncertainty, help us remember our identity as Your beloved sons and daughters. May we find solace in Your loving embrace and purpose in being a part of Your family. In Jesus' name, we pray. Amen.

The Eternal Security of His Sheep

SCRIPTURE: *John 10:28 – "I give them eternal life, and they will never perish, and no one will snatch them out of my hand."*

DEVOTIONAL: He declares, "I give them eternal life, and they will never perish, and no one will snatch them out of my hand." These words speak of the unshakable security we have in our Shepherd's care. We are His sheep, and He is our loving, protective Shepherd.

Loss and trials may come, but our Shepherd holds us firmly in His hand. No circumstance, no power, and no force can separate us from His love or rob us of the eternal life He offers. In Christ, we have an enduring security that transcends the fleeting challenges of this world. As you navigate life's difficulties, hold onto the promise of John 10:28. You are in the hands of the One who gives eternal life, the One who ensures that you will never perish. Take solace in the security that comes from being His precious and protected sheep.

PRAYER: Loving Shepherd, we thank You for the security and assurance You provide. In moments of loss and uncertainty, help us remember that we are held firmly in Your hand, and no one can snatch us away. Grant us the peace that comes from knowing we have eternal life through You. In Jesus' name, we pray. Amen.

Serving Christ and Finding Solace

SCRIPTURE: *John 12:26 - "If anyone serves me, he must follow me; and where I am, there will my servant be also. If anyone serves me, the Father will honor him."*

DEVOTIONAL: To serve Christ is not just an act of duty but a path to closeness with Him. When we follow Jesus and serve Him, we walk alongside Him. We find solace in His presence, knowing that He is with us, guiding us through every challenge and loss.

Moreover, Jesus assures us that if we serve Him, the Father will honor us. This honor transcends any worldly recognition. It's the honor of being embraced by our heavenly Father, a source of profound comfort and meaning. As you face the ups and downs of life, consider the invitation in John 12:26. Serve Christ with a willing heart, and you'll find solace in His presence and deep meaning in being honored by the Father.

PRAYER: Dear Lord, help us to serve You with joy and devotion. May we find solace in Your presence and profound meaning in the honor bestowed upon us by our heavenly Father. In serving You, may we discover the true essence of life. Amen.

Greater Works in Christ's Name

SCRIPTURE: *John 14:12 – "Truly, truly, I say to you, whoever believes in me will also do the works that I do; and greater works than these will he do because I am going to the Father."*

DEVOTIONAL: In times of loss and uncertainty, we may wonder where to find meaning and solace. John 14:12 provides an extraordinary promise from Jesus Himself, offering both. He tells us that whoever believes in Him will not only do the works He did but greater works. This is a remarkable declaration. As followers of Christ, we have the privilege of continuing His work on Earth. The healing, compassion, and love He demonstrated are not confined to His time on Earth; they live on through us. This promise gives profound meaning to our actions, especially when we use them to help others during times of loss and hardship.

Additionally, it's a source of solace to know that we are part of a divine plan that extends beyond ourselves. In our efforts to serve, comfort, and love, we find meaning in bringing Christ's light into a world that often knows darkness. So, take heart. In serving others and continuing Christ's work, you not only find solace and meaning but also the fulfillment of Jesus' promise of even greater works through your faith.

PRAYER: Lord Jesus, thank You for the promise that through faith in You, we can do great works. May we find meaning and solace in continuing Your mission, bringing Your light and love to those in need. In Your name, we pray. Amen.

The Power of Prayer in His Name

SCRIPTURE: *John 14:13 - "Whatever you ask in my name, this I will do, that the Father may be glorified in the Son."*

DEVOTIONAL: This promise underscores the incredible power of prayer. When we approach God through the name of Jesus, we are not only seeking His help but also acknowledging our trust and reliance on Him. It's a reminder that we are not alone in our trials and that God, in His infinite wisdom and love, responds to our heartfelt petitions.

Prayer allows us to find solace in God's presence, knowing that He hears us. It provides meaning as we connect with the divine and seek guidance, comfort, and strength. Moreover, it glorifies God by recognizing His sovereignty and His ability to work through our circumstances, even in the midst of loss. So, during times of uncertainty and hardship, remember the power of prayer in Jesus' name. It's a source of solace, a path to meaning, and a way to glorify the Father through the Son.

PRAYER: Heavenly Father, we thank You for the gift of prayer in Jesus' name. May we find solace, meaning, and the assurance of Your presence as we bring our petitions before You. May Your name be glorified in all that we do. In Jesus' name, we pray. Amen.

Abiding in His Presence

SCRIPTURE: *John 14:23 - "Jesus answered him, 'If anyone loves me, he will keep my word, and my Father will love him, and we will come to him and make our home with him.'"*

DEVOTIONAL: During times of loss, we often seek comfort in the presence of loved ones. In John 14:23, Jesus offers us an even greater promise: that if we love Him and keep His word, He and the Father will make their home with us. This means we can experience the abiding presence of God Himself. In moments of grief and uncertainty, it's easy to feel alone. Yet, Jesus reminds us that we are never truly alone. When we love Him and strive to live according to His teachings, God's presence becomes a constant source of solace and meaning in our lives. It's as if He moves in, setting up residence in our hearts.

This promise isn't contingent on our circumstances; it's about our relationship with Jesus. It's about seeking Him, loving Him, and following His teachings. Through this, we find solace in God's abiding presence and discover profound meaning in knowing that He is with us every step of the way, especially during our times of loss. So, let's invite Him in, keep His word, and find comfort and purpose in His ever-abiding presence.

PRAYER: Heavenly Father, we thank You for the promise of Your abiding presence. Help us to love and follow Your Son, Jesus, and keep Your word in our hearts. May Your presence be our constant source of solace and meaning, especially in times of loss. In Jesus' name, we pray. Amen.

A Glorious Homecoming

SCRIPTURE: *John 14:3 - "And if I go and prepare a place for you, I will come again and will take you to myself, that where I am you may be also."*

DEVOTIONAL: The promise of a heavenly homecoming is a source of immense comfort, especially during times of loss and grief. In John 14:3, Jesus assures His disciples—and us—that He is going to prepare a place for us. He promises to return and take us to Himself so that we may be where He is. Loss often leaves us feeling separated from those we love, yearning for their presence once more. Jesus understands this deep yearning and offers hope beyond the temporal. He speaks of a day when He will return, not only to welcome us into His presence but to reunite us with loved ones who have gone before us.

This promise is a testament to His boundless love and His desire for us to be with Him eternally. In our moments of sorrow and loss, let us hold onto the hope of that glorious homecoming, where tears will be wiped away, and separation will be no more. It's a promise that brings solace and purpose to our earthly journey. As we navigate the challenges of this life, may we find strength and meaning in the anticipation of the day when we will be forever with our Saviour and reunited with our loved ones.

PRAYER: Heavenly Father, we find hope and solace in the promise of a heavenly homecoming with Your Son, Jesus. Help us to hold onto this promise, especially in times of loss, and to live with the assurance that one day we will be where He is. In Jesus' name, we pray. Amen.

Abiding in His Word

SCRIPTURE: *John 15:7 – "If you abide in me, and my words abide in you, ask whatever you wish, and it will be done for you."*

DEVOTIONAL: This closeness fosters a deep intimacy, much like a branch abiding in the vine. As we remain connected to Jesus, we find ourselves aligned with His will, His purpose, and His heart. In this state, our desires and prayers become increasingly aligned with God's divine plan. During moments of loss, we may wrestle with questions, doubts, and pain. However, when we abide in Christ, and His words dwell in us, we can approach Him in prayer with confidence, knowing that He listens and responds according to His perfect will. Take solace in this promise today. Abide in Christ, and let His words guide and comfort you. Approach Him in prayer with the assurance that He hears, understands, and responds with love and wisdom, even in the midst of loss.

PRAYER: Lord Jesus, we seek to abide in You and let Your words dwell richly in our hearts. In our times of loss and need, help us to approach You in prayer with confidence, knowing that You hear and respond according to Your perfect will. May Your presence bring comfort and hope. In Your name, we pray. Amen.

Guided by the Spirit of Truth

SCRIPTURE: *John 16:13 – "When the Spirit of truth comes, he will guide you into all the truth, for he will not speak on his own authority, but whatever he hears he will speak, and he will declare to you the things that are to come."*

DEVOTIONAL: This Spirit of truth is the Holy Spirit, our Comforter and Counsellor. He doesn't speak on His own authority but reveals what He hears from the Father and the Son. His role is to illuminate the truth of God's Word, providing us with wisdom and insight, even in the most challenging moments. When we're faced with loss, grief, or confusion, it's reassuring to know that we're not navigating life's complexities alone. The Spirit is our divine guide, leading us into God's truth, teaching us, and reminding us of Christ's teachings.

As we open our hearts and minds to the Spirit's leading, we discover that we are not in darkness but walking in the light of God's wisdom and grace. We find solace in the fact that He declares to us the things that are to come, assuring us of a future filled with God's promises. Today, let's lean on the guidance of the Spirit of truth. Trust His leading, for He is your ever-present source of wisdom and comfort in every season of life.

PRAYER: Heavenly Father, we thank You for sending the Spirit of truth to guide us. In times of loss and uncertainty, help us to rely on His wisdom and trust His leading. May we find comfort and direction in His presence. In Jesus' name, we pray. Amen.

DAY 322

He Embraces Us With His Love

SCRIPTURE: *Psalm 91:14 - "Because he holds fast to me in love, I will deliver him; I will protect him, because he knows my name.*

DEVOTIONAL: In the darkest valleys of our lives, where grief and sorrow cast long shadows, it's natural to seek solace and refuge. The pain of loss can be overwhelming, leaving us feeling vulnerable and alone. In these moments, we turn to the promises of God, and one such promise can be found in Psalm 91:14:

This verse reminds us that God is our ultimate source of comfort and refuge during times of grief. He is our Rescuer and Protector, always ready to embrace us in His love. When the weight of sorrow presses down on us, we can find strength and hope by loving Him and trusting in His name.

PRAYER: Heavenly Father, I love you, and I trust in your name. I trust in your love, your grace, and your perfect plan, even when I cannot see it. Grant me the strength to endure, to remember, and to heal. In Jesus' name, I pray. Amen.

The Power of Prayer for Joy

SCRIPTURE: *John 16:24 – "Until now you have asked nothing in my name. Ask, and you will receive, that your joy may be full."*

DEVOTIONAL: Prayer is a profound way to connect with the source of all joy and comfort. It allows us to pour out our hearts, sharing our sorrows, hopes, and desires with our Heavenly Father. When we pray in Jesus' name, we align our petitions with His will, opening the door for Him to work in our lives in ways that bring fulfillment and lasting joy.

This verse reminds us that joy is not solely an emotional state but a deep-seated sense of contentment that comes from knowing we are heard and loved by our Creator. Our prayers, offered in faith and trust, become a conduit for God's grace to flow into our lives, filling our hearts with His joy even in the midst of sorrow. As you face challenges and heartaches, remember the invitation Jesus extends to you: ask, in His name, with confidence that your Heavenly Father hears and responds. Through prayer, you can find a joy that transcends circumstances and sustains you through every season of life.

PRAYER: Heavenly Father, we thank You for the gift of prayer and the promise of joy that it brings. Help us to come before You with open hearts, asking in the name of Your Son, Jesus Christ. May our joy be full as we trust in Your loving and sovereign care. In Jesus' name, we pray. Amen.

Embracing God's Love and Peace

SCRIPTURE: *John 16:27 - "For the Father himself loves you, because you have loved me and have believed that I came from God."*

DEVOTIONAL: The love of our Heavenly Father is an unwavering, constant force in our lives. In John 16:27, Jesus assures us that the Father loves us deeply and intimately. This love is not based on our performance or worthiness but on our belief in Jesus Christ as the Son of God and our response to His love. When we love and believe in Jesus, we open our hearts to the incredible truth that we are cherished by God Himself. The Creator of the universe loves us personally and profoundly. His love is a source of unshakable peace, especially during times of loss and turmoil.

As you navigate the ups and downs of life, remember that the Father's love is a constant, guiding force. Embrace His love, let it fill your heart, and allow it to flow through you to touch the lives of others. In God's love, you'll find the peace that transcends understanding and the strength to endure all circumstances.

PRAYER: Heavenly Father, we are grateful for Your deep and abiding love. Thank You for loving us because we have loved and believed in Your Son, Jesus Christ. May Your love be a source of peace and assurance in our lives, and may it inspire us to love others as You have loved us. In Jesus' name, we pray. Amen.

Finding Peace in Christ's Victory

SCRIPTURE: *John 16:33 - "I have said these things to you, that in me you may have peace. In the world, you will have tribulation. But take heart; I have overcome the world."*

DEVOTIONAL: Jesus assures us that despite the difficulties we face, we can find enduring peace in Him. This peace isn't dependent on the absence of trouble; it's grounded in the knowledge that Jesus has conquered the world's brokenness and sin through His death and resurrection. In Christ, we find a peace that transcends circumstances and provides strength and solace during times of loss.

The victory of Christ assures us that darkness and despair will not have the final say. His triumph over sin and death means that we have the ultimate reason for hope. Even in the face of loss and suffering, we can "take heart" because we serve a Savior who has already overcome the world. As you walk through the challenges of life, hold fast to the promise of Jesus. Let His victory be your anchor, and His peace be your comfort. In Him, we find the strength to endure, the hope of redemption, and the promise of eternal peace.

PRAYER: Lord Jesus, we thank You for Your victory over the world. In times of tribulation and loss, help us to find peace and hope in Your triumph. May Your presence sustain us and remind us that, through You, we can overcome the challenges we face. Amen.

Clinging to God's Faithfulness

SCRIPTURE: *Joshua 23:14 - "And now I am about to go the way of all the earth, and you know in your hearts and souls, all of you, that not one word has failed of all the good things that the Lord your God promised concerning you. All have come to pass for you; not one of them has failed."*

DEVOTIONAL: In life, we often encounter losses and uncertainties. The path can be winding, with unexpected twists and turns. Yet, like the Israelites, we can cling to the unchanging faithfulness of God. His promises are a sure foundation that remains steadfast through all seasons of life.

Joshua's words remind us that not one of God's promises fails. Even when we face loss or disappointment, God's faithfulness endures. His plans for us are good, and He works all things together for our good, even when we don't understand His ways. As you reflect on your own journey, take heart in the knowledge that God's faithfulness is unwavering. When loss and challenges come, remember that He remains true to His promises. Just as He was faithful to the Israelites, He will be faithful to you.

PRAYER: Heavenly Father, we thank You for Your unchanging faithfulness. In times of loss and uncertainty, help us to trust in Your promises, knowing that not one word from Your mouth will fail. You are our firm foundation, and we place our hope and confidence in Your enduring faithfulness. Amen.

A Life of Holiness

SCRIPTURE: *Leviticus 21:8 – "You shall sanctify him, for he offers the bread of your God. He shall be holy to you, for I, the Lord, who sanctify you, am holy."*

DEVOTIONAL: Holiness is often associated with purity, but it's more than that. It's about being set apart for a sacred purpose. It's about living a life that reflects the character of God. As we journey through life, we encounter loss, heartache, and challenges. It's easy to lose sight of our calling to holiness amidst the turmoil of this world. But just as the priests were called to be holy because God is holy, so too are we called to live lives of holiness.

Loss and suffering can be opportunities for us to grow in holiness. They refine our character, deepen our trust in God, and draw us closer to Him. As we embrace the call to holiness, we find meaning even in the midst of life's trials. Today, let's remember that we are called to be holy, set apart for a sacred purpose. Embrace the challenges of life with a heart tuned to God's holiness, and you'll find that even in loss, you are growing into the person God created you to be.

PRAYER: Lord, help us to live lives of holiness, even in the face of loss and hardship. May we continually seek to reflect Your character in all we do. In times of suffering, refine us, and draw us closer to You. We trust in Your sanctifying work in our lives. Amen.

Remembering God's Covenant

SCRIPTURE: *Leviticus 26:45 – "But I will for their sake remember the covenant with their forefathers, whom I brought out of the land of Egypt in the sight of the nations, that I might be their God: I am the Lord."*

DEVOTIONAL: In this verse, we encounter the enduring faithfulness of God's covenant. The Israelites faced trials and challenges throughout their history, yet God never forgot His covenant with their forefathers. Loss and suffering can sometimes lead us to question God's presence or His faithfulness, but this verse reminds us that God's promises endure, even in the midst of difficulty.

Just as God remembered His covenant with the Israelites, He remembers His covenant with us through Christ. His faithfulness is unwavering, and His love is unchanging. When we face loss or adversity, we can find comfort in the knowledge that God remains our God, our protector, and our redeemer. As you navigate the challenges of life, remember that God remembers His covenant with you. Your struggles do not go unnoticed by Him, and His love for you remains steadfast. Take solace in the unshakable promise that God is with you, even in the midst of loss.

PRAYER: Heavenly Father, we thank You for Your unwavering faithfulness and the covenant You've made with us through Christ. In times of loss and adversity, help us to trust in Your unchanging love and remember that You are always with us. Amen.

Ask, Seek, Knock

SCRIPTURE: *Luke 11:9 – "And I tell you, ask, and it will be given to you; seek, and you will find; knock, and it will be opened to you."*

DEVOTIONAL: Asking implies a humble reliance on God. When we face challenges or losses, we don't need to rely solely on our strength or understanding. We can ask God for help, guidance, and provision. Seeking suggests an active pursuit of God's wisdom and direction. In moments of confusion or loss, we can seek His answers in His Word, through prayer, and by seeking wise counsel from others. Knocking signifies persistence and faith. Even when doors seem closed, and our prayers may not be answered immediately, we can continue to knock with faith that God hears and will respond in His perfect timing.

During times of loss, it's easy to become discouraged or feel distant from God. Yet, this verse reminds us that God invites us to approach Him with confidence, knowing that He is a loving Father who cares deeply for His children. So, as you face the challenges and losses of life, remember Jesus' words: Ask, seek, and knock. Approach your Heavenly Father with the assurance that He is ready to respond with His wisdom, comfort, and provision.

PRAYER: Heavenly Father, we thank You for the open invitation to approach You with our needs and concerns. Help us to ask, seek, and knock, knowing that You are a loving and attentive Father who cares for us deeply. In Jesus' name, we pray. Amen.

Guided by the Holy Spirit

SCRIPTURE: *Luke 12:12 - "For the Holy Spirit will teach you in that very hour what you ought to say."*

DEVOTIONAL: In moments of loss, grief, or uncertainty, we often find ourselves at a loss for words. It's in these times that we can take comfort in the promise of Jesus: the Holy Spirit will teach us what to say. The Holy Spirit is our guide, our comforter, and our counselor. When words fail us, the Spirit steps in to provide wisdom, comfort, and guidance. He helps us find the right words to speak to God in prayer and to share with others in our time of need.

During challenging times, it's easy to feel alone and overwhelmed. But we are not alone. The Holy Spirit is with us, dwelling in our hearts, and ready to intercede on our behalf. He understands our deepest feelings and needs, even when we can't express them ourselves. As you navigate the difficulties of life, remember that you have a divine Helper, the Holy Spirit. Trust in His guidance and wisdom. Lean on Him in prayer, and allow Him to speak through you and bring comfort to your heart.

PRAYER: Holy Spirit, we thank You for being our guide and our comforter. In moments of loss and uncertainty, help us to rely on Your wisdom and find the right words to express our hearts to God and to others. In Jesus' name, we pray. Amen.

God's Precious Possession

SCRIPTURE: *Malachi 3:17 - "They shall be mine, says the Lord of hosts, in the day when I make up my treasured possession, and I will spare them as a man spares his son who serves him."*

DEVOTIONAL: In times of loss or despair, it's easy to question our worth and significance. We may wonder if anyone truly values us. In such moments, the book of Malachi reminds us that we are God's treasured possession. The Lord declares that His people shall be His, a treasured possession. Just as a loving father values and spares his son who serves him, God cherishes those who belong to Him. This truth carries profound meaning for us.

In moments of grief or loss, when we feel cast aside or abandoned, we can find solace in the knowledge that God values us immeasurably. We are His cherished ones, and He is deeply invested in our lives. He knows our every struggle and loss, and He walks with us through them. Today, remember that you are not forgotten or forsaken. You are precious in God's sight, His treasured possession. Your worth is not defined by your circumstances but by your relationship with Him.

PRAYER: Heavenly Father, thank You for treasuring us, even in our brokenness. Help us to find comfort in the knowledge that we are Your cherished possession, and may we draw strength from this truth, especially in times of loss and despair. In Jesus' name, we pray. Amen.

God's Unchanging Love

SCRIPTURE: *Malachi 3:6 - "For I the Lord do not change; therefore you, O children of Jacob, are not consumed."*

DEVOTIONAL: Change is a constant in our lives. Seasons come and go, people enter and exit our journeys, and circumstances shift like sand beneath our feet. Yet, in the midst of this ever-changing world, we find a comforting truth in the book of Malachi: our God does not change. The Lord's unchanging nature means that His love, promises, and faithfulness remain unwavering. When we face loss and uncertainty, it's easy to feel adrift, as if the ground beneath us is shifting. But in the midst of life's tumult, we can anchor our souls in the unchanging character of God.

His love is steadfast. His promises are true. He will not abandon us. As the prophet Malachi declared, if it weren't for God's unchanging nature, we would be consumed by the trials and tribulations of life. Today, take solace in the constancy of God's love. When you feel overwhelmed by change and loss, remember that the One who holds the universe together remains the same. He is your unchanging refuge in a shifting world.

PRAYER: Heavenly Father, thank You for being our rock, the unchanging foundation of our lives. In times of loss and uncertainty, help us find comfort and strength in Your unwavering love and faithfulness. In Jesus' name, we pray. Amen.

The Power of Faith

SCRIPTURE: *Mark 11:24 – "Therefore I tell you, whatever you ask in prayer, believe that you have received it, and it will be yours."*

DEVOTIONAL: Jesus' words are a testament to the connection between faith and answered prayer. He encourages us not only to pray but also to pray with unwavering belief. When we come before God with sincere hearts, believing that our requests will be granted, we tap into a wellspring of divine grace and possibility.

During seasons of loss, it's easy to lose sight of hope. But faith assures us that God is listening, that He cares, and that He is capable of turning our mourning into joy, our ashes into beauty. Our prayers, fueled by faith, are not in vain; they are a channel through which God's healing and restoration flow. Today, as you face life's challenges and losses, remember the power of faith-filled prayer. Believe that God hears you, trust in His goodness, and watch as He transforms your circumstances according to His perfect plan.

PRAYER: Heavenly Father, grant us the faith to pray with unwavering belief, knowing that You hear our petitions and respond in accordance with Your perfect will. In times of loss and longing, help us trust in Your loving and sovereign care. In Jesus' name, we pray. Amen.

United in Prayer

SCRIPTURE: *Matthew 18:19 - "Again I say to you, if two of you agree on earth about anything they ask, it will be done for them by my Father in heaven."*

DEVOTIONAL: In moments of loss and hardship, we often find solace in the comforting embrace of community. Matthew 18:19 reminds us of the incredible power of united prayer within the body of Christ. When we come together with fellow believers, aligning our hearts and voices in prayer, there is a unique synergy that takes place. Our requests, hopes, and petitions ascend to the Father as a harmonious chorus. This unity amplifies the potency of our prayers.

During seasons of loss, we may feel isolated or overwhelmed. However, it's in these moments that we should reach out to our brothers and sisters in faith, sharing our burdens and lifting them up collectively before God. This communal approach to prayer not only deepens our bonds with one another but also reinforces our trust in a God who hears and answers. As you navigate your own losses and challenges, remember that you are not alone. Reach out to your spiritual community, agree in prayer, and watch as God's transformative and healing power is unleashed in your life.

PRAYER: Heavenly Father, we thank You for the gift of community and the power of united prayer. Help us to come together with our fellow believers, lifting one another up in times of loss and difficulty. May our unified voices bring comfort, healing, and hope. In Jesus' name, we pray. Amen.

Believing in Prayer

SCRIPTURE: *Matthew 21:22 - "And whatever you ask in prayer, you will receive, if you have faith."*

DEVOTIONAL: Our prayers are not merely empty words spoken into the void; they are heartfelt conversations with the Almighty. When we approach God with sincere faith and unwavering trust, something miraculous happens. The mountains of despair crumble, and the rivers of hope flow freely.

During seasons of loss and adversity, it's easy to succumb to doubt and fear. Yet, it is precisely during these times that our faith can shine the brightest. As we pour out our hearts to God, believing that He hears and answers, we open the door to His transformative work in our lives. Whatever burdens you carry, whatever losses you've endured, remember that your prayers, anchored in faith, have the power to move mountains. Approach the throne of grace with confidence, knowing that God is ready to respond to your heartfelt cries.

PRAYER: Heavenly Father, we come before You with faith in our hearts, believing in the power of prayer. Help us, Lord, to trust You even in the midst of loss and uncertainty. May our prayers be filled with unwavering faith, knowing that You hear and respond according to Your perfect will. In Jesus' name, we pray. Amen.

The Promise of Christ's Presence

SCRIPTURE: *Matthew 28:20 - "Teaching them to observe all that I have commanded you. And behold, I am with you always, to the end of the age."*

DEVOTIONAL: In moments of loss, grief, and uncertainty, it's easy to feel abandoned and alone. However, as believers, we hold onto a promise that transcends all circumstances—the promise of Christ's eternal presence. As Jesus concluded His earthly ministry and commissioned His disciples to go into the world, He assured them of His continuous presence. "I am with you always," He declared, "to the end of the age."

His presence is not fleeting; it's a constant, unwavering source of strength and hope. So, when the storms of life rage or when we're navigating the valleys of grief, we can take refuge in the assurance that Jesus is right there beside us. May this truth resonate in your heart today: You are never alone. Christ's abiding presence brings comfort, peace, and hope, even in the most challenging times.

PRAYER: Dear Lord, we are grateful for Your promise of eternal presence. In our moments of weakness and loss, help us to remember that You are always with us, guiding and comforting us through life's storms. May we find solace and strength in Your unwavering companionship. In Jesus' name, we pray. Amen.

DAY 337

Comfort for the Mourning

SCRIPTURE: *Matthew 5:4 - "Blessed are those who mourn, for they shall be comforted."*

DEVOTIONAL: Grief is a universal human experience. At some point in our lives, we all encounter loss and mourning. Yet, in the midst of sorrow, there is a promise of profound comfort found in the words of Jesus. In the Beatitudes, Jesus declared, "Blessed are those who mourn, for they shall be comforted." It might seem paradoxical that mourning could lead to blessing, but it reveals a deeper truth: God is near to the brokenhearted.

God doesn't promise to take away our grief, but He assures us that we won't face it alone. He comforts us with His presence, His Word, and the support of our faith community. He holds us in our moments of weakness and offers the peace that surpasses understanding. So, as you navigate the depths of grief, remember that God sees your tears, hears your cries, and draws near to comfort you. In Him, you find a source of healing and hope that transcends even the most profound losses.

PRAYER: Heavenly Father, we thank You for Your promise to comfort those who mourn. In our times of grief, help us to lean on Your presence and find solace in Your love. May we be vessels of Your comfort to others who are hurting. In Jesus' name, we pray. Amen.

The Blessing of Showing Mercy

SCRIPTURE: *Matthew 5:7 - "Blessed are the merciful, for they shall receive mercy."*

DEVOTIONAL: This beatitude reminds us that showing mercy is not just a virtuous act; it's a pathway to experiencing God's mercy in our own lives. When we extend kindness and forgiveness to others, we mirror the very nature of God. Our Father is rich in mercy and abounds in steadfast love. In a world often marked by judgment and harshness, choosing mercy can be challenging. It means forgiving those who have wronged us, extending a helping hand to the needy, and demonstrating love even when it's undeserved. Yet, it's in these acts of mercy that we discover the depth of God's grace.

As we show mercy to others, we cultivate a heart that is receptive to God's mercy. When we stumble and fall, His compassion and forgiveness surround us. Mercy, given and received, becomes a beautiful cycle that draws us closer to God and transforms our relationships with one another. So, let us aspire to be merciful in our thoughts, words, and actions, knowing that as we do, we open our hearts to the boundless mercy of our Heavenly Father.

PRAYER: Gracious God, teach us the ways of mercy. Help us to show kindness, forgiveness, and love to those around us. May Your mercy flow through us, transforming our hearts and drawing us ever closer to You. In Jesus' name, we pray. Amen.

God's Comfort in Times of Grief

SCRIPTURE: *Matthew 5:9 - "Blessed are the peacemakers, for they shall be called sons of God."*

DEVOTIONAL: Being a peacemaker in times of grief doesn't mean we can erase the pain or the loss. Grief is a journey that must be traveled, and each person's path is unique. However, it means offering the peace of presence, the gift of a listening ear, and the balm of empathy. It means standing alongside those who grieve, even when words fail us. Peacemaking during grief can be as simple as being there, providing a shoulder to lean on, or sending a heartfelt note. It's about creating an atmosphere where healing can begin and where the fractured pieces of a grieving heart can slowly come together.

Just as God is the ultimate source of comfort, we, too, are called to be agents of His comfort, His peace, and His hope in the lives of those who mourn. When we do this, we embody the heart of our Heavenly Father, who comforts us in all our sorrows. Today, if you or someone you know is navigating the turbulent seas of grief, consider the call to be a peacemaker. Extend the comfort you have received from God to others. In doing so, you not only honor your Heavenly Father but become an instrument of His peace in a world scarred by loss.

PRAYER: Loving God, in times of grief, we seek Your comfort and ask for the strength to be peacemakers to those who mourn. Grant us the wisdom and compassion to offer solace, hope, and the gift of your presence. In Jesus' name, we pray. Amen.

DAY 340

The Healing Light of God

SCRIPTURE: *Micah 4:2 - "Many nations shall come, and say: 'Come, let us go up to the mountain of the Lord, to the house of the God of Jacob, that he may teach us his ways and that we may walk in his paths.' For out of Zion shall go forth the law, and the word of the Lord from Jerusalem."*

DEVOTIONAL: Grief can be a long and winding journey, and often, we struggle to find meaning or purpose in our pain. Yet, in our quest for understanding, we can turn to God as the source of eternal wisdom. He is the beacon of light that can guide us through the most profound sorrow.

As you navigate the difficult path of grief, remember that God's teachings are like a comforting light leading you forward. His word, like a gentle whisper in the quiet of your heart, can bring solace and direction. Through prayer and reflection on His promises, you can find the strength to keep walking, even when the road seems unbearably dark. God's wisdom isn't just for the future; it's for today, for this very moment. Seek His ways, even in your grief, and allow His word to be a healing light that pierces the darkness. In His presence, you can find hope, purpose, and the strength to carry on.

PRAYER: Heavenly Father, in the midst of our grief, we seek the light of Your wisdom and guidance. Help us to find solace and purpose in Your word, and let it shine as a beacon in our darkest hours. We trust that You walk with us through every step of our journey. In Jesus' name, we pray. Amen.

DAY 341

Waiting on the Lord

SCRIPTURE: *Micah 7:7 - "But as for me, I will look to the Lord; I will wait for the God of my salvation; my God will hear me."*

DEVOTIONAL: In times of grief, waiting can feel like an unbearable burden. We long for answers, relief, and healing. Micah 7:7 reminds us of the power of patience waiting on the Lord, even in the midst of our pain. When we grieve, it's natural to question and seek answers, but sometimes those answers seem elusive. In our impatience, we might turn to other sources for comfort or solutions, but true healing often comes from patiently waiting on the God of our salvation.

Waiting on the Lord doesn't mean passive inactivity. It means actively trusting and seeking Him, even when the road ahead is unclear. It means surrendering our need for immediate resolution and allowing God to work in His time and His way. During your season of grief, follow Micah's example. Look to the Lord, wait for Him, and trust that your cries are heard. It may not happen overnight, but in His perfect timing, God brings comfort, healing, and answers to those who patiently trust in Him.

PRAYER: Heavenly Father, in our grief, we often seek quick solutions and answers. Help us, Lord, to find strength in waiting on You. Teach us patience and grant us the wisdom to trust in Your perfect timing. We know that You hear us and will bring healing in Your way and Your time. In Jesus' name, we pray. Amen.

Courage in the Face of Giants

SCRIPTURE: *Numbers 14:9 – "Only do not rebel against the Lord. And do not fear the people of the land, for they are bread for us. Their protection is removed from them, and the Lord is with us; do not fear them."*

DEVOTIONAL: In this verse, we see Caleb and Joshua urging the Israelites not to rebel or fear the inhabitants of the Promised Land. Instead, they speak with faith, declaring that the people of the land are like bread to them. Why? Because the Lord is with them. When we face grief and loss, it's essential to remember that we don't walk this journey alone. The Lord is with us, just as He was with the Israelites. The giants we encounter might appear insurmountable, but God's protection and presence make all the difference.

Instead of rebelling against our circumstances or fearing the future, let us, like Caleb and Joshua, face our giants with courage. Let's trust that God will provide the strength and guidance needed to overcome even the most challenging obstacles. In times of grief, remember that your Heavenly Father is your ultimate source of strength and comfort. Lean on Him and face your giants with the knowledge that He is with you every step of the way.

PRAYER: Dear Lord, in moments of grief and loss, help us remember that You are with us. Give us the courage to face the giants in our lives, knowing that Your protection and presence make all things possible. May we find strength and hope in You. In Jesus' name, we pray. Amen.

Transformed by His Power

SCRIPTURE: *Philemon 1:21 - "Confident of your obedience, I write to you, knowing that you will do even more than I say."*

DEVOTIONAL: Grief can be an isolating and overwhelming experience, causing us to withdraw or focus inward. However, Paul's confidence in Philemon reminds us of the power of community and support. When we face grief, there are often people around us who are willing to offer comfort and help. They might not know what to say or do, but their presence alone can make a world of difference.

Just as Paul trusted Philemon to go above and beyond, we can trust that those in our lives, when given the chance, will do the same. It's okay to lean on others and let them share in your burden. Grief need not be faced alone, and sometimes, the healing comes when we allow others to walk alongside us. Today, if you're grieving, consider the people around you who may be willing to support you more than you realize. Reach out, share your feelings, and allow their presence and care to be a source of strength.

PRAYER: Dear Lord, in times of grief, help us to recognize and accept the support of those around us. Just as Paul trusted Philemon, help us trust in the compassion and willingness of others to help carry our burdens. In Jesus' name, we pray. Amen.

God's Faithfulness in Our Journey

SCRIPTURE: *Philippians 1:6 - "And I am sure of this, that he who began a good work in you will bring it to completion at the day of Jesus Christ."*

DEVOTIONAL: In the midst of grief and loss, it can be challenging to see beyond the pain and heartache. We may question the purpose of our suffering or the road ahead. However, Philippians 1:6 offers a powerful message of hope and reassurance. The apostle Paul, writing to the Philippians from a Roman prison, expresses his confidence in God's faithfulness. He reminds us that the same God who initiated a good work within us will see it through to completion. This truth applies to every aspect of our lives, including our grief and the process of healing.

When we face loss, it may seem like the end of the road. But God's work in us is ongoing, even in our most difficult moments. He is with us throughout our journey, shaping us, comforting us, and ultimately bringing us to a place of wholeness. As you navigate grief, remember that God has not abandoned you. He is working in your life, even when you can't see it. The pain you experience is not the end of your story. God is faithful, and in His time, He will bring healing and restoration.

PRAYER: Heavenly Father, we thank you for your faithfulness and your promise to complete the good work you've begun in us. In times of grief, help us to trust in your plan and find hope in your unwavering presence. In Jesus' name, we pray. Amen.

DAY 346

God's Abundant Provision

SCRIPTURE: *Philippians 4:19 - "And my God will supply every need of yours according to his riches in glory in Christ Jesus."*

DEVOTIONAL: Philippians 4:19 reminds us of a beautiful truth: God's provision knows no bounds. The apostle Paul, writing from his own experiences of hardship, testifies that our God is a faithful provider. He doesn't just meet our needs but supplies them according to His unlimited riches in glory through Christ Jesus.

In seasons of grief, when we feel lacking in strength, comfort, or hope, we can turn to this promise with confidence. God knows the depth of our sorrow and the breadth of our needs. He is ready to pour out His abundant provision upon us, filling every void and restoring what was lost. As we face the challenges of grief, let us trust that God's provision is not merely material but encompasses all that our hearts and souls require. In His love, we find the strength to carry on, the comfort to soothe our pain, and the hope to navigate through each day.

PRAYER: Dear Lord, we thank you for your promise to supply all our needs. In times of grief, when we feel empty and broken, we trust in your abundant provision. Help us to lean on your grace and find our strength in you. In Jesus' name, we pray. Amen.

DAY 347

The Peace of God

SCRIPTURE: *Philippians 4:9 – "What you have learned and received and heard and seen in me—practice these things, and the God of peace will be with you."*

DEVOTIONAL: Grief can leave us in turmoil, with restless hearts and anxious minds. Yet, even in the midst of life's storms, God offers us a precious gift: His peace. Philippians 4:9 reminds us that this peace is not just a distant hope but a present reality. The Apostle Paul, who faced countless trials and tribulations, encourages us to practice the things we have learned from him – the things rooted in faith, love, and trust in God. When we intentionally live out these principles of faith amidst our grief, we open the door for the God of peace to walk beside us.

In our moments of despair, let us remember that the peace of God is not a passive absence of conflict but an active presence of calm in the midst of it. It's a peace that surpasses all understanding, guarding our hearts and minds in Christ Jesus (Philippians 4:7). Today, as you face the challenges of grief, practice what you have learned from those who have walked this path before you – trust in God's faithfulness, cling to His promises, and embrace His peace that passes understanding.

PRAYER: Dear Lord, we thank you for the promise of your peace, a peace that surpasses understanding. As we journey through grief, help us to practice what we have learned from you and others who walk in your ways. May your peace be our constant companion. In Jesus' name, we pray. Amen.

Seeking God's Attention

SCRIPTURE: *Proverbs 15:29 - "The Lord is far from the wicked, but he hears the prayer of the righteous."*

DEVOTIONAL: In times of grief, our hearts long for connection and comfort, and prayer becomes a lifeline to the divine. Proverbs 15:29 reminds us of a profound truth: God is attentive to the prayers of the righteous. During seasons of sorrow, it's natural to question whether God hears our cries, especially when grief can make us feel distant from Him. But take heart, for this verse reassures us that our prayers, offered in righteousness and sincerity, reach the ears of our compassionate God.

In the depths of your grief, know that God is not far from you. He is present, listening, and ready to offer His comfort and peace. So, don't hesitate to pour out your heart to Him, for He is ever near, even when sorrow clouds your vision. Let your prayers be a conversation with the One who holds the universe and your tears. Seek His attention, and you will find solace, strength, and the assurance that you are never alone in your grief.

PRAYER: Heavenly Father, in my grief, I turn to you, knowing that you hear the cries of my heart. Draw near to me, Lord, and comfort my soul. Help me find peace in the assurance that you are attentive to my prayers. In Jesus' name, I pray. Amen.

Surrendering to God's Plan

SCRIPTURE: *Proverbs 16:3 - "Commit your work to the Lord, and your plans will be established."*

DEVOTIONAL: In the midst of grief, it can be challenging to see a way forward, to understand why certain things happen, or to find meaning in the pain we experience. Yet, Proverbs 16:3 offers us a profound truth: when we commit our lives and plans to the Lord, He establishes a path before us. Grief often brings with it a sense of helplessness and confusion. It's as if the plans we once had have been shattered, and we're left picking up the pieces. However, in this verse, we're encouraged to surrender the broken fragments of our lives to the One who can rebuild them.

By entrusting our grief, our brokenness, and our plans to God, we open ourselves to His divine guidance and purpose. Though we may not fully comprehend the reasons behind our losses, we can trust that God is working in and through them, weaving together a new plan for our lives. During these moments of surrender, we find a peace that transcends understanding, and we take the first steps toward healing. So, lay your grief and your plans at His feet, and let God establish a beautiful, meaningful path ahead.

PRAYER: Heavenly Father, in my grief, I choose to commit my life and my plans into Your hands. I trust that You will establish a path that is good and purposeful. Grant me the strength and wisdom to surrender to Your divine plan, even when I don't fully understand it. In Jesus' name, I pray. Amen.

DAY 350

Finding Comfort in God's Compassion

SCRIPTURE: *Psalm 10:14 - "But you do see, for you note mischief and vexation, that you may take it into your hands; to you the helpless commits himself; you have been the helper of the fatherless."*

DEVOTIONAL: Grief can often make us feel isolated and abandoned, as if no one understands the depth of our pain. In times like these, it's essential to remember that God sees our suffering and cares deeply for us. Psalm 10:14 reminds us of God's watchful eye and compassionate heart. Even when the world seems unjust, and we are confronted with misery and sorrow, God doesn't turn a blind eye to our pain. Instead, He observes our suffering, our vexations, and our troubles with a loving gaze.

In our moments of helplessness, we can find comfort in committing ourselves to Him. Just as He has been a helper to the fatherless, He will be our helper in our time of need. God's compassion is a refuge for the grieving heart, offering solace and strength as we navigate the challenges of loss. So, when grief overwhelms you, know that God is watching over you, ready to take your burdens into His hands. Trust in His unfailing love and find comfort in His compassionate embrace.

PRAYER: Heavenly Father, I thank You for Your watchful eye and compassionate heart. In times of grief and sorrow, I commit myself to You, knowing that You are my ever-present helper. Bring comfort to my heart and strengthen my faith in Your love. In Jesus' name, I pray. Amen.

DAY 351

God's Faithful Love

SCRIPTURE: *Psalm 100:5 - "For the Lord is good; his steadfast love endures forever, and his faithfulness to all generations."*

DEVOTIONAL: In times of grief, when we may question the fairness and purpose of our suffering, it's crucial to hold onto the unchanging truth that the Lord is good. Even in our moments of pain, His goodness remains steadfast. Psalm 100:5 reminds us that His love endures forever, unwavering and unending. Grief can shake our sense of security and stability, leaving us feeling adrift. But God's faithfulness transcends generations, offering us a rock-solid foundation to stand upon. His promises are sure, and His love is unwavering.

Though we may not always understand the why behind our suffering, we can trust in the character of our Heavenly Father. His goodness, love, and faithfulness are unwavering, even in the face of loss. In this truth, we can find comfort and hope, knowing that we are held in the arms of a God who cares deeply for us. So, as you navigate the journey of grief, remember that God's love is constant, and His faithfulness endures forever. He is with you, offering His unwavering support and comfort.

PRAYER: Heavenly Father, I thank You for Your unchanging goodness, love, and faithfulness. In times of grief, help me to trust in Your character and find comfort in the knowledge that Your love endures forever. May Your faithfulness be a source of strength and hope in my life. In Jesus' name, I pray. Amen.

God's Everlasting Love

SCRIPTURE: *Psalm 103:17 - "But the steadfast love of the Lord is from everlasting to everlasting on those who fear him, and his righteousness to children's children."*

DEVOTIONAL: When we're burdened with grief, it's easy to feel overwhelmed and lost. But God's love is our anchor, a constant in the midst of life's storms. It's a love that endures through generations, reaching not only us but also our children and grandchildren.

As we mourn, let's take comfort in knowing that God's love is a source of hope and healing. It's a love that carries us through the darkest moments, providing strength when we're weak and peace when we're troubled. God's love is everlasting, a reminder that we are never alone in our grief. So, even in times of loss, hold fast to the knowledge that God's love remains, unwavering and eternal. In His love, we can find the strength to endure and the hope to press on.

PRAYER: Heavenly Father, I am grateful for Your everlasting love. In my times of grief, help me to remember that Your love knows no bounds and endures through all generations. May Your love be a source of strength, comfort, and hope in my life. In Jesus' name, I pray. Amen.

Satisfying the Hungry Soul

SCRIPTURE: *Psalm 107:9 - "For he satisfies the longing soul, and the hungry soul he fills with good things."*

DEVOTIONAL: In moments of grief, when our hearts ache, and our spirits feel empty, we yearn for comfort and solace. Psalm 107:9 assures us that God is the one who satisfies the longing soul. He reaches into the depths of our grief and fills us with good things, even amidst loss. Grief often leaves us feeling spiritually hungry, searching for meaning and hope. Yet, God's provision is abundant. He offers the sustenance of His love, His presence, and His promises. In times of sorrow, these spiritual "good things" become a feast for our souls.

As we navigate the path of grief, we can turn to God, trusting that He will satisfy our deepest longings. He fills us with His peace, His comfort, and His unwavering love. His goodness and grace are enough to sustain us through the most challenging seasons of loss. So, when grief threatens to overwhelm us, let us remember that God is our source of satisfaction. In Him, we find the strength to endure and the nourishment our souls crave.

PRAYER: Heavenly Father, in my moments of grief, I turn to You as the One who satisfies my longing soul. Fill me with Your goodness and grace. May Your presence be my sustenance and Your love my comfort. Thank You for the spiritual nourishment You provide. In Jesus' name, I pray. Amen.

DAY 354

Blessings Overflow

SCRIPTURE: *Psalm 115:12 - "The Lord has remembered us; he will bless us; he will bless the house of Israel; he will bless the house of Aaron."*

DEVOTIONAL: Grief can sometimes leave us feeling forgotten or abandoned, as if our pain is invisible to the world. But Psalm 115:12 reminds us that the Lord remembers us. He not only sees our sorrow but also promises to bless us. In times of loss, it's easy to focus on what we've lost, whether it's a loved one, a dream, or a sense of security. Yet, God's promise is that His blessings will overflow. He extends His hand of grace and provision, offering comfort and hope.

Just as He blessed the house of Israel and the house of Aaron, God desires to bless us in our grief. His blessings may come in unexpected ways – through the support of friends, the solace of His Word, or the strength of His presence. Even in the midst of sorrow, let's hold on to the assurance that the Lord remembers us and is working to bless us. His blessings can bring light to our darkest days and peace to our troubled hearts.

PRAYER: Heavenly Father, I thank You for remembering me in my times of grief. Please pour out Your blessings upon me, just as Your Word promises. Help me to recognize Your grace and provision, even in the midst of sorrow. In Your name, I pray. Amen.

Precious in His Sight

SCRIPTURE: *Psalm 116:15 – "Precious in the sight of the Lord is the death of his saints."*

DEVOTIONAL: In moments of grief and loss, we often struggle to understand the deeper purpose behind the pain. Psalm 116:15 reminds us that in the eyes of the Lord, the passing of His saints is precious. It might seem counterintuitive to describe death as precious, especially when it brings us so much sorrow. But in the context of faith, this verse speaks to the idea that when a believer passes away, they are ushered into the eternal presence of God. It signifies the fulfillment of their faith journey and the beginning of an eternity with the Creator.

For those left behind, the pain of separation remains, but this verse offers a glimpse into the divine perspective. God treasures the homecoming of His saints. He welcomes them into His presence, where there is no more suffering or sorrow. As we navigate our own grief, let's find comfort in knowing that our loved ones who walked in faith are now in the presence of the One who loves them infinitely. Their journey has led them to a place of eternal peace and joy.

PRAYER: Heavenly Father, even in our grief, we trust in Your wisdom and love. Help us to see death through Your eyes, as a precious homecoming for those who have placed their faith in You. Grant us comfort and hope as we continue to walk our earthly path. In Jesus' name, we pray. Amen.

The Lord's Words are Pure

SCRIPTURE: *Psalm 12:7 - "You, O Lord, will keep them; you will guard us from this generation forever."*

DEVOTIONAL: In a world filled with uncertainty and shifting morals, Psalm 12:7 serves as a source of great reassurance. It reminds us that while human words may falter and fail, the words of the Lord remain pure, steadfast, and unchanging. In times of loss and upheaval, we can find comfort in knowing that God's promises endure. His faithfulness stands as a guard against the uncertainties of our generation. The Lord keeps and watches over us, providing a sense of stability and security even when the world around us seems to be in turmoil.

When we face grief and loss, the unchanging nature of God's Word becomes a foundation upon which we can stand. His promises of comfort, healing, and eternal life remain reliable and unwavering. We can trust in Him to guide us through the challenges of life. Let Psalm 12:7 remind you that while the world may change, God's love, protection, and promises remain constant. In His words, we find solace and hope.

PRAYER: Heavenly Father, we thank you for the stability and security found in your unchanging Word. In moments of loss and uncertainty, help us to hold fast to Your promises, knowing that You are our guard and protector forever. In Jesus' name, we pray. Amen.

Hope in the Lord's Redemption

SCRIPTURE: *Psalm 130:7 - "O Israel, hope in the Lord! For with the Lord, there is steadfast love, and with him is plentiful redemption."*

DEVOTIONAL: In times of grief and sorrow, we may find ourselves searching for hope, something to anchor our souls. Psalm 130:7 reminds us that our ultimate hope should always be in the Lord. He is the source of steadfast love and plentiful redemption. Loss can leave us feeling empty and broken, but in God, we find abundant grace and restoration. His love knows no bounds, and His redemption is more than sufficient to heal our wounded hearts. When the weight of sorrow presses down on us, we can lift our eyes to the Lord, our source of hope and healing.

It's easy to be overwhelmed by the challenges of life, especially when we face loss. Yet, in the midst of our grief, we can hold onto the promise that God's love and redemption are more abundant than we can fathom. His mercy is deeper than our pain, and His grace is stronger than our sorrow. As you navigate the difficult seasons of life, remember to place your hope in the Lord. In Him, you will find unwavering love, endless grace, and redemption that knows no bounds.

PRAYER: Heavenly Father, we place our hope in You, for with You, there is steadfast love and abundant redemption. When we face loss and sorrow, remind us of Your unending grace and mercy. Fill our hearts with hope, knowing that in You, we find healing and restoration. In Jesus' name, we pray. Amen.

God's Deliverance in Troubled Times

SCRIPTURE: *Psalm 138:7 - "Though I walk in the midst of trouble, you preserve my life; you stretch out your hand against the wrath of my enemies, and your right hand delivers me."*

DEVOTIONAL: The psalmist acknowledges that, even when walking through the midst of trouble, God preserves our lives. He stands as a shield against the wrath of our enemies, defending and protecting us. The image of God stretching out His hand signifies His readiness to act on our behalf.

When we're faced with loss or challenging circumstances, we can take solace in the assurance that God is with us. His right hand, symbolizing His power and authority, is poised to deliver us from the grip of adversity. In our weakest moments, He shows Himself strong. Today, as you reflect on your own troubles and losses, remember that you are not alone. God's presence surrounds you, and His hand is ready to deliver you. Trust in His faithfulness and take refuge in His love.

PRAYER: Heavenly Father, thank You for Your constant presence and unwavering protection. In times of trouble and loss, we find comfort in knowing that Your right hand delivers us. Strengthen our faith, Lord, and help us trust in Your steadfast love. In Jesus' name, we pray. Amen.

The Lord Will Fulfill His Purpose

SCRIPTURE: *Psalm 138:8 - "The Lord will fulfill his purpose for me; your steadfast love, O Lord, endures forever. Do not forsake the work of your hands."*

DEVOTIONAL: In the midst of life's challenges, losses, and uncertainties, it can be easy to question our purpose and God's plan for our lives. We may wonder if our struggles are in vain or if there's a greater meaning behind them. In Psalm 138:8, we find assurance and hope. The psalmist declares that the Lord will fulfill His purpose for us. It's a reminder that our lives are not aimless or accidental. God, in His infinite wisdom, has a specific plan and purpose for each of us. Our trials, our joys, and even our losses are woven into a grand tapestry designed by the Creator Himself.

What's even more comforting is that this divine purpose is grounded in God's steadfast love. His love for us endures forever, transcending the challenges and difficulties we face. It's a love that never wanes or falters, even when we feel abandoned or forsaken. As you reflect on your life's journey, remember that you are a work of God's hands. Your purpose is intricately connected to His eternal plan, and His love will see you through every trial and loss. Trust in His faithfulness, and let His enduring love be your source of strength.

PRAYER: Heavenly Father, we thank You for Your unwavering love and the purpose You have for our lives. In times of loss and uncertainty, help us remember that Your plan is perfect, and Your love endures forever. May we trust in Your unfailing faithfulness. In Jesus' name, we pray. Amen.

Drawing Near to God

SCRIPTURE: *Psalm 145:18 - "The Lord is near to all who call on him, to all who call on him in truth."*

DEVOTIONAL: God's proximity isn't limited by physical boundaries; it's a spiritual closeness that transcends our circumstances. When we call on Him with genuine hearts, pouring out our pain, doubts, and fears, He draws near to us. In these moments, His presence becomes a source of strength and comfort.

But calling on God in truth means being authentic with Him. It involves opening our hearts completely, expressing our thoughts, and sharing our pain honestly. It's in this transparency that we experience His nearness most profoundly. As you navigate the challenges of life, including moments of loss and grief, remember that God is just a heartfelt prayer away. He longs to draw near to you, to embrace you with His love, and to provide the peace that surpasses understanding. Approach Him honestly, for He is always ready to listen and comfort.

PRAYER: Dear Lord, we thank You for being near to us when we call on You in truth. In times of loss and grief, help us to approach You with sincerity and authenticity, knowing that Your presence brings comfort and peace. May our hearts be open to Your loving embrace. In Jesus' name, we pray. Amen.

DAY 361

The Joy of God's Presence

SCRIPTURE: *Psalm 17:15 - "As for me, I shall behold your face in righteousness; when I awake, I shall be satisfied with your likeness."*

DEVOTIONAL: In the depths of sorrow and loss, we often yearn for something that will bring true satisfaction and joy. Psalm 17:15 reminds us of the ultimate source of lasting joy—the presence of God. The psalmist expresses his longing to behold God's face in righteousness. This deep desire for communion with God reflects a profound truth: true satisfaction is found in an intimate relationship with the Creator. In the presence of God, we find solace, peace, and joy that transcends circumstances.

The promise of awakening satisfied with God's likeness speaks of the transformation that takes place when we seek His face. As we draw near to Him, we become more like Him, and in that transformation, we discover a profound and enduring joy. During seasons of loss and grief, when life's troubles weigh heavy on our hearts, remember that true and lasting joy comes from seeking God's face. In His presence, we find strength to endure, healing for our wounds, and a joy that fills the emptiest spaces of our hearts.

PRAYER: Heavenly Father, in times of loss and sorrow, we seek the joy that can only be found in Your presence. Help us draw nearer to You, to behold Your face in righteousness, and to experience the deep satisfaction that comes from being transformed into Your likeness. In Jesus' name, we pray. Amen.

The Inner Fortitude

SCRIPTURE: *Psalm 29:11 - "The Lord gives strength to his people; the Lord blesses his people with peace."*

DEVOTIONAL: The verse begins by telling us that the Lord gives strength to His people. It's a reassurance that, even when we feel weak and overwhelmed, God provides the strength we need to persevere. This strength isn't just physical; it's the inner fortitude to endure trials and navigate the challenges of life, especially in moments of loss. Moreover, the Lord blesses His people with peace. This peace is not merely the absence of conflict or trouble, but a deep-seated tranquillity that resides in the heart. It's a peace that surpasses understanding and can guard our hearts and minds (Philippians 4:7) when life's storms rage around us.

In seasons of loss, when grief threatens to consume us, let us remember that the Lord is our source of strength and peace. He stands ready to provide the resilience we need and the peace that passes all understanding. We can find strength in His promises and peace in His presence.

PRAYER: Heavenly Father, in times of loss and uncertainty, we turn to You for strength and peace. Fill us with Your enduring strength, and grant us the peace that comes from knowing You are with us. May Your presence be our refuge and our comfort. In Jesus' name, we pray. Amen.

Finding Refuge in God's Presence

SCRIPTURE: *Psalm 31:23 - "Love the Lord, all you his saints! The Lord preserves the faithful but abundantly repays the one who acts in pride."*

DEVOTIONAL: In Psalm 31:23, we find a reminder to love the Lord, especially during challenging times. This love isn't one-sided; it's a reciprocal relationship between the Creator and His beloved children. Even amidst loss and difficulties, our love for the Lord can be a source of strength. The verse also highlights that the Lord preserves the faithful. When we face trials and heartaches, it's reassuring to know that our faithfulness to God does not go unnoticed. He watches over us, protecting and preserving us in our times of need. His faithfulness is a rock on which we can stand.

On the other hand, the verse warns against pride. Pride can lead us away from God's path and into a place of self-reliance. It's a reminder that in times of loss, we should humble ourselves before God, seeking refuge in His presence rather than relying solely on our own abilities. As we navigate the complexities of life, especially during seasons of loss, let us choose to love the Lord, remaining faithful and humble. In His presence, we find refuge, strength, and the assurance that He will preserve us through every trial.

PRAYER: Heavenly Father, we come before You with love in our hearts, seeking refuge in Your presence. Preserve us in our faithfulness and guard us against pride. In times of loss, may Your presence be our strength and our comfort. We trust in Your unwavering love. In Jesus' name, we pray. Amen.

Finding Comfort in Troubled Times

SCRIPTURE: *Psalm 34:19 – "Many are the afflictions of the righteous, but the Lord delivers him out of them all."*

DEVOTIONAL: The beauty of this verse lies in the second part: "But the Lord delivers him out of them all." Even in the midst of afflictions and losses, we can find comfort in the assurance that the Lord is our deliverer. He doesn't promise a life free from trouble, but He does promise His presence and His deliverance.

In times of loss, whether it's the loss of a loved one, a job, or something else dear to your heart, remember that you are not alone. The Lord is with you, ready to deliver you from the depths of your sorrow and pain. His deliverance might not always come in the way we expect or on our timeline, but it is a promise that He faithfully keeps. Lean on the Lord during your times of loss, and trust that His deliverance will come. He is our source of hope and comfort amidst life's many challenges.

PRAYER: Heavenly Father, we thank You for the assurance that, though we face afflictions and losses, You are our deliverer. Help us to trust in Your faithfulness, even when life is difficult. Comfort us in our times of sorrow, and help us find strength in Your presence. In Jesus' name, we pray. Amen.

A Benediction for the Journey

SCRIPTURE: *Numbers 6:24-26 - "The Lord bless you and keep you; the Lord make his face to shine upon you and be gracious to you; the Lord lift up his countenance upon you and give you peace."*

DEVOTIONAL: As we come to the close of this year-long journey of devotionals, let us reflect on this beautiful benediction from the Book of Numbers. These words were originally spoken by God to Aaron and his sons, the priests of Israel, as a way to bless and keep the people.

"The Lord bless you and keep you" reminds us that our God is a giver of blessings and a protector. He watches over us and cares for us even in the midst of life's losses and challenges.

"The Lord make his face to shine upon you and be gracious to you" speaks of God's favor and grace. His radiant presence brings light to our darkest days, and His grace sustains us through all circumstances.

"The Lord lift up his countenance upon you and give you peace" offers the gift of peace. In times of loss and grief, the peace of God, which surpasses all understanding, guards our hearts and minds in Christ Jesus.

As we close this year and look ahead, may this benediction be a reminder of God's constant presence, blessing, grace, and peace in our lives. Let us carry these words in our hearts, trusting that the Lord is with us every step of the way, even in the face of loss.

PRAYER: Heavenly Father, we thank You for Your constant presence, blessings, grace, and peace. As we close this year of devotionals, we carry this benediction in our hearts. May Your face shine upon us, and may we experience Your peace, especially in times of loss. In Jesus' name, we pray. Amen.

Conclusion

As we conclude this year-long journey of daily devotionals, we reflect on the many verses, messages, and prayers that have filled our hearts and minds. Throughout this devotional series, we have explored the depths of God's love, the comfort in His Word, and the strength found in His promises, especially in times of loss and grief.

Loss is a part of the human experience, and it touches each of us in different ways. Yet, through it all, we have been reminded of the unwavering presence of our Heavenly Father. He is the God of all comfort, the One who walks with us through the valley of the shadow of death, and the One who offers hope in the midst of despair.

These devotionals have encouraged us to turn to Scripture for solace and guidance, to seek refuge in prayer, and to remember that we are not alone on this journey. God's Word has been a lamp to our feet and a light to our path, providing direction and purpose even in the face of loss.

As we move forward, may the lessons learned from these devotionals stay with us. May we continue to find strength in our faith, comfort in God's love, and hope in His promises. Let us not forget the power of community and the support of fellow believers during times of grief.

While this devotional series has come to an end, our faith journey continues. We face the future with renewed hearts, knowing that our Heavenly Father is with us every step of the way. Thank you for joining us on this meaningful journey of reflection, prayer, and growth. May God's blessings continue to abound in your life.